THE ACCIDENTAL PRESIDENT

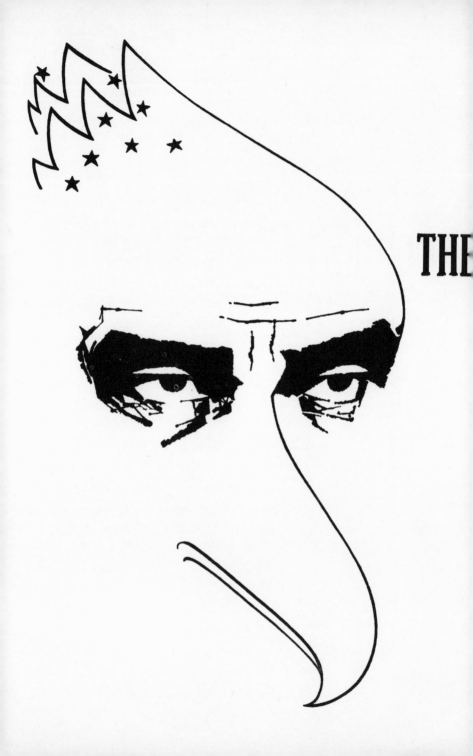

THE

ACCIDENTAL PRESIDENT

Robert Sherrill

GROSSMAN PUBLISHERS ✶✶✶ NEW YORK

1 9 6 7

To Carey McWilliams and Peter

FIRST PRINTING

Preface

Books have been written about Lyndon Johnson to show how powerful he is, how complex he is, how sly and nefarious he is. All of these qualities are rather obvious, but recognizing his power and complexity and slickness somehow misses what I think is the central point for a lot of us, namely: why do we find him such an insufferable and dangerous fellow? Many of us not only voted but worked for him last time and, judging from the sinking bonfires on the Republican side of the river, we'll probably be doing it again in 1968—and hating ourselves for it.

In the last presidential campaign I was assigned by the Fair Campaign Practices Committee to review J. Evett Haley's book *A Texan Looks at Lyndon*. Somebody suggested to Cliff Carter at Democratic National Headquarters that he reproduce my review, as they were reproducing lots of pro-Johnson stuff at the time and mailing it out in bales. Carter's answer was, "Hell, no. If you'll read that review closely you'll see that what he's saying is Johnson isn't *that* bad!"

In presidential years, faced with the alternate choices of a psychotic Wallace or some dull Republican troglodyte, millions of us—effectively de-franchised for lack of a candidate—drag ourselves sullenly to the polls and vote for what those South Korean banners proclaimed as the "Great Texas Giant."

But this is a non-campaign year and this is a non-campaign book. And I think it is a pretty fair review of those portions of LBJ's career that, added up, prompt many of us to look upon the ol' boy as a fascinatingly rousing bastard.

Robert Sherrill

Washington, D.C.
November, 1966

Contents

1 Introduction: A primer of appraisal

*Nobody but the Americans could have invented a
President who poses as a peasant to conceal the
expert ruthlessness that conceals the fact that
he is a peasant all the time.*

—James Cameron in *The
New Statesman*, 17 June 1966

My purpose in writing this primer is to help others enjoy
Lyndon Johnson. Other writers, of course, are also working
in this field, but I find that one thing the critics in the White
House cannot understand is that different writers will be
useful in different ways. Not long ago I was commissioned by
The New York Times Magazine to do a piece on the Johnsons; when the White House learned of this, it exerted considerable pressure on the editors, unsuccessfully, to have the
assignment given instead to either Justice Abe Fortas or col-
umnist William S. White. An unimaginative protest. Fortas,
who was involved in Johnson's election to the Senate in 1948,
could do a splendid little insider's book on whether the 87
winning votes were intentionally stolen; White could hold

us all enthralled with a book on whether or not, as some people say, his columns are ordered by the White House and tailored to its latest line. Other writers will have other purposes. Mine are my own—very modest—only to show one way to enjoy the Pedernales' best-known weekend visitor.

The first thing we must do—and this is absolutely prerequisite to a better appreciation of Johnson—is admit that the man is not likeable and that he is, in fact, treacherous, dishonest, manic-aggressive, petty, spoiled, and above all, accidental.

This is definitely not criticism, no, but merely a suggestion at the outset that if Johnson is fair enough to ask to be measured, we should be no less willing to measure him by a scale of values of our own, though perhaps different from his. Lady Bird's lady-in-waiting, Elizabeth Carpenter, once counseled me, with tears on her cheeks, against becoming known as a "Johnson hater" (I had just written something that made her unhappy) and I earnestly hope to follow her advice. Hate, no; dislike, sí.

Come, let us admit it together: we do not like Lyndon Johnson.

But one should also admit at the outset that any final judgment of Johnson is not likely to do him justice. He is less disappointing than the sum of his defects. One might properly have expected nothing at all—or even worse, an Eisenhower—from a candidate who was elected with the approval of both *The Kansas City Star* and the *New York Post,* both the U.S. Chamber of Commerce and the AFL-CIO. He has risen above those cancellations almost heroically to stand for something—not much, but something. He came to power trailing a long retinue of skeletons, but not all of them are horrible to behold.

Perhaps he did steal the 1948 election, or somebody stole it for him; the man he defeated was a shriveled spirit who would have done nothing for Texas and less for the nation, a man whose hold on life was spelled out all too desolately in the nickname Texans gave him, "Calculatin' Coke." In whatever manner they got Johnson in the Senate, Texans should be grateful they did not instead wind up with an Allan Shivers or a Coke Stevenson.

Perhaps Johnson did win the 1964 presidential election by default, a default to which many liberals and moderates contributed by concluding from the slenderest of evidence that he was a peaceful man. As Senator McGovern has pointed out, if all Johnson's remarks on Vietnam in that campaign were put together, they would scarcely fill a typewritten page; he just kept quiet and let Goldwater make him seem a peacemonger by comparison. So we were misled. But at least Johnson was there to select, instead of Goldwater and instead of, among Democrats, the likes of Symington or Dodd.

Whatever his failings, Johnson is at least no pipsqueak. He is a man who respects power and devotes his whole being to it; he has given Americans a new concept of the tremendous powers with which the presidency is latent—something that for our safety we should be aware of, but which through the dreary retreat of the Eisenhower years and the amateurish, playing-the-game of the Kennedy years we had come close to forgetting. For this, we should be very grateful to Johnson. If he has been a servant of the special interests, he has resisted them more than most Texas politicians. If he came late to the movement of social reform—too late to know how really to participate—he has come part way at last, and for that we should be forgiving if not grateful.

We need to have these things well in mind, but not so much as to keep us from the pleasure of trying to discover why such a successful politician has always been such a miserable failure at the one basic job of a politician: appealing to people.

Take this test. Say that tomorrow he were assassinated.

This, after all, is an idea that some people have been taken with. A Congressional committee heard recently of the way an embittered Mexican-American father—broke and just turned down for a job—greeted the news of the assassination of President Kennedy: "Good. When do they get Johnson and the rest of them?" A speaker at a DuBois Club rally in Washington recently said that if he were drafted for the Vietnam war, "The first person I would like to have in my sights is Lyndon Johnson," to which the audience responded with happy shouts and laughter. The hungry unwashed know what is happening to them. "Negroes," said Claude Brown, Negro writer, appearing before the Ribicoff subcommittee, "really aren't as dumb as we look." The next witness—son of a prostitute, a father at fifteen and grandfather of a bastard at twenty-seven—disclosed to a probably unbelieving white world that the Negroes are well aware that the Norman Rockwell President has given them only a legislative sugar tit. "All the white community has tried to do so far is placate the Negro, keep the Negro cool. Twenty-five years ago they gave us Joe Louis and then eighteen years later they gave us Ralph Bunche. That didn't work out so well, so they give us civil rights bills."

This is the black mood clogging the hypothetical Harlem street down which the President rides on this hypothetical day (very hypothetical: he has *never* risked going into the heart of a slum). The President does not notice the mood; he is happy in his dreams of glory, embracing the multitude to make it whole with his touch. And then the shot. The crowd crests and breaks away. Johnson, who had been reaching for hands, falls folded over the side of the car. The dabbler in divine rights (but no pusher of anti-gun legislation) is gone.

And so we settle down for all the monstrous etceteras that follow such an event. Try to imagine the moment. Would we cry? Would we sit for three days staring into a television

screen or listening to the radio, a shroud of sodden human-
ity around the world? Would a Russian typist, as happened
after Kennedy's murder, come into the U.S. Embassy with a
pot of flowers and announce, half angrily, "No, I don't have
anything to do with America. I brought it because I liked
your President"? Perhaps. There would be some of that. But
I don't think much. We would not be glad that he was gone,
but not many of us would personally feel his going.

We might remember his signing of the education act at
the one-room schoolhouse in Stonewall, Texas, which he
attended; the reconstruction of his birthplace; the setting
aside of parkland across the road, looking to the day when
his ranch would be a national monument—these things done
by him in the spirit of Hadrian building his own tomb, we
might recall, and yet we would remember that we watched
them with the unkind but inevitable question in the backs
of our minds: which crony will get the concession? All that
prefabricated immortality for nothing. The great pity of
the moment would come from the knowledge that Johnson
would have given anything to evoke universal tears.

He knows this is the situation and there was one sunburst
moment in his life when he consciously acknowledged the
awareness; on returning to Washington from what was then
Texas' most recent rifle performance, the one that gave him
the presidency, he sat down and telephoned several officials
in Washington and several political chieftains around the
country, all with the same apology: "I'm the only president
you have." It was a pitiful admission for him to have to make
and for us to have to hear, and we pitied ourselves as we
looked upon the completed political tragedy. The loss, and
the manner of losing John Fitzgerald Kennedy, had led us
into a cave of crudities; the ascension of Lyndon Baines
Johnson, we rightly feared, would not lead us out again.

Reporters of all political persuasions joined the liberals in
dreading the future. Four months after the Dallas murder

the mood was still upon Karl Meyer, writing in *The New Statesman:* "In a sense, the U.S. seems to be drifting in a Gaullist direction of heightened nationalism. But, under Johnson, it would be a Gaullism without *grandeur.* The third LBJ—the exemplar of style—is returning to the old frontier; his presidential prose, one Kennedy aide said, is the worst since Harding's. JFK fascinated and exasperated intellectuals; LBJ has just been designated America's Number One by Arthur Murray, impresario of the dance studios. The White House has gone from Camelot to Johnson City, runs a current wisecrack, and that is about as far as you can go. In turning off the lights at the White House, Mr. Johnson has signaled the end of a brief era in more ways than one."

Henry Gemmill, chief of the Washington bureau of *The Wall Street Journal,* saw Johnson taking the presidency burdened with the latent image of an "opportunist whose mastery of pure politics is devoted not to principle but to personal ambition or even profit."

That mood has continued. Not long ago I was talking to one of the more urbane senators from the east coast about U.S. foreign policy and he explained that "since I am a believer in the political theories of those great men, Adlai Stevenson and John Kennedy, that *automatically* puts me at odds with Johnson." This seemed a matter-of-fact position to take and, if it was supposed to affect me as a monumental pronouncement, it had certainly failed, which the Senator apparently noticed because he thereupon burst out, shouting at me: "It's not so much that Mrs. Johnson reminds me of Lady Macbeth. But the parallel is there. Macbeth was power-mad. Johnson is power-mad. He's good at pulling rabbits out of a hat, but an arrogant bastard. Johnson is in the sere and yellow leaf of his life when he will believe only flattery. People tell him he is great to his face and behind his back they agree he is a son-of-a-bitch." This was a normally sweet-tempered fellow talking; the real Johnson had got under his skin. The man doth make J. Evett Haleys of us all. You hear and read the same reactions everywhere. From the hard-liners and the soft-liners, the cosmopolites and the beats.

Pete Hamill of the *New York Post,* after a long study of the protest movement, said, "One major reason, I suspect, for the virulence of much of the anti-Vietnam war movement can be traced to the character of Lyndon B. Johnson. Not a single student I've talked to in the past several weeks —left, right, and indifferent—respects the President. They think of him as vain, cornball, intellectually muddled, power-mad, paranoiac at times, an agent of the Lawrence Welk gang." A *Washington Star* writer went into Iowa recently and found that while the farms are prosperous and industry expanding, the Iowans did not like Johnson although he carried the state by 62 per cent in 1964. A high Democratic state official complained that Johnson "comes over to the people of Iowa as just a blob. People are distrustful and suspicious of his motives and his looks. Too smart. Too clever. Too slick. Too expedient."

It would be a mystic drudge to attempt to discover on how many Negro and Puerto Rican and half-breed hearts, broken by Johnson's promises, are inscribed the graffiti that Jack Newfield tells of seeing on the urine-splotched walls of Harlem: "LBJ eats it." Here, where rats grow fat and junkies grow lean, some dulled, probably diseased, certainly defeated, bastard son of a welfare digit will sometimes take his stolen chalk in hand and transfer the decal of the slum's broken heart; LBJ eats it. But of course this is an ugly, perhaps even what Bill Moyers would call an obstreperous judgment passed by brutish people who have had no way to judge the man as he really is. Nevertheless, it is the way the slum feels.

So those are the little people. Do the sophisticates feel differently? Yes, they feel even more queasy about the nation's leadership. Senator Morse suggests that there would be justice in Johnson's impeachment; Senator Gruening marks him as the master of deceit; Thomas Boylston Adams ran for the Senate in Massachusetts, with considerable praise and support considering that almost his sole issue was Johnson's "tyranny." Walter Lippmann, the most gentlemanly of columnists, is so stung by Johnson that he writes with uncharacteristic intemperance of the president's "ideological pretensions" that have sent him "off whoring after false gods"; and, after saying it would "take a man of noble stature and of the highest moral courage" to face up to the hopelessness of the U.S. venture in Vietnam, Lippmann realizes sadly that "there is no reason to think Mr. Johnson is such a man." And we have Emmet John Hughes remarking of Johnson's "maudlin sophistry," and the ordinarily tolerant James Reston marking Johnson down as a man somehow deficient in the most basic of civilized ingredients—"No president ever had so many confidants and so few friends." While overseas some see him as a madman (a recent article in a British publication defends Johnson only to the point of admitting that "of course, he is not technically insane"), here at home his myriad critics *usually* do not go beyond downgrading him as a dangerous clod. "Lyndon Baines Johnson is probably unique to the American presidency," writes Stan Cohen in *The East Village Other*. "One cannot imagine an act so small that he would not commit it, nor words so hollow that he would not utter them. He is a crescendo of hypocrisy and pettiness who has managed to congeal in one personality the worst elements of man's most honored traits. He is capable of anger but not passion, he is pious without being religious, tough without being brave, sincere without honesty, and vain without pride." Of course Cohen can be dismissed, by those who wish to do so, as one of those Greenwich Village fellows. But how does one discredit so easily *The Christian*

Century, which prints a less vicious but still comparable appraisal: "Less buoyant than Roosevelt, less upright than Kennedy . . . this man of fearsome rages and somewhat bathetic sorrows can in one sentence fulminate wildly about 'mashing the button' and in another agonize over sending American boys to possible death in Vietnam . . . No President has ever tried so hard to expose himself to the electorate and to win popular support, but no President has aroused such a combination of grudging respect and personal dislike from the public . . . Ruthlessness toward opponents and no-longer-useful underlings, continuous feeling about for new levers of power, lack of patience with criticism, complex wheeler-dealing as a means of ego satisfaction, suspicion of friends as well as enemies, readiness to deceive the public for its own alleged good, acceptance of questionable action rather than permitting a matter to drift without a morally ideal solution—all serve to identify Johnson as a man who has clawed his way to the top of his profession . . ."

The perpetually balanced phrase, the swing and the rhythm of this kind of demeaning—Johnson is this but not that, this but not that; less flip than flap, flap than flip; too much this, and this, and this—has a way of piling up in great spirals until it topples, and the reader comes away dizzy, and suspecting that accuracy was the victim of style; but it is the contradicting qualities of the man, not the necessary balancing and telescoping of phrase, that is to blame. "A man of his word but elusive, a spender but a budget-cutter, an internationalist but a provincial, a Democrat but Machiavellian, a sentimentalist but a cynic, he is many things but he is not a reflective man, not a man of personal grandeur," wrote Ronnie Dugger, editor of *The Texas Observer* in 1960, in an appraisal that still stands very well—with the exception that in the intervening years Johnson has learned how not to keep his word. Alan L. Otten, of *The Wall Street Journal,* four years later, after Johnson had had a year to wash the capital in his personality, saw him still as "an abnormally egotistical man" with "a disturbing tendency to nurture and brood over criticism; his unhappiness roils within him until it bursts out . . ."

Dugger on the moderate left and Otten on the moderate right. In between, Joseph Alsop, who certainly represents the bourgeois theorist at his Brooks Brothers best, has been provoked to a "question that has never before had to be asked in American history: whether it is possible to be a truly great President just by being a 'can-do' President, without the additional ingredient of a certain moral style? For all our truly great Presidents have had both qualities, until Lyndon Johnson came along. . . . And the fact has to be faced that President Johnson has an uninspiring, perhaps even a downright bad moral style."

What did Alsop mean? He specifically denies that he was referring to Johnson's predilection for sub-Snopesian language. "I told you to fix this fucking doorknob," Johnson is said to have yelled down the White House corridor at honest Jack Valenti, but all who have encountered inoperable finery will sympathize. These days, White House transients report, Johnson never refers to Robert Kennedy as anything but "The Little Shit." When the Central Intelligence Agency (CIA), after being discouraged and put off many times by Johnson, finally got him to sit down and be briefed on the Vietnam situation, he listened with iguana-lidded eyes for a while and then ended the interview with the tired question: "How the shit did we get into that place, anyhow?" Not a bad question however it is worded, and that, historically speaking, may not be the most inaccurate way. Johnson has often described his vision and his philosophy of global affairs in the same terms. Late in 1965, when his popular following in the Vietnam crisis was beginning to drift away in great clots, Johnson called in one of the top commentators for a national network and set to work trying to convince him that the Johnson policy was peaceful. As is Johnson's way, he spent most of the time attempting to explain why the best reason for believing in the Johnson foreign policy was that Johnson himself was such a good ol' boy; his motives were right because he had grown up hard; he knew how to get along with good ol' Ev Dirksen and besides all that, he didn't hate anybody. Did the commentator hate *him*? At this point Johnson had got everything, as he likes to do, right down to a personal basis, man to man, and at that level Johnson made the confession of his most intimate feelings about world affairs: "Everything, Joe, that isn't peace is chicken-shit."

The best quote in Michael Davie's book is Johnson's reply to a reporter who had asked a dumb question: "Why do you come and ask me, the leader of the Western world, a chicken-shit question like that?" Commonplace. A United Press photographer takes a picture of Johnson from the wrong profile and, the next morning after the picture has appeared in the local papers, he is singled out at an LBJ ranch press conference as "you sonofabitch." If all the photographers who had taken unflattering or proscribed pictures were gathered together with all the reporters who had written about his administration with timing or completeness that disturbed Johnson and were subsequently sonofabitched or chicken-shitted to their face, and with their colleagues listening, they would comprise an impressively large press corps.

But "if this were the only Johnsonian style problem," Alsop correctly goes on, "it would be enough to say that this style would be vastly improved if he more often showed in public the natural raciness which he displays in private." It would at least do much to counteract Johnson's claims of pious, Lincolnesque humility, which is a side of him, if it exists, that is the LBJ nobody knows.

No, Alsop meant something more dangerously basic; simply that Johnson "is not forthright, either with the country, or with his associates, or even, one suspects, with his nearest or dearest." The fault is not in the act of lying, however, but in his conception of the result. The horror of his misrepresentations is not that he hopes to rearrange reality *with* lies —but that he expects reality to adjust *to* lies, making them the cornerstone of a new reality. And so we are led to the place of national schizophrenia: we are for peace, we are against poverty, our President is an old New Deal Populist, he is masterful in handling Congress. This is all madness. A Texas politician once paraphrased Shakespeare, apropos of Johnson, "O, it is excellent to have a giant's strength; but it is insane to use it like a cardshark." Even worse, Johnson is determined to make us think that deuces are high.

Some people would probably want to add semiliterate to the list of Johnson's defects. Murray Kempton once commented sadly that, "In forty years we have come from a president who read nothing but what was on a fifty-cent piece, to a president who reads the backs of bookjackets he sees in other people's libraries." His authorized biographer notes that since he left college Johnson has probably not read six books through and that his reading consists "mostly of newspapers and memos." Yet it is not illiteracy that is to blame when he says something like this in a speech: "The raging quest and search for bread may bring on the reality of chaos." The turgidity of it, the American Legion armory-braying quality of it has nothing to do with polish or education but everything to do with instinct and spirit. Let us not get bogged down in a comparison of Harvard and Southwest Texas State Teachers College.

Many of us are marked by similar defects but we do not become presidents of the United States and that, like Robert Frost's chosen path through the yellow wood, makes all the difference. For one thing it makes the difference of fascination. A rather dull but persistent intra-office affair which began early in Johnson's life in the Senate and ended after he was vice-president is still discussed by Johnsonphiles as if it were a remembered passion from the court of the Sun King. Being president also makes the difference of forgiveness; what would send one man to prison only lowers the Harris poll for Johnson; what is judged a lie from one man is swathed in sociological cotton ("credibility gaposis") for him. Great conveniences suddenly occur for him. The pretrial hearings of Bobby Baker, for example, are solemnly deferred until after the November elections—for no reason except that it is not in Johnson's disposition to refrain from tampering with the rhythms of justice, and not in our disposition to question the good luck of presidents, luck which, in this instance, includes the amazing spectacle of the U.S. Justice Department rushing eagerly forward to confess that it had violated Baker's constitutional rights by bugging his telephone sixteen different ways, and thereby guaranteeing a very good chance of acquittal; it also guaranteed that much evidence would be excluded from his trial that might embarrass a former majority leader who once called Bobby "my strong right arm."

Because a man of Lyndon Baines Johnson's qualities is also in the world's most powerful political position we are usually prompted, as James Cameron has noticed, to invent another character for him. We say he is The Efficient Peasant, as if this somehow changes the rules of what we had previously accepted as a civilized game. It takes us no closer to an enjoyment of the man, as indeed he can be enjoyed in the manner of historians who play a kind of lusty jackstraw with the bones of Rasputin. Like the noble savage, The Efficient Peasant is a cumbersome myth anyway and better disposed of. Taking his cue from consensus, Johnson's successes have been, considering the demands of the day, no greater than McKinley's, who, as Joe Cannon once observed, had the Johnsonian habit of "keeping his ear so close to the ground he got it full of grasshoppers."

Forget the stereotypes the newspapers and weekly news magazines used to make of Johnson—the legislator possessed, the archarchitect of government—and look back over his career for yourself. After twenty-three years in Congress, Johnson left not one progressive piece of legislation with his name on it, not one piece of legislation that measurably advanced the nation beyond the stage in which he discovered it at the time he entered Congress in 1937.

Of his power there is no question. But where did it take the nation? It was during his years as the most powerful man in Congress that the permanent diplomatic and military establishment and the "New York foreign policy syndicate" were given the funds and the freedom by Congress to gain the overwhelming influence that they still have today and which it is not likely will be taken from them in normal fashion. Both the faculty and graduates of the Dulles School of Diplomacy, men who Galbraith correctly described as having "never raised their hands on behalf of any liberal cause in their life," were given the dominion by Johnson's Senate that they retain today under the Johnson Presidential Administration. Johnson recently said that the principle which guides him abroad is the same principle that guides him at home, and in that he is consistent and successful because in both places—with the profitable cooperation of the giant agrarian cartels, the construction and supply cartels, and the university contract-sociologists—he has, as senator and president, established welfare imperialism.

As for the business-military establishment which President Eisenhower warned of on leaving office in 1960, its linkage was welded permanently by the Johnson Senate. In this work he had ample help—Symington, Russell, Stennis, Thurmond, and in general all the Southern Visigoths—but the guidance and the exquisite cloak of patriotism cast over the effort was his. Although Johnson's Preparedness Subcommittee was supposed to be watching the competition and keeping us in the race, it was in those Johnson Senate years that Russia burst ahead of us in space apparatus development, where they were to remain without challenge for seven years; driven now by what seems to be a paranoiac and unreasonable pride, we will catch up, if at all, only after spending the most extravagant sums. These were the results of the years of Johnson's majority leadership: a couple of recessions, obsessed spending for national prestige, and heightened brinkmanship abroad.

His Great Society achievements have been less damaging. For the most part his program as president has been an adaptation of the Kennedy program, which even Kennedy recognized as only reviving the last ashes of the old New Deal, as the necessary first step to reviving a party that had almost lost its spirit under the Johnson-Rayburn leadership in Congress. Johnson's own touches are typified in a Food for Freedom program that offers tobacco and cotton to the world's hungry, and a teacher's corps for rebuilding the great rot of the central cities.

This latter point sounds like an exaggeration and, in a way, it is because it is quoting Johnson exactly. After the mayors of two cities had told Congress that they would need $65 *billion* over the next decade to save their cities—and dozens of other mayors were still to be heard from—a reporter asked Johnson what he suggested as the best thing to do immediately to save the dying cities. His answer: "The best thing Congress could do is pass my teachers' corps legislation." Thousands of stupefied dope addicts, alleys and hallways that serve mainly as depositories for garbage and through ways for rats, toilets that don't flush, toilets that don't exist, human and animal excretion that clog rivers, transit systems that don't transit, and feeder systems that don't feed—1,700 teachers should be able to fix it.

In less than two years Johnson started nearly a *billion* dollars' worth of construction in South Vietnam, relocated a million peasants, and shipped a small nation of men across the ocean to refashion the mores of South Vietnam. Rivers were dredged, dozens of docks and warehouses and landing fields were built, new sanitary systems and anti-pollution devices were introduced. The face of an entire country was, for better or worse, reshaped in two years. Where, in the same period of time, was a block—one block—transformed in an important slum in this country with federal money? I don't mean merely demolished. I mean made new.

The Johnson philosophy that has guided him for thirty years was loyally stated again by a member of the Attorney General's office on the occasion when highway patrolmen were knocking over the Mississippi marchers with tear gas canisters: "The President does not think we should go too far too fast."

At first glance it sometimes seems that Johnson's *ad hoc* domestic shiftings and neo-Hearst foreign relations have no unifying theme, but actually there runs throughout the steel thread of self-service. Possibly because very few British votes are cast in U.S. elections and because British officials can do him little good, Johnson could not find time to attend the funeral of Winston Churchill; but he slipped away from Washington to attend the funerals of Senator Richard Russell's nephew in Georgia, and Congressman Emanuel Celler's wife in New York, and Senator Harry Byrd's wife in Virginia, signifying his sorrow on the last occasion by kissing Senator Byrd's hand while the photographers asked for seconds.

With his own prestige on the line, Johnson traveled 5,000 miles to give his personal blessings to the regime of Vietnam's Premier Ky, whom Senator Clark accurately called "an evil little dictator, worse than the people we are fighting"; but with only the comfort of some Negroes at issue, Johnson would not walk across Pennsylvania Avenue to discuss the problems of a group of Mississippi sharecroppers who, desperately seeking to attract his attention, had camped in Lafayette Square. He spent $50,000 in counterpart funds to fly pro-U.S. reporters to Vietnam to explain "our side" through the foreign press; but he says he cannot find the counterpart funds to bring war-crippled children out of Vietnam for special treatment in the hospitals of Europe and the United States. He seeks five *billions* of dollars for building a supersonic transport (although most members of Congress acknowledge that its only usefulness is to subsidize the aircraft industry), but he asks Congress to cut the school lunch and school milk programs.

Injustice is a marginal notation on all federal budgets; but as the injustices of this season were consciously shaped by Johnson, with the full light of significant Congressional criticism upon him, they were intentional. Why does he act this way? Because he is a man of sudden eruptions of pity, but without a deep inner well of compassion. He is Old Faithful blowing from the crust only. During the 1964 Democratic convention, a top official of one of the national networks was surprised to receive a personal telephone call from the President himself. The message: "Get your goddamn cameras off the niggers out front [the Mississippi Freedom Democratic Party pickets protesting the seating of the Mississippi white delegation] and back on the speaker's stand inside, goddamn it!" "Niggers" and school children are expected to pace themselves by his fits of helpfulness.

In the opinion of Congressman Wright Patman, who served with Johnson's father in the Texas legislature and has known the President since he was a boy, "he is not a liberal but a do-gooder," and subject therefore to the limited attention and interest span of a do-gooder. He is directed not by a philosophy or a schedule of achievable progress but by glandular gooses, most of them brought on by the approach of November. One year he shapes the die for a better if not a great society, the next year he smashes it while continuing to call it great and, even more absurd, to call it a society. One year, when the Negroes were getting their heads bashed in by Sheriff Clark and Colonel Lingo, he sympathized deeply. The next year, when the Negroes began to fight back, he warned them not to be ugly.

The examples are endless, but one does not need them. It takes no close analysis to strip away the netting of "efficiency" to reveal the naked peasant beneath standing tall and lusty and arrogant behind the erection of his ambitions.

But at least the political peasant is alive in his peasantry. When Robert Lowell fouled Johnson's fine arts festival by orating against his Vietnam policy, Johnson responded later in such a way as to imply that he was being big about it; he used a line of Lowell's poetry, so identified, in one of his little speeches. Unfortunately, as any college sophomore could have told him, the line was not Lowell's but Matthew Arnold's. A New York newspaper called it one of the great presidential boo-boos of all time. A silly inflation of error. At least in that kind of human fumble Johnson comes alive; just as he did when, in signing a Peace Corps bill, he made the mistake of inverting Kennedy's famous "Ask not what your country can do for you, but what you can do for your country," and then catching himself, getting it right at last, and repeating it *five* more times in the same brief speech just to show the folks in the crowd that he really knew the right sequence all along. Only the most foppish Ivy Leaguer could be offended by that peasantry, or by the almost erotic pleasure Johnson enjoys rocking in his very own presidential rocking chair (with seal).

Ordering the presidential seal put on a pair of cowboy boots, and then in panic denying he gave the order; privately ridiculing his daughter's prissy, draft-exempt boyfriend as "Charlie"; unzipping the back of a congressman's wife's dress at a party—this is all trivia—the flattened sun-baked spoor of a wealthy Johnson City daddy—but without it the question might even be raised if he is not also—deprived of the artificial grandeur of office—invisible. Unlike Truman and Hoover and Eisenhower, outside the White House Johnson will be nobody. What reporter in that day of retirement, wanting a wise response to a question about economic matters, civil rights, or foreign affairs, will go to this man whose expression, Norman Mailer once noted, "stirs half-heard cries of death by suffocation of Western Civilization"?

He proved his latent invisibility as vice-president. He had been warned against taking the post. But Johnson was cocky. Thinking the powers relinquished to him by an easygoing Eisenhower and an indolent Senate were his own innate powers, he replied, "Power is where power goes." He went; power did not follow. He discovered there was nothing commanding in his personality or character after all. He discovered that, however awesomely established his name in the Quorum Club, he was not then and had never been to most of the country more than some vaguely feared riverboat politician who was rumored to control some Southwestern turf.

Vice-presidential jokes of today usually portray Hubert Humphrey as a smiling lackey; at least they give him a personality and role. Jokes dealing with Vice-President Johnson simply wiped him out. The CBS-TV program, *Candid Camera,* gave over a portion of one of its shows to the question: "Who is Lyndon B. Johnson?" Nobody knew. Typical was the man who responded, "No, I don't know him. I'm from New Jersey." A woman asked, "Should I know him?" Announcer: "He's a very famous person." Woman: "Well, God bless him." Ironically, he became almost well known for his invisibility. In the comic strip "Beetle Bailey," the Army barrack bookworm, Plato, and Beetle, the typical GI, were talking. Plato: "You don't hear much about the Vice-President any more. He's almost a forgotten man." Beetle: "Who?" Plato: "Lyndon Johnson." Beetle: "WHO?" The question could still be asked today, although Johnson wears the label, if not the cloth, of power with such a tailored arrogance that we are deluded into thinking we recognize the man beneath.

Surely there has never been a more sensual president, in the sense that he seeks to be a physical presence. Campaigning on the road is nothing more or less than, in his words, "pressing the flesh." It gives *him* a sense of identity; touched, *ergo sum*. In private conference, at least half of his persuasion comes from gripping the other person's arm, patting his knee, hugging him, poking his chest, whispering at touch-distance into his ear, shoving his face into the other's face until the warmth of his breath can be felt. For women, it is the kiss. A month after Kennedy's assassination, as the period of official mourning ended, Lady Bird gave a party for her lady friends. There were about twenty women there. Johnson came in and kissed each of them. At Lynda's graduation party, there were dozens of women, and Johnson conscientiously set out to kiss them all. Checking my photo file I find that he kisses Perle Mesta on the forehead, Mrs. John Connally on the mouth, Mrs. Philip Nichols, Jr. on the ear, Mrs. John McCormack on the mouth, Mrs. Chester Clifton on the cheekbone, and is kissed by Mrs. India Edwards on the neck. When the Democratic Women held their convention in Washington in 1966, converging for their final orgy on the White House itself, Johnson came by, though unscheduled, and kissed and was kissed in turn by the score. His pursuit of Courtenay Lynda Valenti, to poke, fondle, and kiss the child has been reported in great detail and frequency. *The San Francisco Examiner* estimated that at the end of Johnson's first 666 days in the White House he had kissed 666 women, but this was a gross undercounting of his activities.

Yet, for all that, for all the patting, hugging, kissing, poking, punching, and holding that the public has been subjected to either in the flesh or in news accounts, no president has been less identified with than Johnson, except, admittedly, by those soulless wanderers in the nether world of business. He simply does not come across.

Johnson has, by his own method of flyspecking history, contributed to our difficulties in seeing him. Somewhere along the line the vacuity of his private life—the sort of tepid new-rich existence that led a long-time acquaintance to describe him as "just a good ol' monolithic Texas daddy" —has been confused with the homeliness of Lincoln. He has helped create this awkward myth, and for some reason we have allowed him to get by with it. In judging his frequent misstatements of political fact, it is usually customary to describe them as being something besides lies. This is traditional leniency. Richard Nixon, for example, made a career of lying about his political deeds, and we weren't too hard on him about that. But we expect politicians to be honor bright about their private lives, and so we gave Nixon hell when he was caught trying to make us believe his wife was born on St. Patrick's Day.

Johnson has strangely escaped the same condemnation, perhaps because around his life he has spun such a cotton-candy web of self-pity and sentimentalism that we feel it hardly worth attempting to penetrate. Actually it can be done quite easily, using his mother's memoirs as a guide. He would not object to that. The elder Mrs. Johnson was by all odds the most intimately influential woman of several intimately influential women in his life. A strong-jawed, strong-willed woman (Johnson says that daughter Luci and Lady Bird are just like her), Mother Johnson pushed her two sons so hard their lives became a precipitous, pell-mell race. Brother Sam Houston Johnson could not keep up; he staggered to the beat of a different drummer. Lyndon made his getaway to

Congress. But he worshiped the domineering old woman ("All vocabularies fail when we attempt to describe Mother's traits"), and she worshiped him ("How dear to me you are you cannot know, my darling boy, my devoted son, my strength and comfort"). The President sometimes gets a little drunk at parties and whacks Lady Bird so hard on her bottom that it brings her up on her toes, and he tells smutty stories until her face freezes and cracks. But he was upright, obedient, and spoiled around Mother. Just as Kennedy revived the mode of the string quartet, Johnson has revived the reverence for the Mother pillow.

Who can help but have a real fondness for the memory of the old lady; although she was a person no less committed to the aggrandizement of LBJ than LBJ himself, she was geared to the old-fashioned motherized notion that what he did was grand enough without the aid of puffery. Bill Brammer, who used to be on Johnson's staff, tells of the day when Johnson, still in the Senate at the time, was escorting a group of reporters on one of those pilgrimages-to-the-family-shrine that were later to become so routine at The Ranch. They stopped in front of a ruined shanty about the size of a chicken coop and Johnson, stretching forth his hand and speaking in hushed and reverent tones, identified it as the place in which he was reared to manhood. His mother, who tagged along a lot with him in those days, piped up: "Why, Lyndon, you *know* we had a nice house over on the other side of the farm."

He has even proposed programs not for their logic or because they were responsive to social needs but only because Mother would have approved of them. Urging a group of newspaper editors to get behind a foreign aid program, Johnson put aside his prepared speech at one point to tell of a visit he once made to an African village where, in one hut, he saw a mother "with a baby on her breast, one in her stomach, and one on her back and eight on the floor." His voice skeetered into a lower register and bumped over the emotional phlegm it found there as he went on: "I thought of my own mother and the trials that she had raising her family. As I looked into this African mother's eyes, I saw the same look in that mother's eyes that I saw in my own mother's eyes when she was determined that her children would have food, clothes and an education." At the time he said that, his planes had already racked up a pretty good score of South Vietnamese mothers (and children), napalmed and bombed in villages thought to harbor, perhaps, a Cong or two. But Cong mammies don't fit into his Al Johnson act so well.

And when his own mother cannot be invoked to make a political point, just any mother will do. At the 1966 Prayer Breakfast, at which he was comforted by Billy Graham for escalating the war in Vietnam (the Reverend Dr. Graham likened Johnson to Christ, bringing a sword unto the world), Johnson likened himself and his needs and the weight of his burden to Lincoln and Lincoln's, after which, in Lincolnesque fashion, he whipped out a letter from a "dear little lady" whose son had been killed in Vietnam and who asked God to bless Johnson nonetheless. His voice thickening with emotion, Johnson told the prayer-breakfasters, "My countrymen, in those words from that dear mother . . ." etc. This was just before his first escalation of the bombings in North Vietnam.

Johnson has dredged up the woeful analogy between his mother and the peasant mothers of the world so often that most Americans probably think his mother was a poor widder-woman who had to scrape for a living. In reality Mother Johnson's situation was so unlike the African woman's as to leave her completely unconcerned about family economic matters. She was so careless with money and carefree with her time that she played at running her own weekly newspaper in Johnson City and whiled away

weeks at a stretch on trips to trace the family's genealogy
(back to the Tenth Duke of Marlborough, she claimed).
Her husband was the inheritor of property, a successful
businessman in his own right, and a state legislator who lived
high enough to have the Governor and other state officials
as guests in his home. "I have known poverty," Johnson told
a group of youngsters come to Washington for summer
employment. His father was so well-to-do that he moved
from Johnson City to San Marcos for no reason but to indulge himself in supervising the college careers of five children; after four years of paying most of the cost to put *five*
children through school, at a time when a college education
was considered something of a luxury, he moved back to
Johnson City and resumed ranching.

We are told repeatedly by Johnson of how he and other
members of his impoverished family were required to work
dawn to dusk in the hard-bitten soil of Central Texas (where
peach orchards flourish), a story somewhat spoiled when we
discover in the family archives the picture that shows they
were one of the few rural families in the area that could
afford an automobile before World War I.

Mother Johnson somehow was unaware that her son had
to shine shoes for a living (as he told a group of students);
she said Lyndon led the "normal, uneventful but enjoyable
life of a popular, fun-loving teenager." After high school he
had the chance to go to college but passed it by to bum
around in California and then return to take a job on a highway gang. To survive? No, for Saturday night money. He
was a trifling, undirected, boozing redneck—no better or
worse than most others turned out by the wretched rural
Texas schools of that day. Finally he decided he'd had
enough. What brought the decision? *He* remembers it as
an evangelistic moment when the woman he worshiped
pleaded with him to forsake his sinful ways; *she* remembers
it as a moment when he got sick of hard work and decided to

seek a softer career. In a *Saturday Evening Post* account of this melodrama, it is said that his parents "kept prodding him to 'make something of himself.' The President remembers the day his mother finally prevailed. He was sleeping late one Sunday morning, after a big night in town. 'I remember her coming into my room just as I woke up. She sat on the foot of the bed, and there was a sad look on her face.' 'I never thought my first-born would be content just to be a road-hand,' she said. 'It hurt me,' the President recalls, 'and I said all right, I'd go to college.' "

His mother, on the contrary, writes: "One raw, cold afternoon, Lyndon came in from a particularly unpleasant day on the highway and announced, 'I'm sick of working just with my hands and I'm ready to try working with my brain. Mother, if you and Daddy will get me in college, I'll go as soon as I can.' "

He recalls that his mother "went immediately to her desk and wrote a letter to Dr. C. E. Evans, an old family friend and president of Southwest Texas State Teachers College at San Marcos" to enroll Johnson. "She signed my father's name to the letter," a good authenticating piece of trivia, if accurate; only his mother said it wasn't so. *She* says she got up and "walked over to the phone" and called the college—their "poverty" not being so great, apparently, as to prevent their having what was then the luxury of a telephone and of placing long-distance calls.

As for the part-time job that he held in college, Johnson perpetuates the poor-boy theme by telling his biographers that he worked as a janitor "practicing oratory as he swept the halls." She has written that his work was not behind a broom but behind a desk "in the office of the president of the college."

There are three portraits of his pre-Congress self that Johnson prizes very highly: Poor Abe Lyndon, which we have already discussed; Lyndon the gay romantic; and Lyndon, Flying Ace. As the gay romantic, he has for years been saying that he proposed to Lady Bird on their first date. This she denies. In fact, she was not at all sure she could take his "intensity," according to one of her closest friends, Scooter Miller, wife of the Texas Gulf Sulphur lobbyist. Even after they were married, Mrs. Miller says, Lady Bird came to terms with her future only by deciding that "she had to do either of two things—get away from him before she was totally absorbed and dominated, or spend her life doing everything possible for him . . ." If his mother could do it, no less would be expected of her.

Lyndon, Flying Ace, wears a Silver Star in his lapel today. A dangerous mission during World War II? That's the legend. When arguing with Vietnam critics he will often gesture toward that pin as he launches into an argument that somehow conveys the general implication that his patriotism, tempered on a war's firing line, is greater than their own. How justified is that medal? Johnson had promised in 1940—true, it was only a campaign promise—that if war came he would resign from Congress and go to the fight with other Texas sons. Well, he didn't quite do that, but he did take an extended leave from Congress, going into uniform as a Navy Lieutenant Commander on December 14, 1941. He had a desk job in San Francisco from then until May 6, when he went into the Pacific as President Roosevelt's personal emissary. He arrived in the war sector on May 14. One month and four days later his tour of duty was over; a fever kept him in Australia a few more days but he was back in the States and out of uniform by July 16, 1942.

During his time in the South Pacific he started on one combat mission as an observer. The best summation of that mission was written by Byron Darnton of *The New York Times* on June 10, 1942: "The plane developed mechanical trouble and was forced to return without reaching its target."

It doesn't sound like the sort of episode one could write a book about, but Martin Caidin and Edward Hymoff, a couple of aerospace writers, managed to squeeze one out for Johnson's 1964 campaign. They interviewed members of the crew on which Johnson flew. They said they had been attacked by Japanese fighter planes. Nobody aboard was hurt; the plane returned safely to base. The only description of Johnson en route told of his looking through a small window on the left side of the plane, then looking through the plexiglas bubble in the plane's ceiling, and a couple of times looking through the cockpit windshield.

For doing this, General MacArthur gave the President's personal emissary a Silver Star for "gallant action" that "enabled him to obtain and return with valuable information." The Caidin-Hymoff book, certainly the most meticulous research done into Johnson's war career, fails to tell what the valuable information consisted of. Nobody on the plane's crew received a medal.

After one month overseas and one incomplete mission, Johnson returned to Congress where he continued to put together another myth, that of Lyndon, the Congressional Creator, and ultimately the Masterful President, myths which this primer is largely aimed at correcting.

2 The exercise of pique

I am the most denounced man in the world.

—Lyndon Johnson, 1965

*Yet, Washington knows him, too, as a warm,
out-going, gentle person whose interest in the "little
things" affecting the families of his colleagues,
friends and employees is legendary.*

—LBJ campaign brochure, 1960

A great deal has been written about Lyndon Johnson's
secrecy, about his manhandling of the press corps, about his
falsehoods and misrepresentations. The picture that grows
out of all this is of a touchy tyrant who does not want anyone butting into what he considers to be his business, even
though others judge it to be the public's business. Senator
Wayne Morse warned recently that it would be hard to find
"another time in the history of the Republic when the danger is as great as it is at the present hour in the development
of a government by executive supremacy and secrecy." There
is such a trend, although it is not quite so threatening as
Morse makes it out to be.

There are several reasons for this, the most comforting being that this ranging, obstreperous land produces too many reporters and too many politicians who won't be shut up and who won't be kept from scrabbling for the facts, and who resent presidents who try to intimidate them. But almost as comforting is Johnson's built-in weakness: he freezes. He can be beaten and when he is beaten (or when he imagines he has been, which is even oftener), he freezes into postures that encourage others to take him on. He is really a rather insecure fellow.

Going back into his homeland for a prime example: before the 1956 national convention, Johnson met secretly with Texas' reactionary governor Allan Shivers and agreed to support Ben Ramsey as Democratic national committeeman if Shivers would back Johnson for the favorite-son nomination. When this deal became known, the Texas liberals were furious with Johnson. Ramsey, then lieutenant governor, presided over the Texas Senate like an old gray hawk. Every time a little wobbly lamb of progressive legislation came into the chamber, he swooped down and disemboweled it. *No* progressive legislation passed through that chamber during the nine years he perched in the chair.

The most furious editorial written in response to Johnson's betrayal of their cause was by twenty-four-year-old Ronnie Dugger, editor of *The Texas Observer,* a liberal weekly. One might have expected Johnson not to be much upset by that. *The Observer* was an impoverished paper, operating then (as now) out of one room; sometimes Dugger had an assistant, sometimes he ran the paper alone, but it was never anything but a minuscule operation. It is true that although he was only a couple of years out of college, Dugger was already the finest reporter in the South; he singlehandedly uncovered enough scandal in Shivers' administration to ruin the man, and his paper was the editorial voice of a quarter of a million fanatical liberals. Nevertheless, the rickety *Observer* has never had a circulation of more than 7,000, and Johnson, then at the very zenith of his power in the Senate, supported by 114 daily newspapers in Texas, could easily have ignored Dugger's blast.

To the contrary, Johnson apparently was devastated. He could not force Dugger's support because *The Observer* had practically no advertising to cut off through pressures. He was nevertheless determined to make a supporter out of him, and so he summoned Dugger to the ranch. All day he held him there, flattering, threatening, pleading, coaxing. "I don't hate *you*," he would say, tapping Dugger on the knee, stroking his arm, hugging him, and leaving the way open for Dugger to give the same assurance in return. But though their statuses are very different, Dugger's ego can match Johnson's any day, to say nothing of his righteous certainty. So long as Johnson was a political sinner, he would say so. When the day was done, Dugger had not budged. He was still his own man. And when the two parted at the gate that night, Johnson was through with him. Furious with him, he was also afraid of him. For years Johnson would not even talk to other reporters if Dugger were present. Even today when top Texas labor leaders, or others who conceivably have some persuasion with Dugger, visit the White House, often Johnson will ask them, "Can't you get Dugger to lay off?" (meaning, lay off the Johnson-Texas machine). Johnson has ridden high and wide in the intervening decade, but he has never been able to get rid of that 7,000-circulation burr, and he has never ceased to be aware of it. The most he can ever hope to do is defame Dugger, and this he tries. "If you look back in that line," he will sometimes say to a visiting Texas politician, "somewhere you'll find a dwarf."

When he meets his match, Johnson invariably reacts in one of two ways: if he is beaten, or held to a standoff, by someone he considers weaker than he is, Johnson becomes a spotted ass; if by someone he considers his equal or his superior, he becomes a sycophant. As an example of the latter response: after Wayne Morse had followed his conscience out of the Republican party in 1952, supporting Adlai Stevenson publicly and eloquently (something Johnson did not do), Johnson agreed to let the Republicans punish Morse in the 1953 Congress if in return Johnson would be allowed to have all the fractional ratios on committees to distribute among the Democrats. But when Morse learned of the horse trade, he refused to lie down and take it. Going to an obscure footnote in the Senate rule book, he insisted that he receive his committee assignments from the Senate as a whole. Johnson, who gloried in a reputation for knowing the rule book, knew nothing of this provision. He turned purple. It took weeks of caucusing to work his way through the Morse "punishment," and thereafter he had a quavering schoolboy awe of the Oregon senator.

A couple of years later Morse went to Texas and made a speech to a Houston meeting of liberals in which he said— and it made front pages all over the state—"Why don't you elect yourself two senators? You have none now. One [Price Daniel] represents the oil and gas industry, and the other represents Lyndon Johnson." Did Johnson become outraged and seek bloody vengeance on Morse? No, he was still whipped. The next time Morse stepped into the Senate chamber, Johnson pulled him aside, grinning, and said, "Wayne, you really did it to me that time! I've got to go down to Texas now and not just mend my fences—I've got to dig some new postholes!" Ha, ha, ha. He can be a real, easygoing sport when he's dealing with someone he can't hurt—a tough senator, the Business Council, Mr. Henry Luce—but when he's dealing with just the wage-earning press, it's the old spotted ass all the way.

He has imposed a news management such as Washington has not seen in modern times. A couple of years ago Ted

Lewis of the New York *Daily News* said, "The clam-up is on an almost unprecedented scale"; about the same time, Alan Otten of *The Wall Street Journal* wrote, "Veteran Washington reporters can't remember when it was so hard to obtain inside insight into an administration's short-term or long-term plans—from the President himself, from the White House associates, or from Cabinet members and other high-level officials. The President and those few intimates who may know what's in his mind simply aren't saying anything much beyond self-serving platitudes; most other federal officials just don't know what the President has in mind." Robert J. Donovan complained, "Proposals regarding the form and dimensions of federal aid to education are guarded as carefully as if they were war plans or diplomatic codes." Johnson was less than three months into his manifest destiny and already the Rose Garden Curtain, as one Congressman called it, had fallen. Since then, things have got tighter.

Yet the government is too big, the places through which news can leak too common, and the stubbornness of the best newsmen too great; Johnson's efforts at secrecy are foiled as often as not. Even the accident at the White House party, in which Mrs. Henry Ford, while dancing with Johnson in a perilously low-cut gown, suddenly found too much of herself exposed on one side—an accident subsequently identified among Washington gossips as "the fall of New York"—even this was duly reported by a couple of the more daring society columnists, in time, though the White House tried to cover it up. Sometimes newsmen must even go so far as to milk foreign journals, even Communist journals, for the facts. Thus it was through the New China News Agency that the U.S. attack on the Plain of Jars became known, and through the Peking news agency in the Congo that the U.S. strikes against rebels in Kivu province were first told. One way or another, the important stuff leaks out.

Occasionally Johnson's hyper-emotionalism pulls the stopper on his own secrecy; thus, carried away by the excitement of a friendly reception in Australia, Johnson let it out that the war in Vietnam was costing us at least $2 billion a month— a figure twice as high as he had ever acknowledged while his feet were on home soil.

Johnson has never been used to dealing with a free press. The longer he was majority leader, the worse his press relations became. After a very brief interlude of calculated friendship for the press during his early months as president, he reverted to his old ways. It is not just that he has his run-ins with reporters, something common to every president's life; with Johnson the trouble gushes up from a deep well of antipathy ("Someone ought to do an article on *you*," he fumed at a team of *Newsweek* reporters, "and your damn profession, your First Amendment!"). When Robert E. Kintner, former president of the National Broadcasting Company, came to work at the White House, Johnson said he didn't want to keep Kintner in any one position too long "because he gets too familiar with you [the press] and familiarity breeds contempt." Johnson believes the feeling is mutual and that only his august position prevents his being torn apart by the bloodthirsty pack. Robert Fleming, who occasionally serves as Johnson's press aide, said that when he came to the White House Johnson told him, "Some of the press respects me some of the time, but none of the press will ever respect you."

His efforts to manage the news have been as ingenious as they have been persistent. Richard McGowan of the New York *Daily News* is convinced that in the days when George Reedy was press secretary at the White House, Johnson had the Reedy office bugged to eavesdrop on the information his assistant was giving out. McGowan said it was a rare day when the Reedy press session was not stopped by a blinking light on the third button, right-hand side, of

Reedy's desk telephone. He would pick it up and whisper yessir, yessir, yessir, put the phone back down and change something he had just said. "It was no secret," said McGowan, "who was on the other end of the line, since all other calls to Reedy were usually held up until the briefing was finished."

No detail of news coverage is too petty to discourage Johnson from pursuing it. It comes as something of a shock to a wire service editor when he receives a telephone call from the President himself with the information that tourists who visit his boyhood home *will not* be charged admission, contrary to earlier reports; but in doing this Johnson is simply continuing a lifetime habit. Years ago when he passed through Corpus Christi, Texas, he noticed that the news photographer took a picture from the taboo side of his face. He called Robert Jackson, editor of the local paper and a roommate of Johnson's in the early thirties, and had the picture killed. With the big name reporters of Washington, Johnson cannot get by with much vengeance, but he still tries heavy persuasion. In his book *This Awesome Challenge: The Hundred Days of Lyndon Johnson,* Michael Amrine has an excellent compilation of the Johnson flattery in the early days of his presidency—fish fries and limousine whoopee rides and chicken dinners and boat rides for the likes of Tom Wicker and Douglas Kiker and Phil Potter and Hugh Sidey; special planes for the bigger guns like James Reston; flattering sit-next-to-me-honey treatment for Hearst's Marianne Means; and special personally-conducted tours through the White House, including peeks at what Mrs. Johnson coyly calls "the presidential potty," for favored women reporters.

Johnson thought to ingratiate himself as one of the boys; out of that misdirection came the ninety-mile-an-hour beer-in-hand ride across the Central Texas hillside—and the resulting publicity that convinced him once and for all that

newsmen are squealers.* For some reason the thought never
occurred to him that he should be ashamed for risking his
life, when, if he had lost it, the nation would have fallen
into the senile hands of a Hayden or McCormack. Somehow
the thought escaped him that the reporters might be com-
mended for not being stoppered by a presidential wink, a
Johnsonian hug, a free guzzle of Lone Star beer, or even a
naked swim with the great man. Management was what he
had been after, and when management hadn't resulted, he
stopped acting the wide-open pal and resumed being the
cold, cold smoothie with the razor blade eyes.

Charles Roberts, who has covered the White House a
dozen years for *Newsweek,* is among the many newsmen
who have felt the edge of Johnson's displeasure at questions that might dislodge a portion of the image he intends
to convey to the world. "On easy or self-serving questions,"
says Roberts, "he can mount a genial filibuster. But on
questions that probe ever so slightly—and politely—at some
issue on which he is sensitive, he bristles and turns scorn-
fully on his inquisitor. I asked him whether he thought the
Vietnamese war would hurt his party—the Democrats—in
the fall election. I thought it was a reasonable question. Certainly it is on the minds of a few voters. The President's
response was to glare at me as though I had just burned a
draft card. 'I don't *really* believe,' he replied, lowering his
voice, 'that any of you want to make this a Democratic or
a Republican army, or air force, or navy, or war . . .' He
continued in that vein for a few sentences, then, having
chastised me for an unseemly suggestion I never made,
went on to answer—or evade—the next question. This was
not an untypical exchange. The fact is, Mr. Johnson, in a

---

* LBJ was back at the wheel in December, 1966, and driving 100 miles
an hour over Texas roads—through fog. Of course it was a front page
story; but the most startling aspect of the public's reaction was that there
was so little. It was almost as though everyone had stopped caring.

news conference, is the most frustrating president of modern times. Ike, despite his tangled five-star syntax, usually told us what he thought. Mr. Kennedy gave witty answers, but was basically an artful dodger. President Johnson, though he has a firmer grasp of issues than Ike, and just as firm a purpose as Mr. Kennedy, is neither candid, nor artful, nor witty."

Roberts had violated the banana-republic mystique that holds the press to be just another tool of the government, like the Bureau of Printing and Engraving, where paper is cranked out to purchase an advantage. By suggesting that there was a division of opinion in the country, Roberts was flirting with treason. It is *not* a Democratic or Republican army; it is a Johnson army fighting a Johnson war, and Roberts had better get behind it.

Constitutional safeguards are neatly ignored to achieve a new utility. Robert Roth, Washington correspondent for the *Philadelphia Bulletin,* put his finger on one of the more critical of these transformations: "The President has taken a position not espoused—publicly at any rate—by any other president. This is that it is the function and the duty of the press to promote and defend the position of the Administration with other nations." When reporters tried to dig information as to why the U.S. had invaded the Dominican Republic, Johnson accused them of putting their nation on trial, a charge he repeated when they got too nosy about the Vietnam war.

When newspapers across the country prominently used a picture of an anti-government Vietnam soldier being shot down while he held his hands in the air, White House aide Fleming protested that this was working against Johnson's efforts to portray the Vietnam government as a responsible outfit, and therefore the picture shouldn't have been used. Charles Mohr, a *New York Times* war correspondent, said the administration was always trying to get reporters not to write about the natives being cooked in napalm or riddled by antipersonnel bombs dropped by U.S. forces. "They want to make it a sanitary war," he said. Of course, Johnson is certainly not the first president to lose sight of the proper role of the press in a time of military stress. Roosevelt "awarded" a White House correspondent an Iron Cross for writing a story which Roosevelt thought aided the enemy, and Kennedy put the squeeze on *The New York Times* to be silent about the Bay of Pigs build-up. Johnson's main problem is that he is just more crude about it.

When Johnson was majority leader, he frequently insisted that news conferences proceed along predetermined channels of inquiry. If a reporter veered too far from that course, Johnson would abuse him and sometimes demand that he leave the group. The same technique, more subtly applied, was used after he became president. Press aide Bill Moyers used to plant questions with certain newsmen before a conference; it was done, he said, because the conferences were for the "convenience of the President, not the convenience of the press" and he wanted to be sure the President was asked the questions he wanted to answer. There is some pretense now that questions are no longer planted, but out-of-Washington newsmen are convinced it is still going on. At a press conference on the ranch, Texas newsmen almost never get to ask a question; Johnson calls on eight or ten of the White House traveling reporters by name, giving them "not an answer but a response," as one nonrecognized reporter described it peevishly, and then the conference is closed. Sometimes the whole thing has the appearance of a dress rehearsal.

Johnson's anger at "leaks" is well known, yet he himself will sometimes let out highly secret defense information in order to help along a budget request or to inflate the polls. At a White House news conference on June 18, 1966, he said, "We must continue to raise the cost of aggression at its source," which many newsmen properly took to mean that Johnson had decided to bomb the North Vietnam fuel dumps, as he indeed began to do a few days later. When they wrote their stories speculating on this possibility, he acted outraged and said he was going to make an investigation of "the leak."

His reaction to reporters' speculations about what he will do next is nothing short of psychotic; he has been known to cancel the planned appointment of an important official simply because some reporter had discovered, and written, that it was about to be made. On other occasions his response is simply to lie. At his first press conference after the 1964 election, Johnson upbraided reporters for speculating that he would shortly escalate the war in Vietnam (although generals at the front were talking about it openly), and that he was about to put Marvin Watson on his payroll. Ridiculous, said Johnson—even though Watson already had a desk in the White House. In March 1966, Johnson interrupted a press conference being held by Agriculture Secretary Orville Freeman to ridicule a just-published news story that U. Alexis Johnson would succeed Edwin O. Reischauer as ambassador to Japan. He hooted it down as a rumor started by "some kid" over at the State Department. Not long after that, U. Alexis Johnson became ambassador to Japan.

Why he does it is anybody's guess. Charles Bartlett thinks it is "part of his Walter Mitty image as the man who has everything under close control"; that is, reality must await his pronouncement.

There are few ways to shepherd newsmen together that Johnson has not tried as a method of influencing them or at least of dominating the moment. He has of course tried the technique of the favored few, a half dozen or eight or ten reporters selected with no eye for geographical distribution of their publications' circulation. It is a kind of

Socratic circle, the wise strongman in his chair, and around him—some of them sitting on the floor, listening to his soft-spoken words, often unable to hear him distinctly, afraid to interrupt with a sharp question for fear of ending the interview—are the uncomfortable, unappeased few. He still uses the technique, but it doesn't work too well; the left-outs are too disgruntled.

More often he uses the "fast draw" news conference, which the twenty or thirty reporters who regularly cover the White House will be able to attend, but not the reporters of specialties who cover the State Department or the Pentagon and whose appearance would mean questions more likely to penetrate the Johnsonian smoke. He once said he most preferred to go to the American people over television, yet a "pool" television team camped in the White House for a year without once focusing their cameras on the President. By selecting the reporters he wants to confide in, and avoiding those he doesn't want to even speak to, Johnson does not do a bad job of managing the news.

One of the oddest methods Johnson utilizes in trying to outwit the press is a kind of Chicken Little hyperbole which, of course, he no sooner gets out of his mouth than the reporters check, and print; and then he is enraged at them for revealing once again his psychotic side. For instance, when Johnson was in South Korea on his Asian swing he told a crowd, according to Marquis Childs, that his great-grandfather died at the battle of the Alamo; Childs commented dryly that this came as quite a revelation to the Texas newsmen on hand. Indeed it should have, for the list of those who died in the Alamo is well known, and if Great-grandpa Johnson was in that fight, he was on the side of the Mexicans.

Probably the best example of the Johnsonian interview extravaganza occurred after he had sent the Marines into the Dominican Republic. Some people were accusing him of pulling a piece of dictatorial intrusion in another country's affairs. Johnson fought back in his press conferences with all the imagination—which is considerable—at his command. With a sob in his throat he told why those gentle U.S. Marines were down there; he told why, "It has been necessary for a few Marines to go out and take an old lady and her little belongings and with a crippled hip, carry her down through the streets where the firing is taking place . . ." Yes, but more than that, they were there to protect United States citizens (he did not mention that a U.S. citizen has not been shot in a Latin-American uprising this century). "There has been almost constant firing on our American Embassy. As we talked to Ambassador Bennett, he said to apparently one of the girls who brought him a cable, he said, please get away from the window, that glass is going to cut your head, because the glass had been shattered, and we heard the bullets coming through the office where he was sitting while talking to us."

That story was told on May 5, 1965. By June 17, he was warmed up to do better. On that day, in a press conference which one reporter called "a truly alarming stream of Presidential consciousness" and another reporter, one of the most respected Latin-American specialists, described as "drunk, if you ask me," Johnson embroidered a bit more: ". . . some 1,500 innocent people were murdered and shot, and their heads cut off, and . . . as we talked to our ambassador to confirm the horror and tragedy and the unbelievable fact that they were firing on Americans and the American Embassy, he was talking to us from under a desk while bullets were going through his windows and he had a thousand American men, women and children assembled in the hotel who were pleading with their President for help to preserve their lives."

Alas, none of this was true. None of it was offered as the truth, or even as a rumor, until Johnson spun it out. William Tapley Bennett, Jr., who had been the ambassador under siege, said later that he could not recall any bullets coming into his office; he did *not* take cover under his desk. The beheadings were imagined. No U.S. citizen was harmed; none was threatened. (Two newsmen were shot by U.S. Marines, though.)

When august hyperbole won't work, he tries forgetfulness. (It must be forgetfulness.) At his press conference of April 27, 1965, he said, "I have always opposed the poll tax"; it had slipped his mind, apparently, that during his Congressional days he voted at least a dozen times (some have counted 16 such votes) between 1942 and 1960 either directly or indirectly to perpetuate the poll tax. Midway through his Congressional career, in a campaign newspaper circulated in 1948, Johnson acknowledged that "I have voted against the anti-poll tax law . . . every time it has come up in Congress." One of his first speeches as a Senator (March 9, 1949) was to proclaim that he would "stand on the floor of the Senate as long as I have the will, the determination, and the breath to oppose . . . the proposed anti-poll tax measures."

Not long before the 1966 November elections, Lyndon Johnson whipped into New York for a little politicking and, while there, paused at the Verrazano Memorial on Staten Island to tell a group, "I like the view from this bridge. Passing over it, I saw the Statue of Liberty where, just a year ago, I signed a law to erase *a shameful period in American history*. Within sight of Verrazano's bridge, we wiped out an immigration policy which was a *standing insult* to his countrymen, and to people from many nations."

The immigration bill which Johnson referred to was passed and signed in 1965, giving Italians, among other nationalities around the Mediterranean, an easier access to our shores. But once again Johnson had shown a knack for forgetting the ugly moments in his life. *He* had helped perpetuate that "shameful period in American history" and that "standing insult" to the Italians. In 1952, when Truman attempted to veto the McCarran Immigration Bill, which discriminated against Italians as well as other swarthy races, Johnson was among those who successfully overrode the veto. And the same year, when the liberals in Congress offered a substitute to the McCarran Act, Johnson voted with those who killed it. The next year Senator Ives specifically offered legislation to liberalize the emergency refugee statutes to permit more Italians into the country. Johnson voted with those who defeated the proposal. Throughout his career in the Senate, in fact, Johnson's record was that of a typical Southerner, voting against the wops, gooks, wogs and spics, of the world.

Sometimes his misstatements are explainable as strategy. When, in August of 1966, Marine Commandant General Wallace M. Greene told newsmen in South Vietnam that Pentagon studies showed the war would probably last between five and eight years longer, Johnson hastily denied that any such studies had ever been made; he also denied that Greene had said such a thing. That kind of lie can be understood. But sometimes he seems to lie just for the practice. Why else did he bother to lie about the political trips which he had planned to take after the Asian junket? "The people of this country ought to know that all these cancelled plans primarily involve the imagination of people who phrase sentences and write columns and have to report what they hope or what they imagine," he said acidly at his November 3rd press conference. His sickness would have been a reasonable excuse, but, no, he had to deny the politicking had ever been considered—although Moyers had told newsmen, before they left Manila, that Johnson planned to stump perhaps as many as eighteen states; privately, Democratic leaders across the country were told of this even before Johnson left the country. On an earlier occasion he had told the press that of 125 peace candidates across the country, not one had survived the 1966 primaries. There had been fewer than 100 peace candidates, and nine had survived. Why lie about such a relatively trivial matter, when the belligerent candidates had indeed dominated the field to a degree that should have been pleasing enough to him?

When Johnson announced on October 15, 1965, his upcoming gall bladder surgery he emphasized that "a thorough examination showed this to be the only trouble." After the operation Johnson's physician disclosed that a kidney stone also had been removed, that Johnson had known about the kidney stones all along, and in fact that there were still some stones rattling around inside the great leader. Why lie about a little ol' stone? Well, why lie about an appointment either? Johnson told reporters on July 27, 1965, that he hadn't the faintest notion whom he might appoint to fill the Supreme Court seat vacated by Arthur Goldberg. The *next day* he announced the appointment of Abe Fortas, who had spun his legal career tightly around Johnson's political life, all the way from the 1948 ballot box imbroglio to the 1964 caper when he went around Washington begging newspaper publishers and an assortment of Establishment newsmen not to print stories about Walter Jenkins' mischief at the Y. Had Johnson just decided—like that—to appoint his pal? Had he no idea he would do this even before enticing Goldberg off the bench? Anyone who believes that, believes Johnson is an honest man.

Some of his best fudging is done by proxy. The Reverend Moyers, his former press aide, for example, was just as good at misrepresenting the President's physical condition as the President himself. Two hours before Johnson announced his post-Far East-tour surgery, Moyers told an inquiring newsman that the President's condition was tip-top, sound as a drum. Later asked why he had said such a thing, Moyers explained with Bible College seriousness that the

President *was* fit as could be, *except* for the growth in his neck and the ruptured inner wall. Moyers did his lying chores with loyal grace, arousing little animosity from the press corps except on the really big lies, as when he said the White House had nothing to do with shaving the steel price increase in early January, 1966. He said he hadn't the wildest idea "with whom any of the steel company officials might have met." It later turned out that the Administration had put tremendous pressures on the steel companies, and that none other than Roger Blough, president of U.S. Steel, had come to Washington to be coerced by Secretary of Defense McNamara.

Early in 1965, after several reporters had complained in print about Johnson's seeming avoidance of news conferences, he retaliated by giving the 2,000 or so newsmen who cover Washington a half hour's notice that he was about to have a conference; then he selected as his site the theater in the basement of the White House. It can hold about fifty persons without cramping; about 200 came that day. White House police warned reporters not to smoke because "we don't have any ventilation in here." Johnson showed up twenty minutes late.

His phobia of being upstaged—the kind of slight madness which resulted in his calling the disastrous Honolulu Conference with Premier Ky on the spur of the moment solely to draw attention away from Senator Fulbright's Vietnam hearings—appears in his handling of press conferences. After the bloody Sunday at Selma, Johnson announced that he would hold a press conference but that it would be in his office and open only to pencil journalists—no mikes, no TV cameras. Then Governor Wallace came to town, had a three hour talk with the President and emerged to tell newsmen about their "frank, forthright, and friendly" chat, and to promise more comments the next day on television. With the show being stolen, Johnson nervously rearranged everything: giving the press corps only fifteen minutes' notice, he shifted the locale for his own conference from his office to the rose garden and permitted not only radio and TV paraphernalia to be at hand, but even permitted movie cameras on the roof of the White House west wing. When a reporter needled him about it, Johnson exploded. *He* would call his press conferences when and how he wanted to! (Nobody would deny that.) The press certainly had a lot of gall complaining, when "I have had forty-six press conferences since I have been president"! He was counting three dozen unscheduled rambles around the rose garden with only the pressroom regulars and the dogs padding along behind, some reporters so far back that they could hear nothing but a faint presidential drone up ahead. At the time he boasted of having had forty-six press conferences, he had had only three regularly scheduled sit-down ones in the past year. That was not the last time he used a press conference just to drown out the opposition; Goldwater came to town to talk to the press at a meeting that had been scheduled for a week, only to have it obliterated by a conference Johnson called on an hour's notice to discuss routine stuff.

And there are other techniques. Reporters who have written things which angered him to an unforgiving degree sometimes find they cannot get White House credentials. *Pravda* reporters can, but not they. I have known several magazine writers whose assignments to do studies of White House personalities were canceled by Johnson pressure. Bill Brammer had the movie production of his novel, *The Gay Place,* nipped the same way. The *New York Review of Books* editors were subjected to a bit of fruitless White House intimidation for using I. F. Stone, one of the sharpest critics of Johnson's foreign policy, to do a review relating to the missile program. Doubleday & Co. bowed to the hysterical complaints of Mrs. Johnson's press secretary, Elizabeth Carpenter—"*Tranquilizers* for Blanco? You just can't write things like that about a *President's* dog!"—and canceled a book about two of Johnson's pets. One of the best television newsmen in Washington tells me that when he and his colleagues persist in exposé-type reporting over the administration's protests, they can expect to hear that certain ones of LBJ's aides have started putting it around that they are "untrustworthy" or "dishonest." Since Johnson does the same thing to congressmen, he cannot be expected to refrain from intentionally damaging the reputation of reporters who, of course, rank much lower with him.

Newsmen who depend on a number of papers to stay in business have lost clients for the same reason. Sarah McClendon asked stiff questions of the president at a news conference; Moyers followed her out of the room and inquired "Why are you so interested in Johnson's business?" She said she had been ordered to by a San Antonio newspaper. Two days later she no longer was a reporter for that paper. Regular White House reporters who do stories that offend Johnson—but not so much that their credentials are taken away—are banished from the Presence for a time. One such reporter, who wrote that Johnson was a "people eater" —meaning, in this case, an employer who consumes the time and spirit of his staff so relentlessly that they must flee into other jobs—received word through the White House underground that Johnson said he would not speak to him again until he had written a pro-Johnson story to cancel the offense.

Johnson has never seen news as anything but a commodity, a quid that can be bartered for some quo up his sleeve. Shortly after he became president, his then press secretary Reedy went around hustling the White House correspondents for a "good story." One of these men, a Houston reporter, didn't know what Reedy meant until he discovered that he was being cut off from news sources and news tips relating to his area. When he complained, Reedy told him, "I haven't seen your good story yet." So the reporter wrote one, so "good" that his editor damned him as a tool, until it was explained that flattery was the coin of Johnson's realm. The story went into type. Stronger newsmen and stronger newspapers would not—consciously—do such a thing.

On no point is Johnson more sensitive than on the coverage he receives from the society writers. In Washington's party world his desire for acceptance and his insecurity reveal themselves as nowhere else. Well remembered is the painful occasion when, as vice-president, he showed up at an embassy party, the only one (other than the butler) to be wearing a white tie. Johnson kept his hand to his throat all evening, sometimes ducking behind Lady Bird to avoid a photographer, seeming to feel that if the nation discovered he had not worn a black tie he would be ruined. This was no exceptional occasion. He reads every line of what the major society writers say about him. Once he called Senator Morse off the floor during an important debate to read to him over the telephone a trivial comment made by *Washington Star* society writer Betty Beale. When the watusiing of Presidential Aide Moyers was photographed at the same party where the wife of a State Department official was sent home to put on some less revealing clothing, Johnson reacted with what for him is standard procedure: the wall went up. Not only were photographers forbidden to attend his next party, but the guest list was withheld from public scrutiny. Taxpayers paid for the food and pleasure of 190 guests, but they never learned who they were. That degree of secrecy did not hold for all parties thereafter, but to this day photographers can rarely get closer to a White House dance floor than they can to an Oak Ridge laboratory.

Was it only coincidental that the *Washington Post,* which gave over its front page and much of its innards to Luci's wedding, put the wedding of Vice-President Humphrey's boy on the second page and the wedding of Defense Secretary McNamara's daughter deep inside (with no picture of the bride, but a picture of the Johnson family entering the church)? Such delicacies of placement and protocol give backdoor entry to the *Post,* and it is aware of what it is doing. So is Johnson, who recently appointed a *Post* executive as ambassador to Switzerland. The *Post* has such a superb stable of reporters that no amount of cocktail-circuit collusion on the part of its editors can keep it from being, along with *The New York Times,* one of the two most influential papers in Washington, and such favors as the editors are capable of slipping in for Johnson—apparently motivated by some vague notion that they should protect Johnson because Philip Graham, the late publisher of the *Post,* participated in the backstage maneuverings that ended with Johnson accepting the vice-presidential nomination—are usually as trivial as they are silly. Example: The U.S. Information Agency used to conduct a World Survey, testing overseas public opinion of U.S. affairs. President Kennedy abused this service by prematurely releasing the opinion poll's results—when it benefited him—and then when Johnson became president, and Leonard Marks (a former employee of Johnson's) was appointed director of USIA, the poll was discontinued altogether. This action was taken, it was subsequently learned, because the last unreleased poll showed Johnson at an abysmal level of popularity in Europe. This kind of cover-up is expected from the USIA, which bought a quarter million copies of Booth Mooney's puffy *The Lyndon Johnson Story,* translated into twenty-four languages, and strewed them around the world, while rejecting, the excellent if sometimes critical *Lyndon B. Johnson and the World* by Philip Geyelin and *Lyndon B. Johnson: The Exercise of Power* by Rowland Evans and Robert Novak. The USIA is in the business of seeing that every one of its offices is well stocked with an adulatory film telling the story of Li'l Lyndon and his upbringing in the Texas Hill Country; it is not in the business of publicizing the fact that most Europeans fear and dislike him. Suspecting the reason for the World Survey discontinuation, Senator Thruston Morton, chairman of the Republican Senate Campaign Committee, decided to get the information anyway, and he hired the Opinion Research Corporation of Princeton to get it for him. Its sampling of 6,090 West Europeans (1,300 more than were sampled by the USIA in 1964) revealed that 46 per cent believed we are farther from world peace as a result of U.S. policies under Johnson, and only 14 per cent (one in seven) thought we are closer (the rest said "no change" or "no opinion"). And to the question, "Under which United States President would you say U.S. world prestige has been greater—today under President Johnson, under President Kennedy, or under President Eisenhower?" the division was sharp: 74 per cent said Kennedy, 11 per cent said Eisenhower—only 2 per cent of the five-country average said Johnson (in France, only 1 per cent). *The New York Times,* for one, reported all of this. The *Post* carried the Europeans' opinion on peace—but omitted their low opinion of Johnson.

With most newspapers he is not so successful, and as a result he customarily meets the press in an ugly mood.

* * *

January 14, 1966:

Q.　Mr. President, in connection with the appointment to the Housing and Urban Affairs Department, there have been reports of a task force headed by Dr. Wood which recommended—

Johnson:　*What* reports? I want to know who reports what.

Q.　There have been published reports in the newspapers.

Johnson:　Whose?

Q.　There have been published reports in newspapers.

Johnson:　Well, who published it? That's what I want to know.

Q.　I saw something in *The Washington Post,* for one.

Johnson: Go ahead. *The Washington Post.* What did *The Washington Post* say?

Q. That a task force headed by Professor Wood had recommended the transfer of the community action program and the Office of Economic Opportunity to the new department, and there have been subsequent reports that you have decided against this. Can you make any comment on that?

Johnson: I would say that, insofar as a report that I have made a decision on the matter, it is more propaganda than accurate. I have made no decision. We will, in the days ahead, consider a good many reorganization proposals, but the best authority for a presidential decision is the President or the press secretary, and you can always get guidance on that if you have the time or the disposition to obtain it.

Q. That's why I asked you.

Johnson: You got it. That's why I told you.

A nice bit of bullyragging, but he wasn't through. Asked if he thought Congress would be able to adjourn in June, he began to grind his teeth: "I came there thirty-five years ago, and the first thing I learned was never to predict when they would adjourn during the day or during the week or during the year. And I have never done that [predicted]. . . . Whether they will go in June or January I don't know. And I have never done it. I have never made any such prediction. And I do get a little bit sensitive sometimes when I see Presidential decisions and predictions being made that I never heard of!"

As a matter of fact, the previous August he had said: "But we look forward to the Congress being able to get out of here early next year—I would say certainly far ahead of the end of the fiscal year in June—so that the members could be at home and could report to the people."

There are at least three reasons why the President treats

the press this way: (1) there is a strong streak of the middle-class bully in him, and since the White House press corps is captive, in a way, he feels it is safe to browbeat it; (2) he enjoys secrecy for secrecy's sake, and always has; (3) he doesn't like to be pinned down with questions, because most of the time he doesn't know the answers until after he has acted.

There is plenty of this bullying to go around; the press corps doesn't get all of it. In dealing with his subordinates he is sudden squalls, dazzling light, thunder, fog; he is as unpredictable, and as unstable, as Texas weather. Those lesser ones who now occupy the marble halls with Johnson must pay for their moment of glory; cabinet and subcabinet members are often put in the position of lackeys, and ignorant lackeys at that. Was Under Secretary of State George Ball deliberately lying when he went on television to say there was no substance to the rumors that the U.S. intended to escalate its bombings—just hours before we began bombing Hanoi and Haiphong—or was he ignorant of the plans? The latter is possible.

From time to time cabinet members, under pressure by Congressional interrogators, blurt out pathetic clues to the way Johnson treats them. Major shifts in the budget are learned by Secretary of the Treasury Fowler when Johnson or a Johnson factotum announces them at a news conference, not before.

Senator Hartke: When did the Treasury first learn it was going to have to pick up the tab for that amount?
Secretary Fowler: Well, those figures first emerged, to my knowledge, when *Mr. Moyers announced them* in late November at the President's ranch.

At issue here was a $4.7 billion supplemental budget for Vietnam. It had all been prepared without the knowledge of Fowler. But surely, you say, the director of the budget is aware of these massive shifts. Here is Budget Director Schultze under interrogation:

Hartke: I am trying to find out whether or not there is any preparation of figures whatsoever in regard to supplemental appropriations.

Schultze: All I can say to the best of my knowledge is, "no." But I simply don't want to speak for the Secretary of Defense on precisely what contingencies he is planning for. I simply don't know at this time.

As a matter of fact, it was common knowledge on Capitol Hill that the Defense Department had for some time been preparing another supplemental budget and, in fact, the size of it generally was known.* Of course, when officials close to the President say they do not know, there is both the possibility that they don't know, and the possibility that they are, either from habit or from the dread that seems to grip all those who surround Johnson, simply lying.

Other upper-hierarchy officials tell similar stories of the hoop-jumping that is demanded of them. With as little embarrassment as might be shown by a trained seal, then Under Secretary Ball admitted that he was accustomed to taking, on presidential command, "one side or another or even to argue each side in turn of a particular question."

It is quite ordinary for Johnson to roust a cabinet member out of bed in the postmidnight hours to come sit with him and listen to him talk, or make him break up a Sunday hike or a summer vacation to return posthaste to the White House for nothing in particular. "Once," recounts John

---

* As early as April, 1966, *Fortune* had made a beautiful estimate that the war costs would run $21 billion a year, or more—about twice what the Administration pretended it would be. By August, Senators Stennis and Russell, both insiders in defense matters, were openly making the same estimate—which Johnson waited another two months before verifying (in Australia), and then another month before making official.

Osborne, a long-time Washington reporter, "he made most of his Cabinet sit in a group for White House reporters, without preparation, in a transparent pretense that they were showing the public how Cabinet meetings go. The President enhanced the humiliation by marching out, with the Secretaries of State and Defense in tow, and leaving a staff assistant to 'preside,' indicating with a pointed pencil the turn of each hapless head of a great department to recite for the embarrassed reporters. The accurate reports of this performance in the next morning's papers threw the President into one of his rages, affecting his temper and work throughout the day. This is the sort of thing that keeps Washington gossiping, and laughing, but also worrying."

Cabinet members are compensated for such embarrassment by being permitted to partake of power at its source. But among White House underlings, with no such balancing rewards, Johnson's harsh capriciousness is taking its toll. Since he became President, seventeen top assistants have fled his payroll—all professing their great admiration for him, but nonetheless hurrying on their way. It is not so much the long hours that turn them out but the atmosphere of psychotic suspicions.

"You could argue with Kennedy," one Kennedy holdover escapee explained, "and if you made sense, he listened right away. With Johnson you always have to waste time first proving you're 100 per cent loyal. Then he'll listen." This is an echo of JFK's complaint that sending a birthday greeting to sensitive Lyndon was like "drafting a state document."

Johnson has a way of constantly testing his staff's loyalty by subjecting workers to various smoker indignities and insults. Johnson likes his most faithful ex-retainer Jack Valenti, in a way. Visiting a college campus, Johnson asked some of the students what speakers had come there recently. Well, for one, they said, Tom Ross, coauthor of

The Invisible Government. And what had he said? asked
Johnson. He had said the CIA is too powerful. That was a
shameful bit of nonsense, said Johnson, and told the students they should be listening to men like Jack Valenti
rather than critics like Ross. But even such dubious praise
as this was not enough to keep Valenti from becoming
weary of Johnson's ragging and cursing him, and kidding
him about questionable and private matters. When he left,
Valenti said he did so with "mixed feelings compounded
of hope and anguish . . . I'd love to stay with the President whom, as you know, I love very much, but I would
then be fifty. And what industry wants to hire a man of
fifty?" What industry would want to hire a man of fifty fresh
from nine years at the very center of power? He couldn't
have been serious. Of course the $125,000 pay was attrac-
tive in the new job, but so was the freedom from badgering.
Once during the old days a friend said to Mrs. Valenti,
"The President certainly does like Courtenay, doesn't he?"
Mrs. Valenti replied in a flat tone, "Yes—it helps."

Other ex-staffers complain of how, in front of company,
Johnson would needle them as being "nobody" or "a mes-
senger." Even his reasons for praising his workers sometimes had a cheapening effect. Of a couple of his speech
writers he once said, "They can cry real good."

He seems to enjoy playing with men's spirits and lives.
He appeared almost pleased in the old days when his harsh
heckling brought George Reedy, for a number of years one
of Johnson's top aides, to the verge of tears. After one such
round, as Reedy was once again writing out his resignation,
Johnson made his well-known remark, "Well, it's time to
give George his Christmas present." When a visitor at hand
asked him why, Johnson said, "You don't give a man a
present when he's up. You give it to him when he's down."

His secrecy is often resented. Government workers are
required to reveal sources of their income and other pri-

vate financial matters, yet for months Johnson has refused
to talk about where the money is coming from to buy the
parkland across from his Texas ranch—parkland that is,
ironically, supposed to protect him from the taint of com-
mercialism. A Texan state senator recently charged that
members of the Texas Parks and Wildlife Commission were
"using the name and prestige of the President of the United
States" to "blackjack contributions," which so far have
come to a couple of hundred thousand dollars. One of the
three members of the commission is A. W. Moursund of
Johnson City, the President's business partner. Another
member, Will E. Odom, is a very close friend. The resentment in Texas toward that deal is so strong that it helped
defeat Waggoner Carr in his recent race for the U.S. Senate.
Carr, as Attorney General, ruled that the commission did
not have to reveal the source of the funds, or how it obtained them.

Finally, there is the matter of Johnson's not knowing how
to answer questions because he flies blind. This has been
a mark of his career. In the Senate he seldom told his plans,
because he didn't know what they were. This infuriated
many of his colleagues, especially the lively liberals. Not
until the 1954 session was *two months* under way did Johnson call a party caucus, and then he permitted only one
topic to be discussed—the triviality of unifying behind the
confirmation of a contested Senate seat. Caucuses were not
for him. He was the slippery, secretive wheeler-dealer. The
strength of his leadership had always depended on the support of Democrats like Richard Russell, who had billion-
dollar pork barrel cravings, and George Smathers of Florida,
a member of the LBJ charm school who was better known
as "Gorgeous George" or "Smooch," and who really didn't
care what went on from day to day. A great deal of lethargy,
self-indulgence and greed made up the majority spirit which
was very easy for Johnson to manipulate, as it would have

been for any strong man who did not let some passionate itch
or his pocketbook sidetrack him from his political ambitions.
It was this period which the *New York Post,* in 1959, saw as
Johnson leadership by "patronage, position, and pork barrel," and warned liberals that "the high price of doing business with him is the forfeiting of their self-respect and the
moral disintegration of their party."

This kind of manipulating was best done, naturally, in
secret; and it was this lack of planning, openness, and co-
ordination that aroused William Proxmire, freshman senator from Wisconsin still full of the belligerency that made
him a boxing champion in college, to take on the mighty
majority leader. Three times Proxmire went to the floor to
do combat with Johnson on the grounds that he was a
despotic, high-handed politician who had risen only through
the unimaginative lines of Southern ascension. "The cold
fact is that Democratic policy in the Senate is made entirely on an ad lib, off-the-cuff basis," said Proxmire on
March 9, 1959. Policy was made neither in caucus nor on
the floor but "in private, over the telephone, with a few of
the top members, by and large."

When Senator Mike Monroney came to Johnson's defense,
Proxmire inquired, "Can the senator from Oklahoma cite
to me a *single* example, in either the 83rd, the 84th, or the
85th Congress [Proxmire was asking this from the promon-
tory of the 86th Congress] when the policy of the Democratic
Party was expressed in any kind of communication to senators, or can he give me an example or an instance in which
party policy was declared in advance and was known?" Monroney could not do it.

The strangely-labeled Senate Policy Committee, giving off
a mist of "consensus" behind which Johnson could act arbi-
trarily while pretending to be seeking the advice of others,
was a feeble and unjust apparatus; it represented in com-
posite only twenty million citizens and had no members from
the Middle West and only old man Green of Rhode Island

from the East. The Policy Committee was so dominated by
Johnson that when he was ill in 1955 it did not even meet.
Naturally he preferred to do his business with this group
rather than make plans with the Democratic party organization outside Congress, for the party leadership included
a number of men and women with strong convictions
coupled with a willingness to fight for them. He avoided the
party leadership, allying himself instead with the Senate
claque that was happy to go along with his furtive, foggy
generalities. Of such was the "program" he laid out on January 12, 1959, in the caucus that so infuriated Proxmire:

"Our controls over the monetary system are now two
worlds old.

"Our budget processes were formed in another day.
"Our tax structure is obsolescent. . . .
"We must not surrender to inflation."

Etcetera, etcetera, a full twenty minutes of hoopla about
"tomorrow's horizons" and "looking into the future," after
which he came to the crucial point of his talk, namely, that
there would be no legislative program. He put it this way:
"There is much that we must do . . . yet for our work, *we
do not come with a checklist in hand to attend only the
pressing problems of the present*." In other words, no par-
ticulars. The very thing Proxmire was complaining about:
another session of secrecy, another session of cloakroom and
swagger.

The press gave Proxmire a loud "amen." Marquis Childs
wrote that, "Public controversy is bad—bad for the party,
and bad for the country. That is the heart of the Johnson
conviction. You have to work things out in the cloakroom;
then when you've got them worked out you can debate a
little before you vote. In the politics of manipulation and
maneuver Johnson, as he proved once again, is a master. But
this ignores the content, the substance, of political give and

take. It draws off the fire, the fight, the conviction, the zeal."
And Willard Edwards in *The National Review* added, "Lyndon Johnson has established speed, unanimity, curtailed debate, and the elimination of record votes as the hallmarks of good legislation. . . . Under his leadership a system of backstage bargaining for votes has reduced debate on the Senate floor to a dull formality. The record of the last session shows that it means to reach 'agreement without discord.' It means brief and perfunctory debate; a lack of intelligent questioning; a sparse attendance; the absence of quorum calls to summon absentees; the omission of record roll calls without which the public can never know which senators were present and how they voted; the approval of legislation in obvious ignorance of its meaning."

There were statistics to prove it: between 1947 and 1952 the Senate passed 2,324 bills, for which work it had 1,034 roll call votes and 1,857 quorum calls. From 1953, the year Johnson took over as Democratic leader, through 1958, the Senate passed 3,248 bills (an increase of 40 per cent) but had only 797 roll call votes (down 20 per cent) and had only 876 quorum calls (down 60 per cent).

These contemporary observations of Johnson's conduct in the Senate are useful in showing that he has not changed, and that the press, the public, and his subordinates are going through what they went through six, seven, eight, nine years ago. He is still discouraging questions, belittling debate, and demanding and getting greater arbitrary powers to act alone and secretly than his office would ordinarily allow (e.g., the Tonkin Gulf resolution).

In part these are the actions and the needs of a dangerous absolutist. But they are also the actions of one who is on the defensive because he does not know where his own impulses will take him. Luci knew what she was talking about: "I can't ever tell what he's going to do. He can't, even."

3 Will the real Lyndon Johnson please sit down?

I never object to anyone being interested in education or health, or any of those things.

—LBJ, April, 1966

Twelve days after John Kennedy was killed, Lyndon Johnson summoned the Business Council, whose membership is made up of about 100 presidents and board chairmen of the biggest corporations. First, in the White House's "Fish Room," he shook their hands and passed a few introductory witticisms, and then, growing seriously accommodating, like a lion tamer with a roomful of strange cats, he counseled them to "banish your fear and shed your doubts and renew your hopes. We have much work to do together."

Reporters were listening to that talk. But later he shepherded the businessmen into the Cabinet Room for a private discussion. One of the businessmen who was there described the group's reaction to that private visit as "impressed and *comforted*." J. Harris Ward, president of Commonwealth Edison of Chicago, said, "I felt so at ease with him . . ."

This became the normal response from big businessmen and industrialists. Wall Street found it liked him. Ralph A. Rotnem, senior vice-president for research of Harris, Upham & Company, Inc., told reporters, "Wall Street looks on Johnson as a great friend of business, and admires him for getting good talent."

Two years later, at the May, 1966 meeting of the Council at Hot Springs, Virginia, you could have walked the corridors of the luxurious Homestead Hotel and mingled in the cocktail parties, stopping these moguls and talking with them all, without finding more than a half dozen who were annoyed with the way Johnson was letting business run. He was proving to be a very understanding fellow.

He had had 150 of them up to the White House for breakfast in March—"a revival atmosphere," one said later—and got them all to shouting and hallelujahing and promising to cut back on their capital expenditures. But then the revival spirit wore off, and within two weeks some, like Pittsburgh Plate Glass, were going ahead quietly with their expansion plans. But Johnson didn't get mad; he waited half a high-spending year before temporarily suspending big business' investment tax credit.

He was always doing little favors for them. Just the month before, when Senator Gale W. McGee of Wyoming introduced a resolution that would have set the Federal Trade Commission (FTC) to investigating price inflations originating in the giant supermarket chains, Johnson immediately had him recall the resolution, and in a presidential letter to the House and Senate asked instead for a "study" of—not the supermarkets, but—"the changes taking place in the American food industry." Unlike the FTC, Johnson's study group would have no power to take action.

The promised big rate inquiry of AT&T was scarcely mov-

ing. There was a sweet harbinger in Johnson's juggling the
Federal Power Commission to reverse the pro-consumer balance; and in the appointment of R. E. Hyde to be chairman
of the Federal Communications Commission, thus assuring
broadcasters of a return to the pre-Newton Minow era of
nonregulation; and in the appointment of Hamer H. Budge,
previously a right-wing servitor of Representative Charles
Halleck, to the Securities Exchange Commission. And then
had come the promise of Attorney General Katzenbach to
the Business Council that there would be a "breathing spell"
in the anti-trust division. Gay and carefree times ahead!
Heady with the sweet smell of profiteering! There was every
reason for *The New Republic* to judge the White House as
"solidly on the side of business—more so than at any time
since Herbert Hoover." About 50 per cent of the ruddy faces
seen in the Homestead Hotel toasting their President on
that happy May day were on record as having voted for him
in 1964, and they still felt they had put their money on the
right horse.

A pattern seemed to be plainly emerging, yet through it
all the nation was generally convinced—having been told so
many times by so many writers—that Johnson, basically,
down underneath the $250 suits and the Hong Kong shirts,
down underneath the $14-million-and-growing bank ac-
count, was just a good old boy from hard-scrabblin' hill
country, grandson of a Populist and faithful to that political
heritage. Even the best reporters couldn't let go of it.
Richard F. Janssen of *The Wall Street Journal,* sensing that
maybe something was wrong, nevertheless would retreat no
farther than to call him a "rather Populist" president. And
even Evans and Novak, after the most prodigious research
of any LBJ biographers to date, could not shake the myth
from their heads. No, they allowed, Johnson was not a true
descendant of the class-struggle type Populist; *his* was "the
Texas-style Populism . . . derived . . . from a dollars-and-

cents economic struggle with Wall Street . . . to bring down interest rates."

Ralph McGill, the bourbon South's chief spinner of authorized fairy tales, sounds like he got his script straight from the Pedernales: "A part of Lyndon Johnson's past is right out of the Populist revolt. He heard it from his daddy, his granddaddy, his uncles and his aunts. . . . There is in the President—out of his past—a feeling that this nation ought to do something about poverty, its unemployed, the slums of great cities and education and care for the needy. *This is in his genes.*" Why Lyndon himself couldn't do much better than that; on his 58th birthday, reminiscing about what a sweet fellow he was, Johnson said: "We are now at [an economic] point that I have envisioned and sought all my adult life—or even as a boy. My earliest memories were hearing my grandfather, who was a leading advocate in this part of the country for social justice, talk about the plight of the tenant farmer. . . . [etc., etc.] That was the philosophy handed down to me by my father, that he expressed all through his political life, and also my grandfather, my mother's father." Man, it's in his *blood.*

It is true that Johnson has often sounded right for the role. Not long ago he told a crowd in New Jersey that he was trying to do things for "the PEEPUL—you know who I mean—the Folks." That was Populist talk, by definition. And a few hours later, in Detroit, he cried out that the "Free Labor Movement's war" is not ended, and he was volunteering to lead it. And in Denver he swore that in all his days as a country boy he "never saw a tenant farmer who could be counted upon to reach his potential knowing that all he does only goes to the landlord."

Out of the past and bounding across the current political landscape has come—like a tumbleweed blown by the hot winds of West Texas—this most burdensome cliché of modern politics. With almost persuasive monotony we are told that while he was a Texas senator, Lyndon Johnson was pressed into serving the economic and social conservatives of his home state, but once he became president he was free to return, and did return, to the inner directions of his Populist soul.

It is a very successful and heartily long-lived myth, but still a myth. Somewhere in Johnson is a compass that holds truest where the cash is piled highest. By temperament and opportunity and conviction, Lyndon Johnson is and has always been a representative of the fat and wealthy merchant who fought the Populist movement with even more energy than did the rich planter, who, in fact, often sympathized with it. Although at odds frequently with the power structure of the old agrarian Texas that was dying after World War II, Johnson's sympathies were not shifted to what used to be easily identified as the submerged masses but to the new-rich businessmen and industrialists.

A millionaire by 1948, he was not, however, graceful with swag. He was no Roosevelt or Kennedy, born to it, but a burgher, defensive about his new clothes and new status, hypersensitive to the grins he knew he provoked in the indolent wealthy. John Kennedy dead, he still fussed with his bones. Johnson told friends more than once in that first year of the presidency that he could trace his ancestry as far back as Kennedy could, an attitude verified by Lady Bird when she disclosed that Lyndon was "disgusted" to learn that his Revolutionary War ancestor was just "plain John Johnson, without even a middle initial." It was, many believed, the burgher in him seeking status that compelled the everlasting monogramming of his life.

At the same time it was this grappling-hook approach to life, this manic scrambling and sympathy for other tough scramblers that gave him his appeal to men such as his multimillionaire pork-barreling friend George Brown, who once pointed out proudly that "Lyndon is the first man in the

White House since Hoover who's had to make a payroll on the first and the fifteenth."

Johnson runs a nonunion television station, and he is tight-fisted with his money. As recently as 1957 he was still publicly complaining about the forty-hour week. He embodies so many of the virtues of thrift and business intrepidity that Henry Ford II confided to a reporter with unembarrassed gusto, "I think he's *terrific*."

It is an opinion which Tom Watson, the redheaded rogue of the old Farmers Alliance and of the Populist movement of the late 19th and early 20th centuries, would not have shared. Tom and his fellows wanted loose money and easy credit, they wanted low interest and an iron bit in the mouth of Wall Street, they wanted the government to regain control of its fiscal and monetary system from the national banks, and they wanted the government to assume ownership of some of the national utilities and the railroads. They wanted to encourage the organizing of the industrial wage earner and his alliance with the sharecropper and the tenant farmer. If Tom and his army had had a slogan to shout like today's rebels, it could have been "Poor White Power!"

Lyndon Johnson, the Drugstore Populist, wants none of these things, nor their modern equivalents.

"There is a gradation in servitude," said Tom Watson, "the laborer, the cropper, the tenant next . . . thousands of people in the State of Mississippi are powerless and homeless, destitute and suffering for food—holding out their hands and asking the National Assembly to give them relief." (1892)

In the fall of 1965, so deep was the misery of the black sharecropper of Mississippi and Alabama that a few of them rose up and tried to beat the system. The "system" in this instance was the white domination of the Agriculture Stabilization and Conservation Service Committees (ASCS) in the

South; these are the community-elected organizations which determine who gets what crop allotments and farm loans, and can thereby keep a farmer penniless or make him well-to-do. The Negroes only wanted fair ASCS elections. With black membership on the committees, the black farmers might be able to stay in business. The white farmers were doing better every year and the Negro tenants were being starved out; some said it was part of a massive scheme to get rid of the black laborer who was becoming an obsolete tool as the big farms became more mechanized. By January, 1966 some 2,000 sharecroppers in Mississippi alone had been evicted.

Joseph Resnick, a New York Congressman, after visiting Mississippi wrote President Johnson, "In spite of the fact that this potential human disaster is well known in Mississippi, *not one single state or federal employee or agency has made plans to cope with the extremely unfortunate situation.*" He asked for emergency food and shelter for the evictees.

When there was no response from Johnson, some of the sharecroppers, who had been living in a tent city, moved into an abandoned army base to get warm. Johnson, deploring "unlawfulness," sent in a general, two colonels and a phalanx of infantrymen to run them out. When a group of sharecroppers pitched tents in Lafayette Park across from the White House to call attention to their troubles, the only official response was a new regulation requiring permission to protest in that park area.

The cotton program passed by Congress in 1965 established a new system—probably accidentally—by which tenant farmers and, to a much lesser extent, sharecroppers, could get direct crop-support and crop-diversion payments from the government; thus they could bypass Charley and his 25 per cent loans, and they could bypass Charley's plantation store, where prices were twice as high as in town. The new program looked like it might give the tenants and the croppers a fractional measure of independence from the thieving landlords. At the White House Civil Rights Conference I ran into one certified sharecropper who told me of how he harvested eighty-two bales for a Prairie, Mississippi landlord, bringing in roughly $16,400—of which the sharecropper got $1,481. But he was lucky, considering what happens to some sharecroppers. George Lardner of the *Washington Post* found a cropper who made sixty bales for his landlord—earning $60 for himself for the year's labor. Similar examples can be found down every dirt and gravel road in the South.

Well, the tenants and croppers didn't get their independence after all. When Secretary of Agriculture Orville Freeman discovered what had been written into the cotton law, he issued an executive order effectively shelving it. For months officers of the National Sharecroppers Fund wrote letters to Freeman itemizing the injustices that federal farm officials in the South not only allow but encourage—and they not only got no reform action from Freeman but often they did not even get a responsive letter.

After the *Nation* magazine, followed by Lardner at the *Washington Post,* gave a full account of the sorry mess, Johnson reportedly telephoned the Department of Agriculture and demanded to know "what the hell is going on"; however, as it turned out, he was angry not with the Negroes' impoverishment, but with the publicity. Follow-up stories written by Lardner never appeared in print.

Getting no relief from the Administration, two dozen ragged sharecroppers and tenants came to Washington and sued the Department of Agriculture for new ASCS elections. The suit was thrown out, the judge claiming he had no right to interfere where the Department of Agriculture clearly had the right to make the rules.

No matter what his feelings toward Negroes, one might suppose that Johnson's sympathies for the Latin-American would be more in evidence. After all, the part of Texas in which he was reared has very few Negroes, and at no time in his life has he had prolonged close dealings with Negroes; but Latins were common in his home area, and later he taught them in Cotulla, Texas. He makes a big point of this in his biographical television shows.

Of Texas' residents 28 per cent are impoverished, making it the largest conglomeration of poverty in the nation; of these a great many, of course, are Latinos. What is being done to get them jobs? When Johnson was a senator, he voted to permit Texas and California farmers to import cheap labor from Mexico, to compete with the jobless Latins in this country; he used the foreigners on his own ranch. And when, as vice-president, he was named by Kennedy to be chairman of the President's Committee on Equal Employment, his attitude did not apparently change. He had the power to cut off federal contracts to any business or industry that was discriminating racially in its employment. Johnson cut off no contracts although, as Franklin D. Roosevelt, Jr., former chairman of the Equal Employment Opportunities Commission, revealed in October, 1966, there are 800 federal-contract corporations in the Southwest with 600,000 employees—not one of whom is a Latin-American.

One of the members of the Committee on Equal Employment under Johnson was Jerry Holleman, former president of the Texas AFL-CIO. Holleman was constantly badgering Johnson to make more use of his power to help the Negroes and the Latins. On one occasion Johnson sought to soothe Holleman by remarking, "You get too upset about the nigras, Jerry." On another occasion Holleman was heard to tell Johnson on the phone, "I'd better hang up before I forget you're the vice-president."

Not long ago Johnson said in one of his boondock speeches that he had "learned the first victims of a sluggish economy are the poor, the Negro, the farmer and the wage earner."

If this were a view that at just one small point touched reality, then it could not only be designated as Populist, but as humanitarian in the deepest sense.

But as a matter of fact Johnson, who is a very learned man in a statistical way, must realize that for four million rural Negroes in the South, many of them living in tenant farm shanties and now many of them living in tents, there has *never* been anything *but* a sluggish economy. To talk of keeping the economy un-sluggish may mean something to a businessman, but it means nothing to these serfs, who wouldn't recognize a fast economy if it passed by as close as Memphis.

In the early autumn of 1966, in a White House press conference, Johnson was asked about the Mexican-American unrest and what he intended to do about it. Well, he said, he had "done everything I could to contribute to a better understanding. I had members of the House who were of Mexican-American ancestry go on a visit with me to Mexico." This is an honest response from his background; it is out of the *jefe* mystique. A Texas politician has traditionally not had to deal with the stoop-working "spics" so long as he had the friendship of their leaders, their profiteering *jefes*, in this instance the Mexicano Congressmen with an eye out for pork barrel. Otherwise, said Johnson, "I have tried to find qualified employees for the government from this [Latin] group. I now have a good many requests out for recommendations." There are only 10 million Mexicanos in the country; he's trying to find a few qualified ones.

*   *
*
    *

No Southerner ever fought for the labor movement like Tom Watson. The mere mention of those rascally Pinkerton strikebreakers would set him to moaning in anguish, and on one occasion, when he was trying to push a pro-labor bill through the House, he shouted an oath. "I will stay here till

*the ants tote me out of the keyhole before I will give up this
fight."*

Johnson's first major pronouncement on labor after he became president set the tone for his administration, unmistakably on the side of management. The Florida East Coast
Railroad (FEC), owned by the duPont Estate, the most
powerful corporate body in Florida, was in the midst of a
labor dispute—one that became the longest railroad-labor
quarrel in history and which still continues. Four years
ago some of the FEC workers struck. Ed Ball, head of
the duPont Estate, responded by locking them out, hiring
scab laborers, and announcing that under no conditions
would he ever rehire the strikers. Thus 1,200 families were
left without an income. As it happens, most of the FEC's
profit comes from servicing the government space project at
Cape Kennedy—a good leverage, one might suppose, for the
government to use to force the railroad to resume negotiations with the strikers. It has not been used. In fact, under
Johnson no government power has been exerted on the company to negotiate. His *only* action was to send in FBI agents
to guarantee that the railroad would not be subjected to
violent protests from the strikers; this Johnson coupled with
a public deploring of "lawlessness." And that was the last
word heard from him.

Johnson has often outwitted organized labor, he has often
helped develop anti-union legislation, he has sometimes
swapped off to get labor's vote; but he has never understood
the union movement. Meany, Reuther, the big shots, he can
handle; they are as susceptible to the mild corruption of a
luncheon at the White House as Henry Ford is. But the
rank and file are beyond his ken. A perfect, though by no
means singular, illustration of that came in August, 1966,
after the airlines strike had lasted more than a month. Now
was the time for Johnson to make one of his dramatic de-
liveries, the kind he is often capable of making when deal-

ing with the authoritarian president of a corporation. After a fast huddle, the usual amount of pinching and squeezing and whispering in the ear, Johnson leaped to the national TV podium to announce his success.

The airline officials, who after all must live with government regulation and cannot afford to offend the greatest regulator of them all, may have agreed to the terms, and the union executives may have also. But the union membership —noting that the cost of living had gone up 5 per cent in the past year, that corporation profits were at an all-time high and going higher, and that many airlines reported profits of 20 per cent during the same year—considered Johnson's talk of keeping wage increases within his arbitrary 3.2 guidelines as slightly silly. They voted down the LBJ proposal. Overconfident, he had moved too fast and had publicly boasted of victory before it was wrapped up—breaking a basic principle of his legislative days. Now he was being publicly taunted by the great dues-paying union members, who annoyed him because he did not understand them, did not know how to deal with them. In dealing with the labor stiffs of Texas, all he had ever had to do was pressure them through their national headquarters. He knew of no way to cope with "the men below" except in this way, through indirect pressures, or by those campaign promises which he tosses into the crowd like a French explorer flinging beads to a strange tribe.

Rattled and afraid and confused, Johnson reverted to his old senatorial razzle-dazzle (unsuccessfully) as a way of meeting a crisis that could have properly been met with more flexible negotiation; he called Wayne Morse to the White House and persuaded him to carry a bill through Congress that would force Congress to end the strike and free Johnson of all responsibility.

But he had lost his touch. He had lost control of the situation and more embarrassments lay ahead. When Labor Secretary Wirtz appeared to testify on the legislation, he ran into an indignant crossfire. Did Johnson favor the bill, he was asked, or didn't he? *Well, did he or didn't he! "President Johnson is asking for it,"* Senator Javits cried angrily, *"or he isn't, or he's neutral or something!"* November was just around the corner and Johnson's psychotic fear of the consensus at such a time had made him send his servant into the arena naked. Wirtz simply sat and took it for his chief. The orders were to offend no one.

This last commandment is, in brief, descriptive of the change in Johnson's moving from a limited to a national constituency. His fears have been enlarged and expanded, but his benevolence has not.

With the exception of one law, raising and expanding the federal minimum wage—which is a law Congress rather automatically passes in some form about every five or six years, whether there is a Whig or Tory in the Mansion—Johnson put no significant pro-labor law through the 1965–66 Congressional sessions. He had repeatedly called this "the best" Congress in history; it virtually ignored organized labor. It is a matter of conversation with all members of Congress and well known to the hierarchy of the AFL-CIO that Johnson expended no effort to pass the other bills he had promised labor for its support in 1964.

In his Denver speech, just before flying off to Southeast Asia, Johnson had said, "Nor is social justice merely a matter of good land tenure system. *It is work at fair wages with the protection of free bargaining.*" But that is easy to say.

In late 1966 in Detroit he *again* promised to push the repeal of Section 14-B of the Taft-Hartley Act—"not because we are poor losers but because we know it is necessary to achieve what Justice Holmes called 'that equality of bargaining power from which freedom of contract begins.'" Labor, probably having no other choice, will pretend that it believes him and vote for him again in 1968, repeating the sour humor of 1964 when one of the well-used sallies among the lunchpailers was, "Tell me again why I'm for Lyndon Johnson. I keep forgetting."

When he was a congressman, Johnson voted to override FDR's veto of an anti-strike bill; he helped shape the Taft-Hartley Act, and then voted to override both of Truman's vetoes of it. But when he sought to claw his way out of the House and into the Senate in 1948, he thought best to embellish these anti-union efforts. Standing on the threshold of the McCarthy era, he threw open the door and pointed at those shadows within: the Communistic Labor Czars. These furtive subversive labor dictators, he said, "have loosed the biggest slush fund in Texas history to defeat me." It was about the only issue he used that year. What labor dictators were these, and how were they imperiling the nation? Lyndon could tell them: "James C. Petrillo, that's who," he said in Dallas. "Dictator of the musicians union. He won't let our children record their fiddle-playing."

His opponent, Coke Stevenson, tried to maneuver attention to Johnson's Congressional record. He asked: "When my opponent landed his helicopter [that was Johnson's mode of transportation] on this very spot, did he tell you of any bill he ever introduced in Congress in eleven and a half years? Did he ever write and pass a bill which would aid the average citizen of the United States? I can't find one. If he has passed one it would be nice for him to point it out. Ask him if he ever even introduced *a* bill. My opponent has been talking about high prices. Did he ever introduce a bill to lower them? There has been a lot of talk about aiding the old folks. Did the other candidate in this race ever introduce a bill which would give the old people more benefits?"

To the question of whether Johnson had introduced *a* bill, the answer was yes. As for the other questions, the answers were no. But the questions were not entirely to the point, since a man does not have to introduce bills to be useful in Congress. There is much to be said, in fact, in support of Mrs. Roosevelt's remark to John Kennedy, "The greatest senators are not those who are most effective in getting bills passed, but those who have great convictions."

For some reason that kind of reply did not occur to Johnson. His general response was to duck the issues raised by Stevenson and keep boasting that he was "no recent convert to the fight against Communism" and keep warning the crossroad folks of those "big labor racketeers, the labor dictatorship who voted to destroy me and other forthright Congressmen who had the courage to vote for the anti-Communist Taft-Hartley bill."

Unionism has flourished during the Taft-Hartley era and even the closed shop provision of the act is, as most union executives will admit, overrated in importance except as a symbol. The remarks made by Johnson in this election would not have been unforgivable to labor if it had turned out to be only campaign talk. But attitudes expressed in the 1948 campaign proved to be his guide throughout most of his Senate career. He wasn't just against the unions; in general, Johnson was stingy with his support of things that helped anyone in the lower classes, organized or not.

To illustrate, let's go back to the year when Johnson was in the very best position of his lifetime in politics to work his will for reform and progress, if that was what he wanted. Skip the years of his Senate leadership up to 1959. Allow him all the excuses he likes for fumbling the first five years: he was too young and too new to spread himself, and then he had a heart attack and had to let down, and then he had to play it cautious in a presidential year, and then he felt he should play along with Eisenhower rather than get a reputation for obstructionism.

But thanks to the Eisenhower administration's genius for fouling up economics, there was a dandy recession in 1957–58 that swept the giant Democratic Class of 1958 into office, and at this point Johnson ran out of excuses.

The *next* year Johnson had nothing but partisan support,

with 62 Democratic senators (34 Republicans) and 282 Democratic representatives (153 Republicans) to bring on a renaissance—as everyone anticipated—of progressive legislation.

The New York Times believed the election must surely be accepted "everywhere as a sweeping victory for liberalism," but as *The New Republic* more realistically remarked, the election actually only signaled the start of an effort by the Democratic liberals "to prevent Senator Lyndon Johnson from kidnaping their victory."

What happened? Nothing.

Was the lamp of social welfare brought out of the Capitol basement, dusted off and stuck in the window again, after five murky years of Ike? No.

After opening the session with a rococo oration on the need to deal with world affairs and outer space, Johnson settled down into his customary cautious posture, agreeing that there must be no "reckless spending," and permitting Senator Harry F. Byrd, of whom he never lost his freshman's fear, to torpedo a Senate-approved workman's compensation measure by surrendering in a House-Senate conference committee. This was only symptomatic of the leadership's malaise.

Nothing came out of that Congress worth mentioning, though it packed more Democratic strength than any Congress since Roosevelt in his heyday.

In one of his slickest maneuvers of the session, Johnson waited until there were only half a dozen senators on the floor and then called up a veterans' housing bill (raising interest rates from 4.75 per cent to 5.25 per cent) that had been passed by the House but had not been sent to a Senate committee because similar features were being considered as part of a general housing bill; at the end of the morning hour when only a couple of potential opponents were on hand, he accepted the House bill for action and rammed it through on a voice vote. Few expected it to come up; the Senate had no advance notice of what LBJ had in mind. Only three senators took part in the brief debate. None of the tough opponents were there. Johnson must have known that the bill would have lost in a fair fight, for the previous year an interest increase in the omnibus housing bill passed only after Vice-President Nixon broke the tie, and several senators who had voted for the previous increase had since indicated a change of heart.

Senator Clark later privately challenged Senator Sparkman (who carried the bill for Johnson) about the greased action, and Sparkman excused himself with the explanation, "this was a bill which Johnson was very anxious to have passed," although according to reports of this conversation, Johnson had admitted it might hurt the chances of the housing bill in conference.

Why would the highly touted "Populist" majority leader want to raise housing interest rates, on veterans or anybody else? Aside from the obvious explanation, on which I must keep insisting, that Johnson is *not* a low-interest Populist, another likely explanation is that his old Texas sidekick Robert Anderson was Secretary of the Treasury; Anderson favored raising government bond interest rates, and if housing interest rates went up, that could kick the bonds upward. Johnson was then—as now—much influenced on fiscal questions by Anderson's wishes.

Some fascinating regressions were also achieved in urban renewal that year. Johnson is much concerned in 1966, he says, about the need for dressing up the cities of America. The problem is not a new one. It was, of course, facing the nation in 1959 as well. What did he do with his awesome Democratic majority in Congress to help out? Note: since the Senate had passed *no* urban renewal bill in 1958 and things were falling critically behind, Eisenhower said he wanted a six-year urban development program initiated.

The American Municipal Association and the U.S. Conferences of Mayors urged a ten-year commitment.

Senator Clark, a former mayor of Philadelphia, introduced a bill calling for a ten-year program of $600 million
a year. The bill passed by the Senate provided for a six-year
program at $350 million to $500 million a year. Over in the
House, a bill had been passed providing $500 million a year
for three years; that is, enough to take up the one-year backlog and continue for two years. But the nation *got,* after a job
of legislative hog-killing in the Conference Committee, only
enough funds for two years, to be stretched over *three* years.
Considering the backlog of needs, the final bill actually provided only for a one-year advance.

This was the Johnson-Sam Rayburn leadership of 1959—
when they had the forces, remember, to do anything they
wanted to do, including override vetoes. What the mayors of
the nation hoped would be a ten-year program, and what
tight-fisted Eisenhower hoped would be a six-year program,
wound up as a one-year advance.

But that really doesn't explain the sellout as well as a
brief look at what happened in the Conference Committee.
Considering the funds on a two-year basis, the Senate con-
ferees went in with a $1.2 billion bill; the House conferees
went in with a $1.5 billion bill. *They came out with a $900
million bill.* That's progress. (The Conference Committee is
where differences are split. How do you split the difference
between $1.5 billion and $1.2 billion and arrive at $900 mil-
lion?) Senator Clark, who was on the Committee, said there
was *no* discussion in conference; it had all been ironed out
by Johnson before they met.

In the same session Johnson ducked out during the fight
to expand emergency unemployment compensation, and
then he returned to help pass the anti-labor Landrum-
Griffin Act.

"So," as one of Texas' young liberal politicians wearily

observed at the time, "in the final analysis, the largest Democratic majority in Congress since 1936 out-did the Republican 80th Congress [which passed the Taft-Hartley Act] in passing anti-labor and in not passing pro-people legislation."

That Congressional year, the year of the hollow man, has never been given the tragic stress it deserves. There was, the session of 1959 revealed, really nothing much to Lyndon Johnson: he was just another conservative Southern businessman come to Congress, to become a sort of ennobled tail-twister for Washington's Kiwanis Club.

By achieving very little during his Senate career he achieved exactly what he set out to achieve, very little. Evans and Novak should be ashamed for calling this the Senate's "golden era" and for saying that under Johnson's leadership the Senate experienced "four of the most productive and fruitful years of its history." Nonsense. In 1951, in a speech in Houston, Johnson had said, "the nation is fed up to the gills with legislation. For twenty years we have been legislating, legislating, legislating. What remains to be done, at present, is mostly a matter of degree, a matter of finishing or improving programs already begun." He had no new visions for the country, no plans to achieve more justice, more safety, more security, more comfort, more ennoblement, more equality, more opportunity. None of this. The nation had, for him, reached a perfection that needed only a little rounding out. For some reason, however, he was constantly on the defensive about having achieved so little, while claiming to have achieved so much. When a national publication scoffed at his inclusion of a poultry inspection bill on a list of "important" measures passed by Congress, Johnson responded sourly, "It is, of course, simple to succumb to the temptation to make a wisecrack about a chicken-feed bill."

And after passing another inconsequential measure which was called inconsequential by the press, he groused, "It is perhaps unfortunate that we did not stage the debate on it in a boxing arena. Had there been blood on the floor, the nation might have been impressed." He explained his unwillingness to fight for any controversial bill by saying that he applied "two standards to almost any proposal. First, would it result in the greatest good to the greatest number? Second, is it attainable?" If he decided it *might* not be attainable, he junked the idea because he had no love, he said, for "fighting windmills." For a favored few, he would make an open fight for a bill; he would do it for the oil and gas interests, for defense or space appropriations, or for old pals like the multimillionaire Klebergs. These owners of the King Ranch—a 1½ million-acre spread, larger than the state of Delaware—had in 1954 been allowed to buy emergency drought-relief feed for their livestock at a $32,585 savings; the purpose of the legislation which made this feed available was to help financially hard-pressed ranchers. The Klebergs were not exactly hard-pressed. In fact, a few days after they got their emergency feed, one of their racehorses won the Belmont Sweepstakes. Three years later, when the drought-emergency bill was up again, some congressmen, remembering the Klebergs' gambit, wanted to make the cut-rate feed available only to those who couldn't pay the full price. Johnson wouldn't hear of it, no sir, because "I don't want Old Muley, out on the range, to starve."

When William A. (Dollar Bill) Blakley was appointed to a brief interim term in the U.S. Senate from Texas in 1957, Johnson assigned him to the Interstate and Foreign Commerce Committee, which handles airline matters. Blakley was then the largest stockholder in Braniff Airlines.

Johnson was very magnanimous in his willingness to do these little favors for wealthy friends, but when it came to developing a program for the nation that would have made an issue of issues and would have challenged the soggy moderation of Eisenhower, he refused. Housing, unemployment, race, health, education, civil liberties, urban decay—on all such issues it was Johnson's habit to advocate a strategy of compromise, evasion, and retreat. If there was even the shadow of a Great Society in his heart in those days he successfully kept it hidden. Thus in 1956 the Democrats witnessed the loss of many urban strongholds that they previously had been able to count on; the loss, also, of great clumps of disillusioned minority groups. Hoping to regain their appeal to these areas and groups, Adlai Stevenson, Mrs. Franklin D. Roosevelt, the liberals in Congress and National Democratic Chairman Paul Butler worked together to set up a 17-man advisory committee which was intended to fill the leadership void; Johnson, of course, boycotted this effort, as did Sam Rayburn, and by doing so they voided any effectiveness the group might have had. The Johnsonian collusion with Dixiecrats and reactionary Republicans became so routine and open that some senators began keeping a record, a kind of losers' scoreboard, of the times when Johnson sided with the Dixiecrat-GOP clique in opposition to a majority of his own party to hold back progressive legislation. Johnson's defense for doing so was that "the majority leader of the Senate must, in effect, try to be a leader of the Senate, not just of the Democratic party." To James Wechsler, editor of the *New York Post,* Johnson at this time was "neither a rabid racist nor benighted reactionary" but "the personification of the spirit of flabby compromise," and his leadership was "dominated by the blurring of clear domestic issues, the avoidance of sharp conflict with the Eisenhower administration on foreign policy, the muting of great causes in the interest of 'party unity'—and the care and feeding of the oil and gas interests." And Richard Rovere, the usually mild correspondent for *The New Yorker* magazine, noted in 1957, when Johnson had steered Congress into some listless backwater, that "if Lyndon Johnson seems to have lost stature, it is not entirely because the President has suddenly become aware of his own strength; it is in part, certainly, because Mr. Johnson has done nothing of consequence, aside from demonstrating, five months ago, his wizardry in beating back the civil-rights bloc. No one who has seen Mr. Johnson at work doubts his skill as a parliamentarian, but it has been quite a while since anyone has seen him use his skill to any interesting purpose, let alone an exalted one, and there is a growing tendency to suspect that no matter how good he may be at holding the Democrats together, he is highly overrated as a statesman. And, of course, there is a growing tendency among Democrats to wish that Mr. Johnson would stop holding them together." This was the year that even Liz Carpenter, today Lady Bird's press secretary, but then a reporter for the *Houston Post,* could see things as they were, writing for the Gridiron Show the altogether accurate lyrics apropos LBJ and Mister Sam:

> *"We run the Hill, together;*
> *Kill every bill, together;*
> *Keep Congress on a tether—*
> *And we both pretend it will never end.*
> *We stop all the fights, together*
> *In Capitol halls, but when Paul Butler calls*
> *We're always away—together.*
> *We shared the pains, together;*
> *Lost campaigns, together;*
> *We're Democrats for the Texas Fat Cats—*
> *And probably will hang, together!"*

*   *
    *

In 1883 Tom Watson addressed the House: "Mr. Speaker, I appeal to this majority; let us assert our manhood one time; let us make the corporations retreat one time; let us stand by the people one time, and we will go home having redeemed in some measure the otherwise discreditable record of the Fifty-second Congress."

From Johnson in the discreditable Congress of 1959 came no such exhortations. And as President in 1965, he was no closer to being an "anti-Wall Street, anti-high interest Populist." An alumnus of the old hardware-store school of economics who believes a "visible" deficit to be some kind of governmental perversion, Johnson was horrified to discover he would be several billion dollars short on income in fiscal 1967. Frantically he sought to cover it up.

The result was the Sales Participation Act (SPA), which allowed Johnson to lump together all government loans—Small Business Administration loans, veterans' loans, student loans, school construction loans, etc.—and sell this paper to banks and other private investors. The money raised from this sale would be set against his budget and, superficially at least, it would look like he had come closer to balancing. Actually it was all a bit of hocus-pocus, with nobody benefiting except the banks. Since the loans are guaranteed by the government and even collected by the government, the banks run no risk and do nothing for their interest payments except, in this case, assist in the paper shuffle that makes Johnson's budget look better. In order to entice the banks to take part in the charade a very high interest rate is put on the marketed paper.

Johnson took the proposal to his friend of forty years, Wright Patman, chairman of the House Banking Committee. Patman, who is a *real* old-time economic Populist, has a disastrous weakness: he sat next to Johnson's father in the Texas legislature, and he remembers Lyndon as a young squirt and takes a paternal interest in him. To Lyndon, he can seldom say no. So, though the legislation violated *everything* Patman had always stood for—it subsidized banks, it raised rates, and it tightened money—Patman agreed to carry the dirty load.

House Banking Committee Democrats caucused the night before the bill was to get a hearing and agreed—in the words of one Texan at the meeting—that it "stunk." They also agreed to support it. Not wanting to call any more attention to their misdeeds than possible, they urged Patman to grease the bill. He did. The White House helped apply it. Presidential aides Henry Wilson and Marvin Watson furiously lobbied the Hill for two days; so did Under Secretary of the Treasury Joseph W. Barr, and so, of course, did Johnson.

The bill was voted out of committee in exactly two hours and twenty-two minutes—no opposition witnesses being given time to testify. Even the two witnesses who appeared for the administration were hustled along by Patman with the reminder that the bill was "kind of urgent." It sped through the House and Senate with the same dispatch.

But Johnson was not trying simply to pretty up his budget. He had a much more disruptive aim. This came out accidentally when Congressman Henry Gonzalez of Texas— a member of the Banking Committee and possibly as intimately familiar as anyone in Washington with Johnson's money thoughts—wrote a letter to a Texas newspaper explaining what the Sales Participation Act was meant to do. "In all," he wrote, "our aim is to move up the ladder from heavy government involvement to *total private loans*." In other words, according to Gonzalez, who had been riding with Johnson on every recent trip to Texas and must have discussed such an important matter with him, Johnson— who once advised REA executives to defend their low rural-electrification loan interest rates by "fighting with beer bottles" if necessary—now wanted to kill not only REA loans and student loans but the *total* loan program.

It was in some ways a startling disclosure, and in other ways not. In his Higher Education Act of 1965 Johnson had started shifting the college loan program out of the government and into private banking; around that time he had also left the Small Business Administration without funds for six months.

But if the Sales Participation Act was indeed his first step toward killing the entire government loan program, he was foiled by his own devices, for the SPA quickly became an embarrassment. Within two months, some of the more alert journalists, such as M. J. Rossant of *The New York Times,* were saying that the extremely high—5.75 per cent—interest rates tagged to some of the earlier SPA sales had triggered a new round of higher commercial interest rates and tighter money.

For Johnson to have sold more of the loans while interests were exploding would have been asking for dangerous repercussions, both in propaganda and in actual deterioration of the money market.

In the late summer of 1966 hardly a day passed that one interest rate or another did not edge up to levels not seen in this country in more than a generation. The mortgage market fell apart. Housing starts were down 40 per cent since Johnson took office. Students needing long-term low-interest loans were being turned away from banks which could do better with their money elsewhere. Municipalities and states were being forced to hold up on needed bond sales.

Not only were the Republicans clubbing Johnson in speeches every day, but so were some key Democrats. "Johnson interest rates," Senator Gore pointed out, "are the highest in forty-five years, the highest since McKinley," and he wondered why Johnson would concoct a program that "fattens the rich and skins the poor." Long of Louisiana was regularly cutting Johnson. "The war on poverty," he stated, "is but a small drop in the bucket compared to the effect on the people that the high interest rates are having." And when that got no response from the White House, Long—who, as majority whip, is supposed to have some truckling relationship to the President—turned a minor technicality into a roundhouse insult: "There is not a member of the

Senate who represents the President of the United States!"
And Proxmire of Wisconsin wondered loudly "why an administration that is always talking about wishing to help
the smaller people is trying to penalize them" by putting a
4.15 per cent ceiling on the working man's E-bonds while
"leaving the lid off for the larger" bonds and the wealthier
investor.

Eggheads at large took up the shout. Dr. Robert Hutchins
said the nation was confronted with "an economic situation
unprecedented in modern history, one in which inflation
and depression threaten simultaneously." The rising interest rates, he pointed out, were staggering the smaller busi-
nesses that had to borrow while having scarcely any effect on
the large corporations, which simply dipped into their unprecedented profits that had escaped the taxgatherer.

Faced with this kind of reprimand and resistance, Johnson finally retreated and threw up a trench of platitudes.
"The tightness of money," he said, "mainly reflects the extreme buoyancy of our economy." And to another gathering
he complained, "Interest rates, interest rates, interest rates,
that's all I hear."

In September, 1966, he announced that he would sell no
more loans, for a while, under the Sales Participation Act.
But he would not take the major step, the crucial step, available to him at this juncture, a step that would have established him as a strong economic reform president. This was
the opportunity to whip the Federal Reserve Board back
into line. Instead, he sided with the Board and double-
crossed his old friend Patman, who had already turned his
own philosophy inside out for Johnson's sake.

In December, 1965, the Board, without even conferring
with Johnson, had raised the interest rates for the federal
reserve system. Johnson's sale of government paper under
the Sales Participation Act had worsened the situation, but
his permitting the Board to get by with the rate raise in

December not only established an official framework for interest escalation but, far worse, seemed to officially commission the Federal Reserve Board as an independent arm of government, co-equal with the Supreme Court, the Congress, and the President—a most powerful fourth arm of government on whose whim recessions and booms depend.

Johnson took the position that he had no control over the Board. But when a seat opened on the Board in January, instead of appointing a "loose-money" advocate, he appointed Andrew Brimmer, a Negro who followed the old tight-money line—thus, ironically, enabling Johnson in one move to gain points with the nation's most impoverished citizens and with the banking community.

In saying he had no control over the Board, Johnson was deserting the Roosevelt-Truman position and siding with Eisenhower. Both Roosevelt and Truman had insisted, consistent with the wording of the Federal Reserve Act, that the Board was theirs to manipulate. They insisted that fiscal and monetary policies were too integral a part of government to leave outside the public sway. But on October 5, 1956, in an historic press conference, Eisenhower had stated that "the Federal Reserve Board is not under my control, and I think it is proper that the Congress did set it up as an independent agency."

Acting with that permissiveness, the Board had caused three recessions during Ike's terms, without a word of complaint from him. And now Johnson was following Eisenhower's interpretation. Furthermore, he was not long in showing that he did not want it otherwise.

In late July, 1966, Patman pushed through the House Banking Committee legislation that would have set a precedent of rate determination independent of the Federal Reserve Board. But in a press conference on August 24, Johnson made it plain that he did not want to be rescued by Patman. He said that even if Patman's bill were passed by Congress—

highly unlikely without Johnson's support—he could promise no more than to "*try* to carry out the terms of the law." He was determined not to move against his banker friends, but still Patman did not give up, warning him that his advisers were "hurting your reputation badly in this area." Finally he pressed Johnson into calling a meeting of opposing sides.

The day before the bill was to go to the floor, Patman met with Johnson in his bedroom in the White House for two hours. Also on hand were Walter Heller, one of Kennedy's economic advisers; Jake Jacobsen, Texas ex-Governor Price Daniel's factotum who had become Johnson's "expert" in many governmental mysteries including finance, although those who recall the fiscal disarray of Daniel's administration will find this hard to understand; Treasury Secretary Fowler; Under Secretary Barr; Marvin Watson, who learned his lean economics under labor-hating E. B. Germany at Lone Star Steel of Texas; and a couple of lesser lights.

Starting with Fowler, who insisted that Patman apologize for calling him "namby-pamby" in public, everyone in the room jumped on Patman, but nevertheless the old man came away thinking he had won an understanding from Johnson that he would not *oppose* the Patman bill. That's all Patman asked: not Johnson's support, but only that Johnson & Company would stand aside in neutral territory and give him a fighting chance with his bill. But Patman was not long in discovering that the President—whom Patman two days earlier had unhappily described as "not the Johnson I once knew"—was going to attack him. In the midst of the House debate on the bill, Johnson held a press conference announcing plans to meet inflation that would make Patman's legislation, he intimated, unnecessary. The timing of the announcement was obviously to kill Patman's efforts.

From early morning, before debate on the floor began, members were being called by the White House and asked not to vote for Patman's bill because the President had come up with another package.

Meanwhile the banking industry was putting tremendous pressures on Congress. *The American Banker,* an industry publication, had rallied the 14,000 members of the American Bankers Association to telephone or send a telegram. Democratic Congressmen softened by this lobbying effort and looking for a way out were now given an exit by Johnson's maneuver. They could vote against Patman and, thanks to the President, keep their party bona fides. And so the bill lost.

Nine years of Johnson following eight years of Eisenhower will undoubtedly convey a common-law power to the Federal Reserve that, the statutes notwithstanding, will leave the nation virtually at the mercy of this shadow agency, whose operational budget is even independent of Congress.

Through Johnson, the private banking industry has won control of the nation's fiscal and monetary policies. The multimillion dollar "Populist" from Johnson City has made the Democratic party respectable as the modern Republican party is respectable; there will be no more Kennedy "s.o.b." witticisms directed at the business community, no more Trumanesque scorning of the industrialist "with a calculating machine where his heart ought to be," no more gentlemanly Rooseveltian reprimands of "greedy" Wall Street. Under Johnson the nabob can be sure that the party of William Jennings Bryan and Pitchfork Ben Tillman will take on new sympathies. There may be some virtues in that, but, as Tom Watson remarked in another day when the Democratic and Republican parties were indistinguishable in their affection for the capitalist, "There is a party for Caesar and a party for Pompey. But there is no party for Rome."

4 The lower kingdom

*The pro-Johnson and anti-Johnson factions are
so violently opposed as to make Texas politics
almost unbelievable. If you haven't seen it,
you wouldn't believe it.*

—Senator Wayne Morse, 1966

For Texas, that proud, fertile desert of social reaction, Lyndon Johnson has been the chief pharaoh. Not that his hand has been felt directly in the life that goes on there: as the great landlords of South Texas rise in the morning and send forth their naked servants to work the earth, and elsewhere armies of laborers raise up the pyramids of industry and the temples of petroleum, the old customs are kept. Annually another generation of Mexicanos and Negroes are sacrificed to the old gods, and the traditional distance is held between the few of great wealth and the many of great poverty. Texas lives and dies beyond the eye of the chief pharaoh; to him, these have been colonial matters, things of the lower Nile, so to speak. His residence, his seat of power, has been elsewhere.

Nevertheless, through it all, even when some of the local rulers, the governors, the lieutenant governors, the officials who regulate the pumping of oil and the dredging of shells— even when these lesser rulers made noises and attracted passing attention to themselves, nobody in Texas forgot that Lyndon Johnson was No. 1. A person was either pro-Johnson or anti-Johnson. There was nothing else to be but some-thing-*Johnson* in Texas.

And that's why John F. Kennedy was enticed into the state. So many slaves were rebelling, it looked like the chief pharaoh was at last in very serious trouble.

*   *
*
*

To an outsider, the constant battle between pro-Johnson and anti-Johnson forces over the years may seem to be only a struggle for power for power's sake. To think so would be a great mistake. The liberals' struggle in Texas has been for the Mexicano who lives with a family of seven in a one-room shanty on San Antonio's West Side, for the Negro child who is still bussed fourteen miles across Houston to a segregated school, for the wage earner who is asked to pay sales tax on his overalls while the giant pipelines companies successfully duck a reasonable spread of taxes.

There are more poverty-level citizens of Texas than of any other state in the nation. Of the 316,194 families in Houston, 18 per cent exist on poverty-level incomes. Twenty-nine per cent of San Antonio's residents live at that level; in this Mexicano mecca where Johnson's Great Society now is spending millions to build a posh international fair, there are 46,000 slum housing units, and in 11,000 of these there is no plumbing at all.

There are 800,000 functional illiterates in the state. The prisons today are better than they used to be, because they are now staffed by decent (though wretchedly paid) men and women, but during part of the period in which the pro-

Johnson crowd defeated efforts at reform, prisoners muti-
lated themselves so they would not have to go into the fields
and be abused by the guards. For most of the years during
which the Johnsonian conflict has gone on, the insane
asylums have been snake pits; they still are, but improved
to a venomless standard.

Labor unions have virtually no rights in Texas. Pickets
can be sent to prison for two years for even threatening to
punch a non-picket. A pro-union bill has not passed the
legislature since before World War I. The legislature in recent years has turned down a *25 cents an hour* minimum
wage proposal.* In Texas there are 1,000 industrial deaths
and 200,000 industrial injuries each year; it is commonplace,
for example, for men in the construction trades to work on
outside elevators, six and eight stories above the ground,
without a guardrail. This is because there are no industrial
safety laws. Safety legislation was killed one session after a
lobbyist told a committee of the Texas House that when a
lumberyard worker loses his hand in an unguarded band-
saw, the company shouldn't be blamed; there was nothing
defective about the *equipment,* for the hand on the ground
proved it was working *perfectly*. This is the kind of tor-
tured logic that has guided state affairs for many years. The
liberals hounded and hounded the legislature to pass a loan
shark control law, and so it did: one that permits 320 per
cent interest on a loan.

---

* To attract public attention to the fact that farmers in the Valley pay
them as low as forty cents an hour, a covey of farm workers hiked four
hundred miles to Austin to lay their grievances at Governor John Connally's door and seek his support in passing a $1.25 an hour minimum
wage law. When they got there, he was out of town, of course. Some of
the farm workers are striking, but so far all they've got for their troubles
is some time in the Starr County Jail. Their leaders have appealed
to Johnson for help, supposing that he just might have some influence
with Connally and other Texas politicos. He has ignored them. When
he went to the Mexican border for a speech recently, the farm workers
showed up and tried to get close enough to give him a brochure listing
the problems arising from having to live on about $1,000 a year—but
Johnson couldn't seem to see their waggling arms.

The tax legislation that is passed by the legislature is openly written by the Texas Research League. And who are the members of the TRL? They are top executives from the likes of the Shamrock Oil & Gas Company, Southwestern Bell Telephone Company, Brown & Root, Humble Oil & Refining Company, Neiman-Marcus, Texas Gulf Sulphur, Mobil Oil Company, and the First National Bank of Dallas.

This is the Texas that the local liberals have been trying for a dozen years to wrest from the hard fist of the Johnson machine so that they can turn it into a pleasant land, supported by those best able to pay.

And because any revolutionary change of this kind would endanger his power base, Johnson has opposed the liberals at every move. His most effective opposition has come in the form of destroying liberal themes and in corrupting and destroying liberal idols, since to permit their existence would be to give the liberals something to build around.

For example, there was a time, not long ago, when Henry Gonzalez was the most courageous radical politician in Texas. In 1957 he stood almost alone in the Texas legislature filibustering against the anti-Negro bills. But then he was elected to Congress, the first Latin-American to make it. Johnson helped him get elected; and recently he helped pass through Congress a $6.7 million boondoggle, HemisFair, for Gonzalez' home town. His part in the Faustian pact completed, Johnson demanded repayment. Thus in 1966 Texas was presented with the weird sight of Henry Gonzalez breaking with his old liberal supporters, calling them "undiluted fools," doing what he could to tear up the liberal organization, and urging the election to the U.S. Senate of one of the South's most opportunistic racists.

And then there was Jerry Holleman. In 1960 Holleman, president of the Texas AFL-CIO, vowed he would stick to the end with the liberal coalition opposing the candidacy of Johnson as Texas' favorite son. At the last minute he backed out, destroying the coalition and giving labor a

reputation for treachery in Texas politics that it is still trying to live down. Holleman's reward was an under secretary-
ship of labor—until he borrowed $1,000 from Billie Sol Estes,
the dishonored fertilizer king, to help pay for a banquet
honoring Johnson. The loan discovered, Holleman went
out. Today he is a "management consultant," advising industrialists how to beat his former comrades at the bargaining table.

National politicians could learn much from the Texas
microcosm. They could learn, for instance, that to have fun
in LBJ's bed, a political leader must come to it as one of
Lyndon's lusty kind; seduced liberals, if they are not ruined,
never do very well. Gonzalez and Holleman are little men,
but what happened to them, if he had noticed it, might have
made Hubert Humphrey, one of the great liberals of the
recent past, think twice before he crawled between the presidential sheets.

The one important liberal in Texas who has withstood
the sorceries of Lyndon Johnson is Ralph Yarborough, better known to his east Texas neighbors as "Raff." He was
attending labor union conventions when no other important
Texas politician dared show up. He went to Young Democrats conventions when the word was being spread that they
were run by communists. He campaigned as a liberal when
nobody else would, took the abuse, gathered a nucleus of
affection. He is inept and inarticulate and, perhaps justifiably, politically paranoiac: his mail has been mysteriously
opened, his phone in the Senate Office Building has been
found bugged. Texas newspapers print the wildest sort of
gossip about him, without bothering to check their sources.
He shouts and rages at his office staff over trifles, until the
girls weep and the men quit, and then he complains that he
is deserted. Not only has he been opposed by big oil money
and by Johnson and every Texas governor since he entered
politics, but also he has been undercut by politicians from

whom he properly could have expected full assistance. Yet through it all he has survived, grown pricklier and flowered, like the barrel cactus.

And because Yarborough won't succumb, Johnson has of course done his best to ruin him. 1956 was the year in which Johnson really launched forth with a vengeance to turn back Yarborough's promising career. Perhaps to call his career promising when he had lost two previous campaigns for the governor's office may be stretching it a bit, but his doggedness as well as his popularity was increasing, and it seemed that nothing could hold him away from a major political victory, eventually. In 1956 he ran again for governor. His most important opponent was Price Daniel, retiring as U.S. senator. In some ways this was a crucial race for the entire South.

Texas was ending three terms of extremely reactionary leadership under Governor Shivers; if it had obtained a breathing spell, perhaps even an upward progressive shove, with Yarborough in the mansion—if the seemingly unbreakable chain of conservative rule had been snapped for even one two-year term—Texas could have been an example, a political talisman which would have given spirit and aggressive hope to the small clumps of embattled progressives across the South at a time when the racial boil was beginning to break and spoil the whole environment. Little Rock was just a year away.

Out of a Yarborough victory something in the way of a regional antidote might have been managed. Yarborough, although he has voted for most of the civil rights bills that have come up since he went to the U.S. Senate in 1957, and made a rousing "Shame on you, George Wallace!" speech in the Senate in 1965, is no great integrationist. But his followers have been the rural county officials who got the Negro vote because they did not use the race issue and were the ones who fought the racist sheriffs.

Daniel, on the other hand, campaigned against the NAACP, minority-race "Communists" hiding behind every bale of cotton, and the usual 1956 racist kit. Under his governorship and with his approval, Texas was to produce some of the rawest anti-Negro legislation written in the South. Johnson was the key to Daniel's winning. He used his influence in South Texas, the purchasable home of the Latins, and especially he used his influence with the Rural Electrification Administration (REA) officials. With them he traded off: he would push a Niagara power bill then before the Senate (and he did) in exchange for their support of Daniel. In largely rural Texas that was important help. After the Establishment had counted the ballots for three weeks, Yarborough lost the race by 3,000 votes.

But the next year Yarborough (again with the opposition of Johnson, who was working behind the scenes this time for the candidacy of Martin Dies, the former chairman of the House Un-American Activities Committee) went to the Senate.

Now at last the aroused Texas liberals had a hero to rally around, and the split in the Democratic party began widening at such a rapid pace that, by 1963, it seriously threatened the Johnson-Connally control of the party. The liberals now had a leader who, publicly, just a few weeks before the Kennedy visit to Texas, was willing to shout his defiance and contempt for Johnson: "A number of people have asked me how I was kept off the appropriations committee when I was senior senator applying for it! This happened last year also! It happened after the *lackeys and henchmen of a powerful Texas politician* had lobbied with other senators against me . . . I did not go to the United States Senate with a ring in my nose, nor to be the sniveling satrap of a *power-mad politician!*"

Eager to keep national liberal themes and national liberal leaders from tying on to the Texas "red hots," as he called them, Johnson has never been subtle about it. In fact, during the Stevenson years he was downright brashly antagonistic.

Late in September, 1955, a side door of Lyndon's farmhouse opened and three men came out into the dazzling morning light to hold a press conference: Rayburn, Johnson, Adlai. They sat down in canvasback chairs before a battery of microphones and awaited questions.

Someone asked Stevenson if he thought Texas would switch back to the Democratic column the next year.

"It's my opinion—" Stevenson began.

Johnson cut in: "I think Sam and I can answer that question. Texas will be in the Democratic column by a substantial margin."

That was Adlai's first and last chance to say what he thought of politics on that Texas visit: it was symptomatic of the squelching he regularly received from Johnson. He knew what he was up against and he passed it off in his style. "I'd like to come back to Texas and either talk or listen— whatever they'll permit me to do," he said. The reporters laughed. Rayburn smiled slightly. Johnson squinted into the sun.

In 1952 Johnson had made one (1) speech in Texas *sort of* on behalf of Adlai Stevenson. He spent far more time in Missouri campaigning to help Stuart Symington than he did in Texas campaigning for the national ticket. In fact, in the one radio talk he gave at home, he spent most of the time saying nice things about "the Southerner on the ticket" (Sparkman), denouncing those who would "rob Texas of her tidelands" (thus disassociating himself from the Adlai-Truman position, and siding with the oil companies, on the tidelands issue), and praising his own record in the Senate. He claims today that it was a pro-Adlai speech, but if he even so much as mentioned Adlai's name, no one remembers it.

His important betrayal of Adlai had taken place at the

1952 national convention in Chicago. Sam Rayburn, presiding, did not at first want to seat Texas Governor Allan Shivers' delegation because he did not think he was a loyal Democrat; Rayburn had good reason to think so, since it was known that Shivers had taken oil money to lead a bolt to the GOP.* A scanning of the Shivers' delegation would have told even a political novice that most of them were the same men who had gone Dixiecrat four years earlier and had fought Roosevelt in 1944. As a group they weren't just passively reactionary; they were violently so, and everyone in Texas politics knew it.

Their seating was being challenged by another Texas delegation, led by Maury Maverick, a certified loyal Democrat, as Rayburn and Johnson and everyone else were very well aware. Rayburn at first wanted to seat the Maverick group, but Lyndon met Shivers at the airport and brought him to Rayburn's room in the Blackstone Hotel where he persuaded the old man that Shivers could be depended on to stay true blue to the party.

So Shivers was seated; whereupon his outfit voted against every Democratic candidate at the convention with a hope of winning the nomination. Shivers then not only went home and personally deserted the Democratic nominees, but also led a mass exodus of all important Texas officials out of the party. Eisenhower won Texas.

Once again in 1956 Johnson betrayed Adlai. It takes a pretty fast talker to address a group of Democrats for an hour on national politics and on the national political campaign without once mentioning the presidential candidate by name, but Johnson managed to do it every time.

Money which was supposed to be used to promote Stevenson's candidacy by the Texas State Democratic Committee was instead spent on reprinting and distributing a Holmes

* See "Shivers of Texas, a Tragedy in Three Acts," D. B. Hardeman. *Harper's Magazine*, November, 1956.

Alexander column which knocked Stevenson and praised Johnson as "the tall traveler [who] came to Congress as a follower of Franklin Roosevelt but a number of years later . . . was riding in the first-class coach of arch-Republicanism, the Taft-Hartley Act." (At least Johnson took it as praise.) And just to be sure that Stevenson would have no chance of carrying the state, Johnson and Rayburn advised him that he didn't need to come to Texas because it was "in the bag."

Coupled to Johnson's basic dislike for the Stevenson wit were now added his own presidential ambitions. In 1956 Johnson was already rolling the taste of the nomination in his mouth, he wanted it so very much. He was repeatedly told by his Southern colleagues in the Senate that he could get it. Russell and George, the Georgians who had made Johnson majority leader, told Johnson that he could become the South's favorite son. Said George publicly, "If he can be persuaded to do so [that is, take the nomination], he might well become the effective candidate for the party because of his strong support through the South, as well as in other sections of the country." Russell said on the floor of the Senate: "I cannot refrain from observing that when Johnson's name is presented to the convention as a favorite son candidate from the great state of Texas, *it will be impossible* to prevent delegations from other states adopting him as their favorite son." And again he said that Johnson could easily become a favorite son of the South.

Who else liked Lyndon? Senators Harry Byrd and Willis Robertson of Virginia, economically the two most reactionary men in the Senate at the time, proclaimed Johnson as being of "presidential stature," and George Smathers of Florida, who five years earlier had won his seat from Claude Pepper in the dirtiest racial campaign in modern times, and Strom Thurmond of Dixiecrat notoriety, and Russell Long of Louisiana, who disagreed with Johnson on some economic matters but thoroughly agreed with him on protecting the oil industry (since Long owns oil property) and on how to keep the Negroes down—*they* all came out strong for their majority leader.

Johnson, of course, believed them; believed that rank and file America was no different from these soiled politicos. He thought that at the very least his strength at the national convention would be as Mike Mansfield predicted: ". . . enough to have strong influence on the ultimate selection of the nominee." Johnson believed them because he is a man of closet vision. That's one reason why he was a rather good manipulator in the Senate. To him, the world was no bigger than the Senate. He has never had any interest in the intimacies of Texas government—the condition of the penal system, the condition of the schools, the justice of the state welfare payments. A Johnson friend of many years told me that "he's bored with state affairs. He's bored by all the things that make up life within the state. A Texas Congressman once talked to him about going back and running for governor and he said, 'Why? You've got a better job up here. State politics is a dead end.' " To Johnson, Texas was a thing to hold in his hand, like a doorknob, but only because it opened the door of the Senate.

So when his cronies in the Senate told him in 1956 that he was a shoo-in as regional favorite son, he thought he heard the world speaking. A politician could not have a graver defect, but few have noticed it. Hugh Sidey, political reporter for *Life,* is one of the few who has put it down in print: "There is a persistent legend that Lyndon B. Johnson is the world's best politician. He is regarded by many of his enemies as well as his friends as having almost mystical ability to understand the polls and the pols, to know how to wage and win elections, to pursue and persuade the indifferent and the doubtful. But in fact, this evaluation is imprecise and highly misleading . . . it is still a matter of wonder-

ment to students of L.B.J. that a man so adept in other
forums can remain so clumsy in national campaigning. Back
in 1960 when all those Democrats were seeking the presidential nomination, Johnson was the most inept of all the
losers. While Kennedy went out into the country and gathered the delegates, L.B.J. relied on his Senate cronies—most
of whom had long since lost touch with their states—to de-
liver the goods to him. He accepted political advice from the
likes of Bobby Baker, who may have known how to wheel
and deal in the Senate cloakroom but had no understanding
of how to work in the open spaces. Johnson always has had
a singular reluctance to believe bad news. In 1960 he preferred to rely on the dubious promises and evaluations of a
host of second-raters who had attached themselves to him in
search of power. He was, of course, clobbered."

Exactly. And if Sidey were a little older, he would have
applied the same description to Johnson's tactics in 1956:
relying on his Senate cloakroom buddies who didn't know
how the country felt, didn't know even how their own regions felt. He was accepting assurances of Walter George,
for example, although there were many counties in Georgia
which George, by his own confession, had not visited in fifteen years (one reason he was about to be bluffed out of his
seat). He relied on the assurance of Strom Thurmond, who
had just got through beating the Democratic machine in
South Carolina in a spectacular write-in campaign that left
the machine Democrats furious and just waiting for a chance
to get even. It is indeed doubtful that Thurmond knew how
his own clique felt. Jimmy Byrnes, the man who had made
Thurmond senator, when asked by Shivers at the 1954 Governors' Conference at Boca Raton to support Johnson in
1956 had hotly refused to do so, calling LBJ "an upstart."

The highly unprofessional reluctance to believe bad news
that Sidey noticed in later campaigns was then, too, an
amazingly impacted defect. Popular? Gallup had just polled

the country and found that among Democrats, 39 per cent wanted Adlai, 33 per cent Kefauver, a few (6 per cent) would go along with Averell Harriman, even fewer (4 per cent) would be willing to give their vote to the implacable Georgian, Russell, and only 3 per cent of the national Democrats liked Johnson. As for the independents of the country, Gallup found Johnson so unattractive among them that he did not get a high enough percentage to be listed.

The attitude of the liberals in the Democratic party was indicated in the announcement of Joseph Rauh, then national chairman of the Americans for Democratic Action (ADA), that if Johnson got the nomination he would just sit out the election because so far as he could see Johnson was "running the Democratic party for the benefit of the Southern Conservative viewpoint." Rauh need not have worried. The cloakroom soap bubble did not last to Chicago. Aside from Texas, only one state threw its delegation to Johnson—Mississippi. Just ol' Mississippi, hatchery of Bilbo and Barnett, given to Johnson by Governor James Coleman, for which quixotic gesture he was later rewarded with a federal judgeship. Johnson is not always grateful to those who have joined him in embarrassment, but he was on this occasion.

So neither Democrats of the South nor of any other point of the compass, wanted Johnson as their presidential nominee. But surely he came closer to getting the vice-presidential nomination? Alas, no; for that he received only one-half (½) of one delegate vote, the least popular response to any of the thirteen candidates who received votes.

Having failed to get the nomination, Johnson used his control of the Texas convention votes like a drunken card sharp and lost everything. Early in the week, when the Texas delegation would have clearly swung the nomination for Stevenson, Johnson tried to push too far. In return for his support, Johnson demanded that Stevenson name a member of Johnson's staff as head of the Democratic National Committee (which would give Johnson a head start on the 1960 nomination). Johnson also tried to make him promise a weak civil rights plank, and guarantee that Johnson would have a voice in the vice-presidential nomination.

Adlai said no.

So Johnson held out; after the first ballot, if it looked like his own chances were gone, he would throw the delegation to the strongest candidate other than Stevenson. The trouble with this plan was that there was no second ballot. When it became clear to everyone that Stevenson would get the nomination on the first ballot, the Texas delegation tried to climb on the bandwagon, but Speaker Sam Rayburn—who was chairing the convention and who had predicted all along that Stevenson would get it on the first or second ballot—was so disgusted with the strategy of his protégé Johnson that he would not even recognize the delegation to allow it to shift its vote.

Having deprived Texas of a voice in the nomination of the presidential candidate, Johnson next went to work to manipulate the vice-presidency. He instructed the delegation to vote for Governor Frank ("How long, O how long?") Clements of Tennessee, a racial reactionary. When Clements withdrew, Johnson instructed the delegation to switch to Senator Gore of Tennessee. The idea was to vote for a Southerner to save face in Texas and then, on the second ballot, to go for Humphrey, whom Johnson considered on the side of the South and "the most misunderstood man in the Senate." At this point there were some rumblings among the Texans. One said Johnson was asking them to "act like a bunch of eunuchs." Tom Connally, the ex-senator, told Johnson "you vote like you damn please and I'll vote like I damn please. Gore is a tinhorn. If you're gonna vote for anyone from Tennessee, why don't you vote for Kefauver?" The answer, of course, was that Johnson hated Kefauver, who had frequently bucked Johnson's policies in the Senate.

On the first ballot, Humphrey finished fifth. Now it was clear the choice was between Kefauver and Kennedy. The Texans caucused again, and Johnson talked them into backing Kennedy. "You sent me here as your leader. I've worked in the Senate with these men, and I want you to know that I favor Kennedy." Kefauver won.

As old Tom Connally shuffled out of the place he sighed with almost treacherous relief, "Once again the Democratic Party has saved the nation from Texas."

It may have been embarrassing to have been led over the cliff by Johnson in Chicago, but the Texas liberals were about to discover that the Big Betrayal of 1956 was just beginning.

In those days Texas Democrats held two state conventions each year, one in May and the other in September. Johnson wanted the May convention to support him as the favorite son in Chicago, but to achieve this he would have to side with the liberals against his old friend, Governor Shivers. He didn't mind doing this because by now Shivers was thoroughly discredited, leaving office that year trailing great clouds of scandal from his administration. Significantly, when Johnson publicly denounced Shivers (they have since made up) he did not damn him for these scandals, nor did he condemn him for allowing an armed mob to succeed in keeping Negroes out of a school in Mansfield, thus setting a pattern for other rebellious governors to follow (as Faubus did, even mentioning the Texas incident, the next year). No, the only thing Johnson had against Shivers was his "personal attack on me and my patriotic reputation."

To say that the liberals were skeptical of Johnson's help at the May convention is putting it very gently, but they accepted him because while they had the muscle to take the convention, they did not have respectability. Liberals were not respectable in Texas in 1956. They needed a front man to give them respectability and, uneasily, they agreed to team up with Johnson, take the convention, and send him off to Chicago with unanimous, if grudging, support.

But now they learned that Johnson had vowed his loyalty to the liberals *only* to get their support in Chicago, nothing else. He had wanted to go to the national convention with the faint aroma of liberalism around him, in order to entice any susceptible northerners. When he did not get the nomi-nation, when in fact he was humiliatingly turned down for it even by Southern delegates, he and Rayburn returned to Texas and stole the September state convention by refusing to recognize the legally elected liberal delegations, who sat out the convention in a neighboring cow barn. They turned the party machinery back to the oil-insurance-banking con-servatives who have held the controls ever since. Adding in-jury to insult, they even hired a goon squad, headed by a former Texas Ranger, to throw out liberals who complained.

Mark from that day the liberals' permanent estrangement from Johnson. The depth of bitterness felt by them was modestly expressed by W. O. Cooper of the Democratic Organizing Committee of Dallas at that time: "I have left my last entrail on the battlements under the leadership of Johnson and Rayburn. I have never seen people kick their political friends in the teeth with the kind of vengeance that was done this day."

A more accurate measure of the bitterness lodged in the hearts of Texas liberals is the remembrance of Dave Shapiro, one of the young, bloodthirsty generals in Yarborough's camp: "That was the year, 1956, that Lyndon first really came to the front as the enemy of organized liberalism in his home state. His game was, pure and simple, to keep the new and growing urban liberal organizations in Houston, San Antonio, Fort Worth and in other industrial sections, and the ape-shit country Ralph Yarborough-types, from getting control of the state Democratic party apparatus, and to keep the post-Shivers Establishment finks in control of the party. Up to this time I had a mild distrust of Lyndon. After the fall 1956 convention I hated his ever-loving guts."

That was the liberals' last real chance to have a significant role in the operation of the Democratic party in Texas. Because Johnson betrayed them on that occasion, they have never forgiven him, never trusted him, have indeed despised him to this day, and do so even though he has wagged the standard of liberalism from the White House in an effort at appeasement.

* *
   *

It is said that Kennedy was surprised that he did not fare stronger in 1960 with Johnson on the ticket. Apparently Kennedy failed to draw conclusions from the treatment Johnson had received at the 1956 convention, when he was supposedly at the very peak of his power in the Senate and of his popularity in the South. Even so, Kennedy could have been spared surprise if he had done some elementary investigation before inviting Johnson aboard. If Kennedy had talked to a few workhorse politicians around Texas instead of drawing his conclusions from the tired, out-of-touch U.S. Senate hands, he would have easily found that Johnson has never been much admired by any constituency at any level of politics.

Johnson has climbed by successes so small that the accumulative grand success seems an accident, as indeed in more than one way it is. He has never had to face serious opposition except in his first race for the U.S. Senate, when he lost, and in his second race for the Senate, won with votes which most historians now designate as of questionable authenticity, to say the least. Otherwise he has won because he was unopposed or opposed only by unknowns, or by painfully clumsy fellows like Goldwater. Both in the elections that sent him to the House and then to the Senate, he received less than a majority (if we acknowledge theft on the latter occasion).

In 1937, the first time Johnson ran for Congress, he received only 27 per cent of the votes. This was enough because it was a high-man-win race, and he had eleven opponents chopping up the rest of the votes. It was in this race that the myth of his liberalism was first established—a myth that will be unwound as we go along—when he, as most biographers insist on saying, courageously supported the Franklin D. Roosevelt program. Courageous is not the proper word; it was clever . . . Not devilishly clever, certainly not a display of genius; just good political strategy. How does one win in a plurality twelve-man race? Become the target of *all* the others. This Johnson did by not only supporting Roosevelt but also by singling out the most controversial point in the FDR program, the court-packing plan, to praise. Since this was the Roosevelt proposal least understood and least sympathized with by the general public, the other candidates took the bait. They started attacking FDR to get at Johnson.* In 1937 Roosevelt was still generally popular in Texas, and it does not say much for Johnson that, although he was the only candidate to wear the Hyde Park colors, he was able to obtain slightly more than one-fourth of the votes cast (representing about one-eighth of the adult population).

In 1941, when he made his first try for the U.S. Senate, President Roosevelt publicly endorsed him, but this was not

* Accounts of Johnson's closeness to Roosevelt are getting a little out of control these days, as LBJ goes about encouraging these myths of the "inheritance of history." A good practical illustration of how close they were occurred when Tom Miller, mayor and for many years patriarch of the Austin political structure, came to Washington with but one desire: to personally meet Roosevelt. Miller was on the third rung of Texas politics, but he was an important man in Johnson's Congressional district. For two days Johnson tried to get Miller in for just a brief handshake, but without luck.

enough burnishment for a state-wide race. He lost to the flour salesman W. Lee (Please pass the biscuits, Pappy) O'Daniel, who ran on the Decalogue, the Golden Rule, and the most transparent kind of hokum. To offset such an attraction Johnson had FDR's faded endorsement, but little to offer personally in the way of a record or imaginative proposals. Most of the great New Deal innovations had been advanced and settled before Johnson arrived in Congress.

At that time Johnson's "liberalism" consisted of voting for rural electrification, various New Deal farm programs, and various public works programs—the kind of federal assistance that Senator Theodore Bilbo of Mississippi and a majority of other Southern Congressmen were entirely will-ing to support, inasmuch as about one-third of the total federal expenditure for these programs was coming into the South. This was the notable Beggar's Opera liberalism of many who backed Roosevelt in those days, and it had noth-ing to do with civil rights or civil liberties. Even as limited as this liberalism was, it had deserted Johnson's make-up by the time he again considered running for the Senate. By that time—1948—he had, as the great political historian V. O. Key noted, "lost much of his crusading sheen." Be-ing only sheen, it was easily lost.

Throughout his career Johnson has used the New Deal like a reversible vest. During the 1930's and early 1940's he was pro-New Deal because that's the way the country felt too. During the 1960's he has again worn the pro-side of the vest on the outside because it is now politically camp to do so. But in the late 1940's and through most of the 1950's when asked about his connections with the New Deal, he often sounded like Peter with a whole barnyard of cocks crowing in the background. After World War II had ended and the nation was a bit hung-over from its Rooseveltian orgy, Johnson seemed amazed and disturbed when taken for a New Dealer. Him, a New Dealer? Pshaw! Oh, he might have mentioned FDR's name once or twice in getting elected in 1937, and he might even have been heard to say that Roosevelt "was like a daddy to me," but that certainly shouldn't be construed to mean that he believed in the Roosevelt philosophy. He told the Associated Press on April 23, 1947, that "the term 'New Dealer' is a misnomer. I believed then and I still believe in many of the causes Roosevelt backed. That includes development of water power and other natural resources. I believe in the REA and think all-weather roads should be built to every farmhouse. But I believe in free enterprise and I don't believe in the government doing anything that the people can do privately." Just roads and rural electrification? This could have been Cotton Ed Smith talking, or Jim Eastland. It was certainly no liberal talking.

It was the announcement by the grand chameleon that he was preparing to change his coloration. The new-rich of Texas, the industrialists who had waxed fat on wartime contracts, the insurance companies and banking houses that were building a new skyline in Dallas and Houston, the international oil giants, these—not the small farmer—were to be the new power levers in Texas and he was not at all against pulling them.

Of course, it depended on what audience he was addressing. Even as late as 1957, however, in speaking to a Farmers' Union convention in Abilene, he glossed over his ties to the old New Deal. He spoke nostalgically of the Roosevelt revolution that "brought the professors and more crackpots and dreamers to Washington that you ever saw—but what's important a nation was saved." But, he hurried on, "I have to admit, I am perhaps more conservative than I once was. But I see no real change in my philosophy. When I was a young man of adventure with more guts than brains I did some things I don't do today." It was a typical bit of Johnsonian pro-and-con ping-pong, but the friendly references to

Roosevelt's "crackpots and dreamers" hardly disguised the fact that Johnson had recently voted against 200,000 public housing starts, against cutting corporation taxes on small companies and against raising the taxes on large corporations, and against tight money controls. By 1957 the Johnson who had become a cuff-links cowboy with a pasture full of prize bulls, the Johnson who could come in any door of the Petroleum Club and be welcome was many REA light years away from the "young political natural on the make who had nailed his flag squarely to the mast of what was, after all, the national government then in power," as Selig S. Harrison once described him. He had become the middle-aged political natural on the make who had run his very Jolly Roger up a different economic mast.

Harrison, associate editor of *The New Republic,* with plenty of leg work and perception did a study of Johnson in 1960, when everyone was curious as to what sort of scrambler this was seeking the presidency in earnest. Among those Harrison interviewed was Ed Clark, then thoroughly established as the most powerful lobbyist in Austin and today Johnson's ambassador to Australia. Clark told Harrison that Johnson consciously decided after the death of Roosevelt that the only way to the top then was to win the favor of the moneyed of Dallas (Clark meant Houston, too). Thereafter this would be Johnson's comfortable, sympathetic power base, "where the people of substance," as Clark put it in his folksy way, "have this type of working political relationship to each other. You know, not like it's schemed out, but everybody just gets the idea and they go the same way."

In Johnson's favor it must be said that he had enough self-awareness to doubt his abilities to inspire the public. Ego he had even then, abundantly, but not confidence. When the U.S. Senate seat opened up again in 1948, a group of young veterans, wanting to get Texas off to a progressive postwar start, met privately in Austin to decide on a candidate. In those days it did not take much to qualify as a progressive in Texas; if one was not a neo-Republican, which is to say (by Texas-Republican standards) if one was not Neanderthal, then one was prima facie a progressive. Thus, and only thus, Johnson qualified. As a Congressman he had not only voted for the labor-crippling Taft-Hartley Act, he had also helped shape it. He stood adamantly against all civil rights legislation. He had given the oil industry of Texas full and loyal support on every issue potentially affecting it. Yet he was considered more liberal than most of the Texas politicians of that time, and so the young turks wondered if he cared to run. He said yes, finally.

Johnson's claimed motivation for agreeing to run is wonderfully illustrative of the way he twists history. For his authorized biographer, Booth Mooney, Johnson recalled that he went to Austin ready to announce that he would not run because "he wanted to make money, which he knew he would never be able to do in politics" (sic). Mooney quotes Johnson as saying:

> I got down there and called in a few of my close friends and told them what I planned to do. There wasn't much talk about it, no display of disappointment on their part. They seemed to accept my decision . . .
> Then about four o'clock in the afternoon a group of young men came to see me. I had known some of them since the NYA (National Youth Administration) days. They had helped me in my 1941 race for the Senate. Some of them were making good records of their own in public service.
> They told me I had been the cause of their taking an interest in public affairs and working for better government. They said that gave me a certain obligation toward them. They asked me, quietly and without any argument, to change my mind about the Senate race.

Because of their persuasion—Johnson writes through Mooney—he did reconsider.

Others remember the motivation somewhat differently.
Mooney is an innocent prevaricator; he couldn't be expected
to know what was going on because *he* was working as a public relations man for Johnson's *opponent* in that race. Stuart
Long, a pro-Johnson newspaper reporter who has been cov-
ering Austin politics for thirty years, was actually one of the
young turks who met that day to decide on a candidate. *His*
recollections move over this enchanting course:

> Maybe it takes vanity to carry one to the top of the polit-
> ical mountain. In 1948, Johnson came home to assay his
> chances for the U.S. Senate seat which was being left open
> by W. Lee O'Daniel, who had beaten Johnson by 1,311 votes
> in 1941. Everywhere he turned he read signs that convinced
> him he could not win. One night a group of us gathered to
> try to get him to run. He said "no" and went to bed.
>
> We sat and talked, eight of us, all convinced that former
> Governor Coke Stevenson could be, and should be, defeated.
> Finally we agreed that John Connally should run. He would
> have been a good campaigner. He was big and handsome
> with three brothers who were even bigger and more hand-
> some, and their father looked like Old Man Texas himself.
> They would all have campaigned for Connally. Most World
> War II veterans would have voted for him. Stevenson spent
> the war years at home grousing about everything, including
> gas rationing. We sat up late mapping his campaign. Next
> morning, some of us advised Johnson of our decision and
> asked his support. He was popping mad, of course, and that
> afternoon he announced as a candidate.

This campaign that began with Johnson accusing his
friends of treachery and opposing their plans out of pique,
ended in theft, so blatantly done that it takes on all the dark
appeal of a crime of passion. Johnson came out of the primary trailing by 73,000 votes his opponent, Stevenson, a
miserable reactionary who as governor had almost ruined
the University of Texas with one of the nation's first campus
witch hunts. It was obvious to everyone that the run-off

would be a squeaker, and Johnson made preparations for that eventuality. He went to South Texas, the habitat of Mexicanos who were openly sold through their *jefes* to the highest bidder in every state-wide election, just as the Boston Irish used to be sold, and just as the dead constituency of Gene Talmadge's home county, Telfair, were once "borrowed" in some of Georgia's closer elections.

Johnson was not doing anything new—new, to Texas, that is. In Duval County, the South Texas political fortress of George Parr, the "Duke of Duval," Johnson received 99.1 per cent of the run-off vote. This was standard lopsidedness for Duval, which in the five previous gubernatorial elections had never cast less than 95.4 per cent of its votes for the candidate who had Parr's support. Stevenson had himself solicited George Parr's support and benefited by the same kind of lopsided majorities in four elections in the previous ten years. Parr's friendship was worth having, for he seemed to have mystical influences over the ballot boxes not only in Duval but seventeen other counties.

This time, however, Johnson added an unusual bit of garnish, even for a South Texas deal. With the votes all collected, but not yet officially tabulated, Johnson knew he was in trouble. For several days the lead seesawed back and forth and it was clear that the winner would not come out ahead by more than one hundred votes or so. It also was becoming increasingly clear that Stevenson would probably be the one to come out with that margin. And then the folks over in Jim Wells County got to scratching around in Box 13 and, by gosh, discovered another 203 votes—all but one for Johnson! Ah, strange things are done 'neath the south Texas sun. Some of this misty constituency had marched to the polls to vote in alphabetical order, all their names signed to the poll list in blue-green ink (the rest of the list was black ink), and, such was their regard for Johnson, some had even arisen from the grave to cast their ballots. Thus, after all the stuffing and unstuffing of ballot boxes, all the canvassing and re-canvassing of votes was over—Texas had a new senator on his way to the presidency by the margin of eighty-seven mostly-dead Mexicanos out of nearly a million votes cast. Before an official investigation could be completed, the votes were accidentally, they said, burned. The subsequent court hiatus is, like this recount, a matter of often repeated history, and I repeat it here once again simply to give it a place in the cumulative evidence of Johnson's somewhat dubious popular support.

Thereafter he had no real challenge, no test of his strength, for twelve years. Nevertheless his entire career through these years seems to have been motivated mainly by fear and insecurity. Anything that looked like organized opposition in Texas made him respond like a political squid, first throwing out a billowing cloud of obfuscating ink and, if then he discovered that the opposition was trivial, enveloping and crushing it with unreasonable fury. Having slipped into office in 1948, he lived in dread of 1954. From 1952 to 1954 especially, his voting record in the Senate spells out his awareness that pro-McCarthyite Governor Allan Shivers, or someone like him, could beat him; and so he set about methodically to be more pro-Republican and, within the allowable limits of taste, more reactionary than Shivers.

In mid-1966 Johnson remarked, in what was understandably not a happy way, since the memory of his neo-Republican days must still be an embarrassment, that "I supported Eisenhower so much there were some people who thought I should join the Republican party." When it looked like he would be opposed in 1954 by oil man Dudley Dougherty, such a political unknown that today not one Texan in 500 could tell you Johnson's opponent that year, Johnson responded characteristically. Dougherty said he supported the Bricker Amendment; therefore, Johnson voted for it. He also began to jaw as loudly as the McCarthyites against the admission of Red China to the United Nations. And even though his victory over Dougherty was so total as to make light of Texas politics, Johnson returned to the Senate hound-dog-grateful to the rich interests for not having turned him out. He came back to Washington debased by the awareness, as Murray Kempton put it, that the big business-men of Texas had saved him from more rugged opposition only because they had "found him useful by a measure they would have applied to a used car salesman."

The next time he was up, things were different. Money could control the Democratic party, but the Republican party was such a runty thing it could get no big money sup-port. Therefore it had nothing to lose by bucking the Estab-lishment at that time. As if out of nowhere holes began to appear in Johnson's armor and the hot wind off the steppes of West Texas made the most discordant sounds through them. Was this an erosion in his popularity? Not at all; it was merely a slight abrasion of assumed popularity. And so, while it was dramatic, it was not really unexpected when in 1960 John Tower, a nondescript, ineloquent Republican professor from a lower middle-class college, running in a state that had not seriously considered electing a Republican in three generations, polled 900,000 votes to Johnson's 1,306,600 in the general election.

If the creators of the Johnson image were stunned by that, they were equally stunned when Texas in the same ballot-ing came within 46,233 votes of turning down the Kennedy-Johnson ticket. In fact, the outcome of that race was so vigorously challenged as rigged that the Democratic victory may have survived only because the lawsuit brought by the Republicans to contest it was handled (gingerly) by a John-son-dominated board sitting in Austin. The Republicans charged that 100,000 votes had been illegally thrown out. It is unlikely that a re-count would have changed the results, but in any event there was not likely to be a re-count from a three-man canvassing board of which two members—the governor and the Secretary of State—had been key speakers at a Johnson fund-raising dinner a few months earlier and who now claimed, literally, that they did not know *how* to re-count.

There are several explanations for the near catastrophe of this election, but the most compelling one is that Texans did not like the way things had been changed around to suit Johnson. A special law, quite openly nudged from the Texas legislature by the Houston and Dallas "interests," gave Johnson the privilege in 1960 of running both for re-election to the Senate and for election to the vice-presidency. Even more to the point, it set up the date for the primaries so he could have the Democratic nomination for the Senate—which in those days was considered tantamount to election—wrapped up before heading off for the Democratic national convention. Running for two offices at the same time had not previously been permitted, but the corporations who owned shares of Johnson did not want to risk his being without an office.

While the "favorite son" bills made it through the legislature, Johnson paid a devastating prize for the victory: feelings that had been generally suppressed or spoken only over beer at the Scholtz Garten had now been given a kind of legal existence by being stated and restated on the floor of the Texas legislature. For the first time in his career an organized effort had been made (for there *are* liberal legislators in Texas and some very eloquent ones) to convince the people that indeed the emperor was wearing no more than a gold-lined G-string. Heresies were uttered, and nobody died for uttering them; Texas politicians never again had quite the same awe of Mother Baines that they had had in the past.

Henry Gonzalez, now as quick as any congressman to take LBJ handouts, was then a state senator still motivated by a fighting liberalism. He opposed the passage of the early-primary bill with the warning that "sinister elements and forces are taking advantage of the name of Lyndon B. Johnson to prevent poor candidates from having a chance for political office." This was indeed what the bill did. The cutback in campaign time put the wealthy incumbent at a tremendous advantage, at such an evident advantage that nobody ran against Johnson in the Democratic primary in 1960. But the bill did one more thing: it abolished the second sequence of precinct and county conventions with the result that the May delegates would also constitute the September state convention. Previously the liberals had had two chances—usually frustrated—to capture control of the party. This move would, as Gonzalez pointed out, "facilitate rigged conventions—more and better rigged conventions." It was difficult to imagine more rigged conventions than Texas had already witnessed, but there *was* this possibility.

As another prominent legislator stated in the debate, the bill "will only help Jake Pickle and the Republican faction of the Democratic Party that he represents. Jake Pickle is one of the slickest convention thieves you ever saw in your life." This is no overstatement. Pickle—who today holds Johnson's old Congressional seat and is one of the President's most intimate advisers—had been Johnson's organization chairman in the disputed 1948 race and had been behind some of the classic smear campaigns of Governor Allan Shivers, but he was at that time best known for having mapped out the strategy by which the conservatives, working through Johnson and Rayburn, stole the party apparatus away from the liberals in the famous convention brawl of 1956. (This was the convention at which feelings became so bitter that Johnson was heard to tell his college roommate in a nostril-to-nostril piece of savagery that if he didn't help depose Mrs. Frankie Randolph, the liberal national committeewoman, in favor of a woman who had backed Eisenhower in 1952, the old chum would never get the federal judgeship that Johnson had promised him previously.)

The damage to Johnson's position was increased because among the legislators, even those who supported Johnson, there was a feeling of having been trotted before the public as cheap hirelings, and they resented Johnson for putting them on exhibition. What, after all, could they say in response to *The Texas Observer*'s criticism: "Is it not depressing that a legislature which cannot, in four months, pass a tax bill for students, mental patients, old folks, and mentally backward children can pass in two days a bill for Lyndon Johnson?" Nor could Johnson, for that matter, answer the other *Observer* questions: "Is it not strange that our great liberals in Washington—Rayburn, Johnson, Thornberry, Wright—get exercised about a bill to help Johnson, but never bother to place a telephone call against, say, the Texas House-approved resolution to abolish the income tax and leave the nation helpless in a world burning with communism and revolt? Is it not contemptible that Johnson, who is always telling liberals what a liberal he is, sells out his friends to his enemies in his home state again and again and again?"

In the 1960 election, as was the custom in the previous elections and has been in subsequent ones, Johnson's appeal was monstrously overrated by the political professionals and by the big money contributors. Texans barely wanted him in one office; they almost rebelled when asked to vote him into two. Thus the only logic for Johnson's being on the Democratic ticket—to guarantee the solid South for Kennedy and to put Texas' critically-needed electoral votes deep in the bag—appeared on the morning after the election to have been something less than sound. Texas was hardly past the lip of the bag, by a vote of 1.16 million to 1.12 million for Nixon, and four states of the Old Confederacy (Virginia, Louisiana, Tennessee, Florida) had not viewed Johnson's presence on the Democratic slate to be any commanding inducement to turn away from the Republican path they had learned to follow under Eisenhower.

It is useless to speculate on how much damage Johnson had done the ticket in the Negro-heavy and South-hating enclaves of the urban North and West, but it certainly occurred, since liberals from these regions had expressed almost hysterical opposition to Johnson at the Democratic national convention. Labor leaders, Negro leaders, liberal leaders almost to a man fought his nomination for president, and when he was proposed as vice-presidential candidate, "We replied," Louis Lomax recalls, " 'No thanks, you-all. But we'd rather not.' Johnson cost the Democrats thousands of Negro votes. Had the ticket lost, Johnson would have been one of the reasons why."

To the nation's tepid response to him in 1960 was now added the imminent danger of his losing control of his power base in Texas. The indigenous liberal movement in Texas—which has little relationship to the national liberal movement and is, in fact, little understood by liberals elsewhere—was gathering strength. Furthermore, Tower's amazing support showed that some of the conservatives were beginning to waver in their addiction to the time-honored one-party arrangement. If, in 1962, the next gubernatorial election year, the liberals took the state house and the state Democratic executive committee, it would mean that at the 1964 convention Johnson would very possibly fail to win the endorsement of his home folks, and that would be curtains for his career. For Johnson it was absolutely mandatory that the conservative Democrats come up with a strong gubernatorial candidate in 1962. All of which was easy to say, but as a matter of fact the Democratic conservatives had no strong candidate waiting.

So Johnson and his backers set out to make one. Their choice was a convenient one: John Connally, a smart, hand-

some, vain, mean veteran of many Lyndon campaigns, and
a hobnobber with the rich "Air-Strip Set"—as newsman
Stuart Long named them after he heard one oil man invite
Connally to drop by for a Johnson fund-raising party at the
ranch in 1960, and Connally responded: "Sure—if you've got
an air strip long enough to handle a DC-3." A very, very
good man at plucking contributions from the indolent
wealthy.

Back in his National Youth Administration days, Johnson
was one of a fraternity of Texans that included Connally,
Jake Pickle, Ed Clark, Bob Phinney, Willard Deason, Walter Jenkins, J. C. Kellam, and others. Most of them went
into the service at about the same time, kept in touch and,
the war over, converged on Austin, where a group of them
set up, with Johnson's help, a new radio station, KVET.

After that they began to spin off into politics. Clark became one of the most powerful lobbyists in the state. Jenkins
went all the way to the White House with Johnson. Deason
became a member of the Interstate Commerce Commission.
Phinney became a very handy director of the Internal
Revenue Service. Kellam, now president of the LBJ Corporation, was chairman of the Texas State Colleges Board of
Regents. Homer Thornberry, who came into the fraternity
later than most, took Johnson's Congressional seat when he
moved up to the Senate. When Johnson appointed Thornberry to a Federal judgeship, Pickle, having proved his
worth as an excellent campaign propaganda provocateur *

* Best known as cocreator of the television documentary, "The Port
Arthur Story." The other creator was Phil Fox, former Ku Klux Klan
publicity writer and convicted murderer who handled publicity for
Johnson in his 1948 campaign. "The Port Arthur Story," directed
against Ralph Yarborough, told of how Communist agents were flocking
to Texas to infiltrate labor unions and help take over the state for
Yarborough. At the 1958 state convention, police acting under Pickle
roughed up and threw out a sixty-four-year-old state senator with a
heart condition who wanted to present a resolution against supporting
Johnson for president in 1960.

and strong-arm man on the state Democratic executive committee, moved into the old Johnson-Thornberry seat in the House and, simultaneously, took his place on the right hand of Johnson in the inner councils of Washington. It is a tight, loyal group, a cactus-patch Mafia.

It was quite obviously fitting, then, that Johnson and the old gang should tap Connally to be the next governor. But Connally had a handicap: he had played his role so subtly over the years that few Texans knew anything about him. Not that he was a stranger to politics. He had managed most of Johnson's campaigns. He had most infamously managed Johnson's campaign for the presidential nomination in 1960, as the one who "revealed" to the nation, with a somewhat hysterical note, that John Kennedy was suffering from a "fatal" illness and would surely die in office, if elected. Kennedy, he said, "was staying alive only through massive doses of cortisone"—a bit of propaganda meant to offset public awareness that LBJ was operating on a bad heart.

Nevertheless, Connally was almost an unknown to the average voter. A 1961 poll showed that only 1 per cent of the Texas voters would back him in the following year's election. Money and a massive publicity campaign ("Connally Go-Ahead vs. CIO Red") took care of that, however. He had also been helped by a swift bit of polishing in the role of Kennedy's Secretary of the Navy, a post obtained for him by Johnson, before returning to Texas as the new front man for the conservative Democrats. His job was to re-recruit the defectors to the Republican party and re-establish one-partyism. He made no secret of his objective. Reporters who traveled with him in the 1962 campaign say he was furious with then Governor Price Daniel for "letting the party get away from him." He won the nomination—but by a margin of only 27,000 out of 1,100,000 votes cast.

It was hardly a notable victory. The race was not so much a test of Connally's popularity as it was a test of Johnson's popularity. Although his opponent, Don Yarborough, a young Houston attorney who is no kin of Senator Yarborough's, had only one daily newspaper (out of 114) on his side and had the entire financial and industrial community arrayed against him, although Connally conducted the best-financed campaign in Texas history, although Yarborough was working against Connally's past connections with a national administration that was popular among the minorities, although Connally's campaign workers openly purchased votes in the border counties and in San Antonio— with all this going against Yarborough and for Connally— such was the feeling against Johnson and his crowd, such were the sidewalk passions illustrated by the "Scratch Lyndon's Boy John" bumperstrips, that a shift of only 14,000 votes out of more than 1,000,000 cast would have upset the machine and defeated Connally.

Connally paraded his prior, brief affiliation with the Kennedy cabinet when he was addressing Negro and Latin groups; to conservative audiences he presented another side. While Connally opposed almost the entire Kennedy program, Yarborough stood for all of it. National liberals predicted that a Don Yarborough victory would ignite flurries of progressive effort even in the eddies and back washes of the Deep South, in the stale sinkholes where the idea that a liberal might win had long ago been given up. It would have been a stimulus for the Kennedy program everywhere, for if a Kennedy liberal could beat the Johnson machine in Texas, all things were possible.

But a deal had been made with Johnson, and Kennedy kept it, although the manner in which he disregarded those who had fought for him and now sought his help was considered a bit raw by observers such as *New York Post* editor Wechsler, who conjectured that the 14,000 votes needed to establish a new way of life in Texas could have easily been got "by even a word or a sign from President Kennedy or

sympathy for the man who was running on his program.
. . . There were Negro and Latin-American areas in which
Mr. Kennedy's voice would have been decisive and where
the Johnson-Connally operatives made inroads that would
have been inconceivable if the President had made a gesture
for the candidate who supported his program. Instead it is
even reported that the President tried at one point to persuade some Texas labor chieftains to desert Yarborough and
endorse Connally."

The gullible young President, tricked and confused, had
only succeeded in heightening the disharmony that a year
later Johnson would ask him to come back and lessen. If he
had only asked some of the Texans who believed in him,
they would have told him that nothing he said or did could
have lessened the underlying cause of the trouble: tired of
being drummed out of state party conventions, tired of being bypassed on patronage, tired of the dominance of labor-
baiting, witch-hunting Lyndon—who even in the late fifties
was sometimes heard to call them "red-hots" and "dead-
marx"—the Texas liberals were moving toward a rebellion
that would not be stopped.

In the general election many thousands of liberals so
opposed Johnson—and therefore Connally—that they voted
for his Republican opponent even though he had a most
wretched platform. There are about a quarter of a million
progressives in that state who literally despise Johnson, and
another 100,000 who can take him only in the smallest of
doses,* because they consider him guilty of the sellout, the
buyout, the priority of self and cronies over state, and now
over nation. This is the way they have felt about him for
years. And it was this rage, exploding more and more often

---

* And about an equal portion of Republican Johnson-haters out of
Texas' 3 million potential voters. The remainder are the undefined
mass, the shifters, the stay-at-homes for whose support the pro-Johnson-
ites and anti-Johnsonites fight.

into visible fires, that prompted Johnson, fearful of his future, to bring Kennedy into Texas for his last trip.

Oddly unquestioning, the Warren Commission accepts the explanation of Governor Connally that "the President (Kennedy) wished to resolve the factional controversy within the Democratic Party in Texas before the election of 1964."

This is the kind of nearly-truthful statement that is disastrous to history. There was a controversy raging within the Texas Democratic party, true enough, but Kennedy could not possibly have resolved it; if he wasn't smart enough to know that, then the supposed canniness of Kennedy and his advisers was woefully overrated. It was the same controversy that had been shaking the Texas Democratic structure for a dozen years, but in that year of Kennedy's death it had taken a new turning; the liberals believed they were within only a few months of smashing the Johnson-Connally Washington-Austin axis. They were in a tigerish mood. They wanted to disembowel the old body politic. They did not *want* the controversy resolved—except at the polls.

These were no ordinary passions motivating them. This was a sanguine whoopee mood. Sweet revenge was, maybe, just around the corner, and no Kennedy would swing them away from it. The liberals wanted revenge for Lyndon's disruptive use of pressure through the labor brass in Washington, through the REA hierarchy, through the Establishment press, and revenge for various kinds of subtle pressure, including money and jobs, and just plain brute force.

They had reason to think they were in good shape for the battle. On the morning of the assassination day, the *Houston Chronicle* published a poll conducted statewide by Bo Byers, its top political reporter, and seven other newsmen showing that Kennedy-Johnson popularity was trailing Barry Goldwater 48 to 52 per cent; that, because of a general upheaval and a straining of old allegiances within the conservative ranks, Governor Connally could have real difficulty being re-elected the next year if he again faced Don Yarborough, who had come so close to defeating him in 1962. The poll also showed that Senator Ralph Yarborough, the liberal's lochinvar, had become virtually unbeatable.

It hadn't just happened. Senator Yarborough had flown back to Texas to make speeches and shake hands and mend fences *every* weekend that year. He was up for re-election in 1964, and ready. Johnson was doing his best to recruit a strong candidate to run against Yarborough. Significantly, when he put the proposition to ex-Governor Allan Shivers, at one time the most powerful politician in Texas affairs, Shivers turned him down. Senator Yarborough was too strong.

When the trend became evident, a reporter commented to Yarborough that it looked like he wouldn't be having any trouble the next year, and asked if that didn't please him. Yarborough, in that furious raving way of his, began beating the table and roaring, "Let the bastards run somebody against me! I *want* the bastards to run somebody against me, so I can beat the living hell out of 'em!" That's how the liberals felt, *eager* for a showdown.

And they weren't just imagining their strength or their chances. Allen Duckworth, political editor of the hyperconservative *Dallas News,* a 100 per cent pro-Establishment newspaper, in the early fall of 1963 wrote that a big switch of conservative Democrats to the Republican primary, which many anticipated, "could be disastrous to those who control the state Democratic Party machinery," and he went on to say what was already all too much in Johnson's mind: that if Connally and Johnson did not have control of the next state convention, and if it did not endorse Johnson for a second term as vice-president, "he might not get it."

—A new liberal organization called the Democratic Coalition—Negroes, labor, independents, liberals, Mexicanos—backed by a hefty foundation grant had done an excellent job of registering and organizing voters in the big city precincts.

—A gratuitous remark in mid-1963 by Governor Connally, deploring the public accommodations section of the proposed Civil Rights Bill, had not exactly endeared him to Texas' Negroes, the most politically active group of Negroes in the South.

—Labor, often divided, had patched up its differences and was united again. On November 21, on the same night that Kennedy and his entourage were toasting Congressman Albert Thomas at a party in Houston, the top labor executives of Texas were clinking glasses at another Houston party, swearing fealty to the cause of defeating Connally in the next election. Even the steel workers, often at odds with the state AFL-CIO, were there, and that meant strength.

—The Republican party, seriously organized for the first time since Reconstruction days, would pull through its primary election at least 300,000 conservatives who normally voted for the most reactionary Democrat on the ballot. This was a phantom gift of 300,000 votes to the anti-Johnson-Connally Democrats.

Against this background, the belligerency, the jeering and the challenges were more open than ever, and it was very clear that a great quantity of intraparty blood would flow in 1964. There is evidence that Kennedy wanted no part of it. That hadn't been in his bargain with Johnson.

Kennedy had agreed to stay out of Texas affairs even when it would have been to his advantage to participate and when it would have been to liberal Texas Democrats' great advantage. He had agreed to allow Johnson to pad the vacuum of the vice-presidency with his old senatorial privileges of appointments and veto over appointments, despite the fact that this was a great embarrassment to Yarborough, who became Texas' senior senator after Johnson moved up. "Just speaking very frankly, when Johnson was elected vice-president, he told me the people had elected him senator, too, and they expected him to be senator, too," Yarborough recalls with no mellowness. "There was violent disagreement." But Kennedy supported Johnson in this fuss. Now Johnson wanted support in the wider violence of disagreement at home, although the other half of his deal with Kennedy had been that he—Johnson—would handle Texas, keep the Democratic forces unified and compact, ready and easy to swing behind the national administration. Johnson had not been able to carry out his part of the bargain. Texas was getting away from him. The leaders of the Republican and liberal Democrat factions were teaming up in a purely Machiavellian way.

Already there was national talk of the desirability of dumping Johnson from the ticket in 1964. He had foundered at the one role in which everyone had conceded he might be useful to Kennedy—helping the New Frontier program through Congress. If to the normal antagonisms he aroused in northern Democrats was added the visible proof of his growing weakness at home, Johnson might indeed—despite Kennedy's public assurances to the contrary—have been removed from the ticket. That would have been the end of Johnson's hopes for the presidential nomination in 1968 or in any other year.

The man who had built a reputation as the giant of Texas politics needed, with ironic desperation, the help of the frisky lightweight from Boston. Kennedy was modest enough to be baffled. He was also angry.

By the time Kennedy arrived in Texas, tempers on both sides were at a flash point. When Yarborough refused to ride with Johnson in San Antonio and again in Houston, Kennedy asked the senator what was wrong. Yarborough explained he had heard that Connally intended to humiliate him by excluding him from the head table at the Austin fund-raising banquet. Kennedy made Connally promise not to throw any protocol bombs and the procession came under a momentary outward calm. When the group arrived in Fort Worth, Yarborough rode from the airfield to town with Johnson,* and he was riding with him again the next day when the shot was fired.

With that shot, Texas politics changed completely. The developing balance was destroyed. Texas liberalism as a force to be reckoned with was all but killed, and Johnson was out of trouble.

Riding with the President, Connally took a crippling bullet and was elevated to semi-martyrdom. The clothes he was wearing on that day, put on display, were treated almost as religious relics. Getting shot may not have made him a better politician, but it certainly made him unbeatable. A thoroughgoing country club conservative, he nevertheless now shared, in the minds of many ignorant Texans, the mystique of the fallen liberal President. Connally was re-elected in 1964 by the biggest vote ever given a governor of Texas, running against the same young man who had come within a whisper of beating him only two years earlier, and despite the fact that his administration during that term was anything but brilliant; he received, in fact, more votes than Texans gave Johnson for the presidency. In less than four years—dating the transformation from the year he returned to front for the machine—Connally, his image re-created by an assassin, has moved from being a political nonentity

* Les Carpenter, husband of Mrs. Johnson's lady-in-waiting and a correspondent for a number of Texas newspapers, happily used a planted story—that later got wide currency—to the effect that when the troupe prepared to move into Dallas, Kennedy told Yarborough, "You'll either ride with Johnson, or you'll walk." It would have been absurd for Kennedy to make such a remark since Yarborough had the night before shown his new willingness to ride with Johnson, and Kennedy was aware of it.

to become the most powerful governor in Texas' history.

In 1966, elected for a third term, he will have his men in every seat on every appointive board and commission. Connally men, among other things, now control the most important regulatory body in the state, the Railroad Commission, which determines all things in the oil and gas industry. From the White House Johnson has contributed greatly to the establishment of almost dictatorial one-man rule at home by protecting his old friend from those who might otherwise threaten his administration. With Connally in the mansion appealing to their former allies, the Republicans, and Johnson in the White House making at least the gamesmanship sounds of a progressive, the Texas liberals are barely breathing.

A few days before Texas' first primary election in 1966, LBJ landed in Houston and climbed from the bowels of Air Force One with his arm around a congresswoman. At the bottom of the gangway he disengaged himself from her long enough to give a kiss to another congressman's wife. Thence the joyous celebrants followed their leader into the Shamrock Hilton, where 900 wealthy backers—who had paid nearly $1,000,000 for the pleasure—watched and listened with mellow approval while Governor Connally called Johnson "the most dedicated, able, compassionate President of this century," and Johnson, moist-eyed, responded with an unhurried and intimate eulogy of the Governor as "my John . . . my John."

One might suppose this hugging and kissing and sweet-talking and money-collecting made all Texas Democrats happy. To the liberals, the day's doings were indicative of all the hopes that were gone, all of the things that had fallen wrong since Kennedy's death; but especially it underlined that since then, all the money and all the glamour had been for "the others."

The two men have their little spats, but on the major

issues the Austin-Washington axis is unbreakable. When Connally goes to Washington, he stays at the White House; when Johnson goes to Texas he often has Connally out to the ranch, and it is probably true—as the chairman of the Texas Democratic Executive Committee insists—that "there is a deep affection between the two, like father and son, or brothers. The only differences that may arise is because they see things differently. One sees the valley from the mountain top, the other sees the valley from halfway up the mountain. They are as close personal friends and associates as any two men or as two officeholders can be. The President feels that when the ship goes down, the last two aboard will be he and John Connally."

He has supplied here a figure of speech that would be very appealing to most Texas liberals, who have for years been trying to sink that ship, but who, witnessing such occasions as the Houston banquet, realize now that there is not much hope for a real, lasting, "useful" split between Johnson and Connally. The overriding conclusion is that each needs the other too much, and the Texas Establishment needs both. Texas liberals now concede that as long as Johnson is president, he will have through Connally—or somebody like Connally—an unshakeable hold on Texas government, and the longer it is unshakeable the more the fortunes of liberal Democrats will decline. The withering away of this wing of the party, born in the reform economics of the 1890's, is now seen as a real possibility.

In Texas, all is the way it has always been: conservative. The Negroes and the Latins still live in near-peonage, the big corporations still successfully duck taxes. It is only one state and the rest of the nation may not get too excited by what has happened there, but Texas liberals who have fought the good fight and lost believe that what Johnson has done to them, he is canny enough to do everywhere.

★
★ ★
★

For the nation, there must have been no special comfort in watching Johnson surround himself with White House troops recruited from his reactionary Texas reserves. They come and go—all the original gang he surrounded himself with on coming to the White House have since departed, being subject to the same limits of human endurance—but the criterion for recruiting is constant. The most important recent addition is George Christian, press aide. He was formerly press aide and executive assistant to Governor Price Daniel for six years and for three years to Governor John Connally. His services were varied, from lobbying the Texas legislature for the governor's pet bills to propagandizing. Such services in these two governors' administration is significant. When Daniel was in the U.S. Senate he was almost comically subservient to the oil and gas interests, and his regard for them did not diminish when he became governor, of course; but his service as Texas governor is perhaps best remembered for the anti-Negro laws and the consumer sales tax (while skipping taxes on the big outfits) that were passed. Daniels' successor, Connally, has run Texas like a trust company for special interests. In Christian, Johnson has a superb liaison with the right people back home.

A product of much the same background was Jake Jacobsen, in the White House inner circle for more than a year before returning to his Texas law practice. Jacobsen was administrative aide to Governor Daniel; he was also one of the smoothest "fixers" to operate at Texas political conventions, always to the disadvantage of the Texas liberals. Here and there in Jacobsen's background there appear to be faint whiffs of conflict of interest. He was, for instance, one of Johnson's closest advisers on economics in 1966, a year that saw Johnson permitting banks to charge the highest interest rate in forty-five years. According to the last registry issued by the House Banking Committee, Jacobsen was a director of Citizens National Bank in Austin, Texas, and held 889 shares. (Other major stockholders include Brazos Tenth Street Company, the Lyndon Johnson Foundation, and the LBJ Company Profit Sharing & Incentive—all fronts for presidential business activities.)

Johnson slipped up on Bill Don Moyers, his former press aide, who had all the credentials and recommendations of a red clay conservative—but turned out to be a pretty decent fellow after all. Before he hired Moyers as a temporary staff member several years ago, Johnson called Millard Cope, editor of the Marshall newspaper in deep East Texas, to ask if Moyers was "our kind of man." Yes, indeed! said Cope, a creative racist who favored the town's selling its park and swimming pool rather than integrate. Billie Don had worked as a reporter for him and, in fact, he looked upon the young man almost as his son. Eastern newspaper biographers usually relate with sincere gusto how Moyers "jumped into the fight" to help Johnson in his 1954 Senate race against a wild conservative. What race? What fight? Johnson had so little opposition he did not even campaign. But in 1956, 1957, and 1958 there *was* a fight—liberal Ralph Yarborough against well-heeled and well-known conservatives; during those campaigns Moyers was conspicuously missing from the workers who turned out to help the liberal side. In fact, in 1958, when Moyers was working for Johnson's KTBC in Austin, he signed one of those Young-Men-For ads supporting Yarborough's opponent, "Dollar Bill" Blakley, a notorious reactionary. Moyers has no liberal credentials in Texas. And that undoubtedly was what sent him to the top of Johnson's staff, but once there he began to exert a humane influence that had been rather foreign to Johnson's inner group up to that time. Much of the "Great Society" thinking was his, as was much of the *less* rambunctious White House thinking on Vietnam. It was one of Johnson's redeeming acts that, although he didn't permit Moyers to serve as much more than window-dressing, at least he did keep him around for that and, from time to time, appeared to be temporarily influenced by him although too often it was the other way. "The trouble is," Moyers is reported to have remarked wistfully near the end of his servitude, "he doesn't get more like me, I get more like him."

But the staff member who seems to fit in most comfortably with the Johnson way of operating is Marvin Watson, a blocky steer-faced pleasant fellow in his early forties, who is proving extremely adroit as the White House's No. 1 hatchet man. For nine years Watson was an official at Lone Star Steel in deep East Texas. In the steel industry, which is notoriously anti-labor, Lone Star Steel is renowned as the toughest company of them all. Its image is improving a little bit these days, but it will take years of cosmetic applications to make Texans forget what the company was like under E. B. Germany, long its president, now retired. Solely as the result of Germany's unwillingness to give a fraction of an inch in union negotiations, Lone Star Steel was hit by a strike in the late 1950's that, in bitterness, can only be rivaled by the Kohler strike in Wisconsin. Families, churches, civic clubs were split; some still are, almost a decade later. At about the time the strike started, Watson became a Lone Star Steel public relations assistant, and shortly thereafter personal assistant to Germany, specializing in political affairs. Germany, whose political views are far right of Genghis Khan's, recently said Watson's political views are "about the same as mine." Watson served as Germany's ambassador to the hyper-anti-union Texas Industrial Council and, like Jake Jacobsen, did some expert manipulating at state Democratic political conventions. Liberals accuse him of being the rigger of the credentials committee at the state convention in 1964, which handed the state machinery over to the Connally gang *in toto*. Maury Maverick, Jr. voiced their irritation by calling it "a common pig-sty steal."

Washington didn't know quite what to make of Watson.

There had been plenty of bureaucratic spying around town in other days, but it had never flourished at the White House until Watson instituted the regimen of requiring that all incoming phone calls be logged as to who was on each end. He also required that the White House chauffeurs make a full report of where they took any staffer, and in other ways he started keeping dossiers on his fellow workers. If that had been the end of it, Watson's White House muck-up would have been put down as merely a bad/good case of Lone Star Steel-type public relations. But, as Joseph Alsop noted in spring 1966, "It is of course an open secret that the telephone and limousine checks are only parts of a much wider system of surveillance that now covers most of the city of Washington. It is informal, but it works very efficiently. In brief, a great many sleazy persons are now aware that the quickest way to make Brownie points at the White House is to pass the word that X has been seen talking to Y. Thus it is now an odds-on bet that any X-Y meeting, in a restaurant or other public place, will soon be added to the White House's dangerous associations-list."

Watson not only got by with that, he was soon to have a hand in a much more fearsome job. This was the notorious elimination of Abba P. Schwartz, a Kennedy appointee as administrator of the State Department's Bureau of Security and Consular Affairs. He was a well-known liberal lawyer around Washington, an ADAer, a frequenter of Eleanor's lyceum, but adventurous enough to have a number of conservative friends. It was because Schwartz could name a few of these in his circle that Kennedy had the conscience to throw him into the State Department job, a sticky post, the kind where a liberal might feel like a foreign agent in his own country, doing his work slyly behind an outer shell of tailored conformity. Schwartz helped liberalize the McCarran-Walter Act, he helped bring to this country foreigners who, under a more cautious director, would have had to spend months trying to excuse some political indiscretion in their past. He had tried to relax the rigor mortis that had set in in the policies of issuing passports to Americans, and he had been trying to negotiate with the North Vietnamese for the release of American prisoners of war.

But peeking through Schwartz' keyhole were Watson and Mrs. Frances Knight, head of the Passport Office, who carries on a secret pen-palmanship with J. Edgar Hoover in which they discuss subversive tendencies and suspicious persons within the government. After months of secret planning, Watson was ready to do Schwartz in.

Secretary of State Dean Rusk, after first rehearsing his statement with Watson, told Schwartz that he was being let out because of a reorganization plan. Schwartz had never heard of the reorganization plan before; but he had, a few hours earlier, been tipped off by a newspaper reporter that he was about to get it. That was his first word of what was up. Rusk confirmed it. Reporters asked the White House what was going on. Johnson said it was an economy move; he figured they would save a quarter of a million dollars by abolishing Schwartz' office. Schwartz quit. Congressional liberals were outraged, convinced that Johnson was throwing Schwartz into the right-wingers' maw by way of a deal allowing Johnson to change the immigration quota system. Like Adam Yarmolinsky, Schwartz was auctioned from Johnson's Congressional liaison block.

The economy abolishment of Schwartz' office never, of course, took place. When Johnson saw that Congressional liberals were just itching to investigate and shred any reorganization plan he submitted—an investigation that Schwartz was promised he would be called to testify in—Johnson quietly called off what undoubtedly was from the beginning a bogus proposal. Johnson, who had accepted Schwartz' resignation without comment, also refused to explain why, with the departure of Schwartz, he was no longer interested in saving money. It looks like there will be no investigation.

If Johnson was unhappy with the conduct of the boy from Daingerfield, Texas, he gave no sign of it. Watson, he said, is "as wise as my father, as gentle as my mother, and as loyal as another East Texan I know, Lady Bird."

The most important man in Johnson's shadow cabinet, regularly in touch with him through private channels but seldom seen at public White House gatherings, is Robert Anderson, a Republican who was Secretary of the Navy, Deputy Defense Secretary, and then Secretary of the Treasury under Eisenhower; he is now a member of a New York bond house. His influence in White House affairs was most recently seen in the tight money policy that brought the home building industry to the brink of chaos—similar to, but worse than, the tight money period he triggered under Eisenhower. Anderson is an ultraconservative Texan with a deep oil background; a former president of the Texas Mid-Continent Oil and Gas Association and thereby one of Johnson's best ties with the oil world, as we shall now see.

5 That isn't unction, boy, that's petroleum

Joe McCarthy had strength, he had great courage, he had daring . . . There was a quality about the man which compelled respect, and even liking, from his strongest adversaries.

—LBJ eulogy to "fallen comrade," 1957

This is *not* an assassination conspiracy theory. But oil, after all, has sloshed around rather freely in Johnson's background and—even though some people seem to be avoiding the topic these days because they feel that to talk of Johnson/oil raises unfair suspicions about his role or the industry's role in Kennedy's death—it is relevant to any understanding of the pressures that have put a right-wing imprint on Johnson's character and on much of Texas' population.

The conspiracy theorists were still some distance from the scene of President Kennedy's assassination when several of them began to sniff what they thought was oil. Upwind, downwind, the acrid odor came to them. Every one of them a vigorous amateur sleuth, they of course looked first for the motive to explain the murder. What Texas politician would benefit most from the assassination and could in turn be expected to move heaven and earth, if need be, to benefit the major oil companies? A nasty thought, but there it was. Thomas G. Buchanan, whose *Who Killed Kennedy?* was perhaps the most widely read of any assassination account in Europe, plainly blames the deed on oil billionaires who did not like Kennedy's fiscal philosophy but approved of Johnson's very much indeed. By innuendo a few newspaper reporters in this country built a foundation for the same suspicions, and the public was not slow to pick up the ugly conclusion and nourish it, not always silently.

The suspicions were made much easier to develop because of the proximity of H. L. Hunt's office, on the seventh floor of the Mercantile Bank Building about ten blocks east of the murder scene. No responsible person suggested that Hunt actually pulled the trigger; but it was suggested that anything that could be bought was within reach of the nation's richest citizen and the country's most powerful propagandist for the extreme right. Hunt's radio program, *Life Line*— sponsored not only by his own oil companies but by others such as Gulf Oil, Sun Oil, Standard Oil, Standard of Indiana, Ohio Oil Company, as well as by some nonoil industries—had been building to a crescendo of anti-Kennedyisms in recent days, warning its listeners over 331 stations that Kennedy's tyrannical administration was bypassing the laws of Congress, following a line ordered by Moscow, suppressing the chief spokesmen for freedom in the land, and forcing American taxpayers to subsidize Communism around the world.*

* Whether or not these broadcasts stirred up the right wing is not known, but they apparently stirred Jack Ruby, Oswald's killer. On the night of November 22 he turned up at radio station KLIF in Dallas, where he showed one of the station's reporters a reprint of a *Life Line* program (entitled "Heroism"), which, according to *The New York Times*-McGraw-Hill version of the Warren Report (p. 319), "was appar-

Three days before the shot was fired, *Life Line* had begged its listeners to show "extreme patriotism." Then, on the very morning of the assassination, *Life Line* warned that it might soon be too late for action, because if Kennedy succeeded in communizing the country we would find that "no firearms are permitted the people, because they would then have the weapons with which to rise up against their oppressors."

A ghoulish coincidence.

One *Life Line* commentator, hearing of Kennedy's death, wept and said he would have nothing to do with murder. Many Americans were similarly offended. The radio propaganda, coupled with the fact that one of Hunt's sons helped pay for an advertisement in the *Dallas Morning News* greeting Kennedy as a traitor, stirred passions high enough so that the Dallas police advised Hunt to get out of town and hide for a few days.

What justice was there in linking Lyndon Johnson to H. L. Hunt? Well, *some* justice. Booth Mooney, who was Johnson's aide for half a dozen years, had for some time written scripts for Hunt's program, unquestionably with Johnson's knowledge. Furthermore, even when Mooney was not directly on Hunt's payroll, he was looked to for assistance. In a 1959 letter to Wayne Poucher, *Life Line*'s best-known commentator, Hunt had suggested ways to plant letters in newspapers around the country; in this letter he advised, "Booth Mooney could be of great help in figuring out other connections."

But there were other, better-known, ties between Hunt and Johnson. Hunt, who had once backed MacArthur for president and General Edwin Walker for Texas' governor,

---

ently one of the scripts that had come into Ruby's hands a few weeks before." Ruby urged the radio station to editorialize against "them," but according to this account he didn't make himself clear as to whether the editorials should be against the sponsors of *Life Line* or against left-wingers.

was wild to get Johnson nominated in 1960. Kennedy had gone on record as favoring a review of the oil industry's tax benefits, including the depletion allowance. A "review" could only mean a lessening of benefits. Kennedy must be stopped. Hunt paid $10,008 to reprint a local Baptist minister's sermon, in which it was proclaimed that "the election of a Catholic as President would mean the end of religious liberty in America"; he mailed out 200,000 copies, which, he felt confident, would launch a wave of angry Protestantism across the country that would wash Kennedy out of the running. Instead, it only aroused great animosity among editorial writers. The U.S. Senate, noting that there is a federal law against distributing anonymous political circulars after a campaign is officially under way, began an investigation. Hunt panicked and went into hiding. Then, when the Senate decided that the mailings had preceded the formal opening of the campaign, Hunt sheepishly emerged to apologize that he had done it "only to help Lyndon."

One of the most widely circulated pieces of campaign literature in the 1960 campaign, the Hunt leaflet, did Johnson much more harm than good. This was the usual result of Hunt's political support. Texas Attorney General Crawford Martin said in 1963 that Hunt had done more, in a financial way, "than any other one man" to shape the contemporary politics of the state. Martin was fooled by the Hunt myth. The old billionaire actually was a tightwad in his support, seldom giving more than $250 or $500 to a candidate. But he was a great talker. A couple of weeks after the assassination, Hunt, depressed by the thought that people could blame him for the assassination, pointed to the toy flag on his desk (it was at half-staff) and then, looking out his office window and across the prosperous towers of Dallas, observed, "If the Constitution of the United States could incite to assassination, then *Life Line* could incite it." Having disposed of that, he went on to say how happy he was that Johnson was president. He assured me that he (Hunt) had played a determining role at the Democratic national convention in getting Johnson to accept the vice-presidential nomination. Hunt said he was terribly regretful now that he had "alone and single-handed, by telephone, letter and personal talks" been responsible for the ratification of the 22nd Amendment (no third term) because it would prevent Johnson from staying in longer. "Johnson," he told me, his puffy pink cheeks glowing in the soft light, "is the kind of president who can lead Congress around by its nose. I wouldn't mind seeing him in there for three terms." *

These things show that Hunt—who had nothing to do with Johnson's accepting the vice-presidential nomination and, with the exception of *Life Line* propagandizing, nothing to do with forcing state legislatures to ratify the 22nd Amendment—is the Major Hoople of the oil world. A genius at playing either poker or oil, he is an ineffectual dreamer in politics, and Johnson should not be strapped with him.

Eliminate cherubic HLH from your suspicions. Do this so that we can get down to Johnson's *real* connections with the oil powers that do count in Texas and national politics. If one is seeking circumstantial evidence to play with, it can be found. But it has to come by a circuitous route.

Every politician who intends to make a serious bid for success in Texas must, of course, genuflect before the derrick, no matter what his personal feelings are toward the industry. But with Johnson, the cooperation goes beyond a mere politico-religious ritual. It always has. On the surface Johnson's support in Texas now appears to be no more oil than industry. There are, for example, Jim Ling of Ling-Temco-Vought, a fat contributor to the President's Club and to Johnson's lieutenant, Governor John Connally; and Erik Jonsson of Texas Instruments, who is a Yankee and nomi-

* For more of Hunt's philosophy, see *The Nation*, Feb. 24, 1964, "H. L. Hunt: Portrait of a Super-Patriot."

nally a Republican, but nevertheless a part of the Dallas business establishment that supports Lyndon; and the various generous fellows heading the insurance companies and banks. But these brownies cast in the corporate-management mold are the latter-day Lyndon-lovers. In these later years Johnson has not been above taking support, a subtle kind of kickback, from men grown rich largely from government contracts; but in the early years his spreading domain was purchased with the aid of men who made their money from plundering the state's natural resources or from other normal cutthroat enterprises. The old steadies who have been around from the beginning are contractors like the Brown brothers of Houston and H. B. Zachry of San Antonio, and the oil men—John Mecom and Wesley West and Leonard McCollum of Conoco and Gardner Symonds of Tenneco and the Murchisons and always, but always, the late Sid Richardson. These are his kind of men, and he theirs. Between them there is a rough-hewn camaraderie which has not always produced the most burnished examples of statesmanship.

Within the hour after his return to Washington after taking the oath in Dallas, Johnson (according to *The New York Times*) was talking by telephone with his old confidant Robert Anderson in New York. He asked Anderson to come to Washington; Anderson, another of Johnson's key links to the oil fraternity, is always happy to answer his country's call. He and Johnson talked several hours that Sunday and, *The New York Times* reported, they resumed their conference the next day. The consultation, in a manner of speaking, still continues. For some reason, the Johnson-Anderson relationship is often treated as something almost clandestine. Way down in one of Walter Winchell's early-1964 columns, following bits about Eartha Kitt's "top-he-cret" and a "charming brawl" in front of the Pakistan embassy, was the revelation: "Ike's ex-U.S. Treasury chief (Robert Anderson) is LBJ's No. 1 financial adviser." The only surprising thing about that tidbit was that Winchell considered it such inside information as to be worthy of space in his gossip column. Anderson's powerful influence over Lyndon Johnson, and the position Anderson was marked to play in directing the financial policies of the Johnson administration, were both known and predictable from the beginning. They have been intimate allies for thirty years of politics in Texas and Washington. They were especially intimate in the creation of an oil program which, without much public awareness, had developed to a controversial crisis that was effectively quashed only by Kennedy's death.

The seed of that program was really planted, more than a quarter of a century ago, on a passenger train clacking through the night. There are several accounts of what happened, but one goes this way: oil millionaire Sid Richardson, and President Roosevelt's son Elliott, and Bill Kittrell, a kind of protégé of Sam Rayburn's and a well-known man about Texas, were keeping each other company on a trip to Washington. But the conversation was beginning to droop, so Richardson sent Kittrell into the chair car to scout for a fourth for a round of bridge. By and by Kittrell came back with a young Army colonel in tow, an open-faced fellow by the name of Dwight Eisenhower.

From the train trip developed a strong friendship between Eisenhower and Richardson; after the war, when Eisenhower was being rushed by both political parties, his Texas oil pal showed up in Paris to tell him that if he ever did get into politics he could count on plenty of Richardson money.

Exactly what generosity Richardson showed has never been more than wildly hinted at, but it apparently was enough to make Eisenhower moderately grateful. When Richardson and other Texas oil men recommended Robert Anderson, Eisenhower named him Secretary of the Navy. The importance of this to Texas oil men is a matter of almost comical stress. Anderson, a resident of landlocked Fort

Worth, knew nothing of naval affairs before he got the post, but that hardly matters; all he needed to know was that Texas is the largest oil-producing state and that the Navy is the largest consumer of oil as well as leaser of valuable lands to favored oil firms. From this producer-consumer relationship things work out rather naturally, and it was this elementary knowledge that later made John Connally (who had for several years, through the good offices of his mentor Lyndon Johnson, been serving as Sid Richardson's attorney and who later became executor of the Richardson estate) and Fred Korth, also residents of Fort Worth, such able secretaries of the Navy, by Texas standards. But this, perhaps, is beside the point.

Anderson is a very smart, very religious man. He sometimes keeps a picture of Jesus on his office desk. Scandal has not yet touched his name. Years ago he was on the Texas Horse Racing Commission, and there he struck up a friendship with one of Texas' wealthiest horse-loving families which, after pari-mutuel racing closed in Texas, hired him as general manager of half a million oil acres. It was on this hillock of special interest that he became friends with all the influential oil men in Texas. As president of the Texas Mid-Continent Oil and Gas Association, he became one of the most eloquent lobbyists for the industry's fiscal plums, including the oil depletion allowance.

One of his close friends was fellow Fort Worthian Sid Richardson, who counted his wealth in the hundreds of millions. The two men agreed that it might be well to have a Texan of Anderson's instincts on Ike's staff, and so he went.

After Anderson had served for a time in the Navy job and then as Assistant Secretary of Defense, he retired, late in 1955, to re-enter private business, leaving Ike's bosom with strong assurances that eventually even better things lay ahead for him in politics. Eisenhower meant what he said. The "better things" were spelled out in a conversation with

Richardson, during which Ike hinted that Bob Anderson would make a fine running mate in 1956, in place of Nixon. Just to keep Ike thinking so, Richardson flew back to Washington a couple of days before Christmas, 1955, with his DC-3 laden with quail, ducks and steaks for the president; at this time they again agreed that Anderson would make a dandy running mate for Ike the next year.

By this time they could talk more firmly because things had been "worked out" with Anderson, who, when first approached by Richardson with the idea of taking the vice-presidential spot, had said he would do so only if he had a million dollar capital gains nest egg to make up the difference. He was tired of puny federal salaries. So Richardson arranged the million dollars in an oil deal affecting several companies.* (See footnote on page 271.) Unfortunately for their plans, the professional politicians decided to keep Nixon on the program after all and Anderson's windfall appeared to have profited nobody but him, which had not been the scheme.

Or could he still be useful?

Eisenhower, on the urging of Richardson and Lyndon Johnson,† named him to the office of Secretary of Treasury, and on June 21, ten days after selling his gift oil property, Anderson was free and clear to tell the Senate Finance Committee that he held no property that would conflict with his interest in the cabinet post.

A few weeks later Anderson was appointed to a cabinet committee to "study" the oil import situation; out of this study came the present-day program which benefits the major oil companies, the international oil giants primarily, by about one *billion* dollars a year.

Although Standard of Indiana, one of the companies involved in Anderson's million-dollar windfall, used the re-

† Whom Ike owed plenty for botching the 1952 and 1956 presidential elections in Texas.

sulting import program to great success, moving in a few years from a company with no foreign holdings to one of the largest overseas oil explorers, there was nothing illegal in this mutual benefit. Anderson could be charged with nothing more than poor taste.

Nor was Anderson held solely responsible for the oil import program's formula; not at all. Industry insiders believed—and their beliefs were printed in industry publications—that equally influential in the shaping of the program were Lyndon Johnson and his ally in all things pertaining to oil industry legislation, the late Senator Robert Kerr of Oklahoma.* Kerr, an owner of the Kerr-McGee Oil Company, did very well under the new oil program, but his attitude toward conflict of interest was singularly easygoing. "Hell," he once remarked, "if everyone abstained on grounds of personal interest, I doubt if you could get a quorum in the U.S. Senate on any subject."

(The fight over the terms of the import program was between the billionaires and the multimillionaires on one side, and the millionaires on the other—which is not the kind of fight that is likely to interest the average wage earner who senses, properly, that however the profits are split up, none will come to him. But the issue is really more important to him than he suspects.)

Although the outcome of the fight seriously hurt the independent oil men of Texas, especially the smaller ones, it was only natural to find Johnson siding with the big-big oil companies against them. He is a cinch player, and always goes with the stronger side. The most important fact to remember as a spectator is that the cost of imported oil, from source to gasoline pump, is from $1.25 to $1.50 a barrel cheaper—but you and I don't pay any less when we buy our gas. The benefit from the cheapness stays in the pockets of the im-

* See Jim Collins in *The Oil Daily*, June 21, 1963.

porter. It is a bonanza. Oil importation is now 2.5 million barrels a day. That's nine hundred million barrels a year. The annual profit—to the importers, not the consumers—is between a billion and a billion and a half dollars.

Surely, you say, there must be some way to let the average taxpayer benefit from the cheap oil. Yes, there is a way. In fact it was being proposed in 1958, at the time the present quota system was agreed on in its place. The other proposal would have provided that the Interior Department first figure out how much oil it wanted to allow to be imported, then put import quotas up for competitive bidding—with the proceeds to go to the U.S. Treasury. In addition to benefiting the treasury it would have given every oil company in the country, large or small, a shot at the quotas.

Johnson, Anderson, and Kerr went to work and squelched that, persuading Congress to leave the whole thing up to the President (and his advisers) to determine.

Early the next year Eisenhower imposed the program they wanted. Under the formula still operating, companies that import oil are supposed to have refinery facilities—a requirement which knocks out all but one hundred and fifty oil companies and "sets it up" for the very largest, because, beyond that, their import quotas are linked to the amount of domestic production and domestic refining they do—so the largest companies get bigger. Twenty oil giants bring in 85 per cent of the foreign oil.

There was never any evidence that Johnson personally benefited from the program he helped shape. But there was trouble ahead. The smaller companies, the traditional wildcatters, were being ruined by the competition from the imported oil. While the big companies prospered as never before, the smaller companies were going out of business. In the first years of the oil import program, thousands of wells were shut down in this country, thousands of oil field workers were thrown out of jobs.

He may have really sympathized, and on the other hand he may have been making campaign talk only, but on numerous occasions in 1960 Kennedy had said the kind of thing the independent oil man wanted to hear. In Wichita Falls that presidential year Kennedy commented, "Here in this old community, Sam Gray, who sells shoes—from 1955 to 1960 he sold 60 pairs of oil safety shoes a month. Do you ˶now how many he sold last month? Two. Eight days an oil well works in the state of Texas. Eight years ago it was twenty days."

By 1962 President Kennedy was making what the oil industry, especially the major companies, must have viewed as ominous signs of imminent reform. On July 12, 1962, a Treasury Department official acknowledged that "it is no secret that we are collecting financial data on percentage depletion in the oil and gas industry, and that we are considering this issue in connection with tax reform." This meant the 27.5 per cent oil depletion allowance, the industry's most treasured piece of governmental favoritism, might be reduced or abolished altogether. By May of 1963, Attorney General Robert Kennedy was talking openly of "an apparent tendency toward concentration in this industry" and the need for an anti-trust probe. A cabinet-level Petroleum Study Committee, after noting dangerous implications in the oil import program, suggested radical changes which many industry observers believed would certainly be put into operation by January 1, 1964, when a new import quota period was scheduled to begin.

Meanwhile, in Texas, minor politicians, representing the smaller oil operators who were in troubled straits, were preparing a last-ditch effort to get fast action out of Kennedy. State Senator Charles Herring, one of three Texas senators who had attended the 1963 World Petroleum Congress, returned to write a furious report setting forth the Texas independent oil man's troubles in competing with the im-

port program dominated by the international giants. It was
a thirty-six-page report spelling it all out: how the program
came into existence, who was profiting, who was being put
out of business. Herring and other representatives of the
independents obtained a firm commitment that when Kennedy reached Austin on November 22, the report would be
put in his hands along with a confidential letter from Herring which talked of the import program's having the
"potential for scandal . . . perhaps dwarfing the Teapot
Dome scandal of yesteryear" and of how

> . . . it now seems impossible to overlook certain aspects of
> the program which seem peculiarly conducive to inferences
> of political scandal. I refer, for example, to the multiple ill-
> defined bases on which companies may qualify for import
> quotas, to the variations and exceptions within those formu-
> lae—and in general to the arbitrary and flexible manner in
> which oil import allocations . . . worth perhaps $1 million
> per day are passed out by federal officials who so far have not
> been required to explain their decisions. Charges have been
> made, and never challenged, that import quota tickets are
> "sold" in violation of the import order. Indeed, quota tickets
> are apparently awarded some non-importing companies which
> enter into undisguised paper "exchange" transactions with
> leading importers for no purpose except to award them sub-
> sidies through the import program. Etc.

In short, scandalous favoritism. The report and the letter
never were seen by Kennedy.

It is absurd to suppose that Kennedy, who was anything
but a talented manipulator in Congress, could have taken
away the oil depletion allowance. But this form of favoritism
is not at all popular with many Congressmen, and it is not
unthinkable that he might have trimmed the allowance, say
down to 25 per cent.* Once shaken, the allowance would

---

* Senator Proxmire got 31 votes (against 58) on a proposal to cut the
depletion allowance for the big operators to *15 per cent.*

never again be secure, as it has been for more than a generation. And think what even a 2.5 per cent reduction in the
present allowance would have meant to the Treasury. Suppose further that Kennedy might have been able to wangle
some adjustments, even minor ones, in the depletion allowances under which favored oil companies based in this country operate abroad—allowances which now permit some of
these billion-dollar companies to escape any U.S. taxation
whatsoever. Suppose also—which is the most likely possibility of all—that he had decided to adopt the quota-auction
system, with the proceeds going to the U.S. Treasury. This
was a proposal under consideration at the time of his death.
Put all of these possibilities together, and it adds up to several billions of dollars that the government is now missing.

If any relief was felt within the oil industry at Kennedy's
assassination, it was not felt in vain. Five days after the
assassination, Senator Herring wrote Walter Jenkins at the
White House, "Powerful forces doubtless are seeking to
utilize the present period of transition to delay further the
overdue shake-up in the oil import control system." Whether
or not it was due to "powerful forces," the delay certainly
did occur, and does to the present time.

Under President Johnson the situation has steadily
worsened. With a great show of playing fair, of keeping his
hands out of it because he was from an oil state, Johnson
ordained that the import program would be left strictly up
to Interior Secretary Udall. Ominously, the American Petroleum Institute, chief lobbying agent for the oil industry,
hailed the transfer of authority as "entirely logical," and
the *Oil & Gas Journal,* official organ of the industry, reported that "industry spokesmen were quick to voice approval of President Johnson, pointing out that he has placed
authority in the hands of government officers who know
most about oil."

To this group of knowing officers was added, within a few

weeks, another—or almost. The appointment of Joe T. Dickerson to be head of the Interior Department's office of Oil and Gas was sent to the Senate for confirmation, but the Senate gagged and could not go through with it. It would have been Dickerson's job to "police" the oil industry. Some cop. A former vice-president of Shell Oil Company, Dickerson was receiving a $20,000 yearly pension from Shell, given with the written provision that he do nothing to hurt his former employers. He has also been a paid lobbyist for the Mid-Continent Oil and Gas Association, whose membership includes Humble, Gulf, Phillips, Shell, Socony, Standard of Indiana, Texaco and the like.

This was Johnson's first oil-oriented appointment, and it was blocked only after a great outcry, led by Senator Proxmire, who likened it to "putting the foxes in charge of the henhouse." The foxes, unfortunately, were already in charge. Udall does not make an appointment touching on oil matters without first checking with the National Petroleum Council.

The controversial oil import program, which Kennedy had been depended on to tighten up, has under Johnson become even looser. Restrictions on the importation of residual fuel oil have been eliminated almost altogether. In his first year a franchise was granted Phillips Petroleum Company to build a refinery in Puerto Rico which was to send an additional 25,000 barrels daily to the U.S. market, despite the fact that the oil import program as originally written states that Puerto Rican oil refining can be increased only if the products are consumed locally or sent to a foreign country. This was a $25,000 a day windfall for Phillips. Johnson said the decision was out of his hands. But it is possible that Secretary Udall might have been influenced by the fact that Abe Fortas, one of President Johnson's closest advisers, was counsel for Puerto Rico (which wanted Phillips to come in) in this case.

Under Johnson the trend toward monopoly and amalgamation goes on unchecked. When Pure Oil Company and Union Oil Company proposed a merger in Johnson's first year as president, the Justice Department quickly gave its approval, without even a close study of the case, although it was one of the largest corporate transactions to be proposed in recent years and would eliminate a solid competitor from the oil market. Observers of a more suspicious nature said it probably did no harm to have Houston attorney J. A. Elkins—one of Johnson's most powerful political allies back home and a former lobbying employer of Johnson's crony, Ambassador Ed Clark—initiate the merger.

When a San Francisco federal court dismissed an antitrust suit against Standard Oil Company of Indiana and Tidewater Oil Corporation, who joined to pay $385,000,000 for Honolulu Oil Corporation, the Justice Department at once promised to appeal to the U.S. Supreme Court. But then, in a curious reversal, it announced that because of the "particularities"—which were not explained—of the case, the appeal was being dropped. This sort of thing happens so often that an observer runs the risk of seeing something sinister in the ease with which the government surrenders. There really is nothing sinister about it. The major oil companies have always prospered with Johnson's help. Now, as president, he can help without impediment. Even as senator he *tried*—as we shall see—even when the hanky-panky became embarrassingly open.

*
* *
*

For eleven of the last fourteen years Johnson has been the most powerful member of the Democratic party, which is supposedly the more libertarian party; yet during the period of his leadership the nation has become, often with his public approval, less tolerant of its mavericks. If Johnson cannot be held accountable for the drift, neither can he be credited with trying to hold it back. He has pilloried honorable public servants and consented to and assisted monstrous smears. He voted in 1943 to extend the life of the Dies Committee; he voted the ten Hollywood writers in contempt when they refused to say whether they were Communists in 1947. He said, and often repeated, that he wanted nothing to do with "extremists—neither the KKK *nor the ADA*," which is as nice a job as was ever done on that bland group of institutional liberals. On other occasions liberals were hailed by him as "red-hots, pink-eyes and pinkoes."

During his last year in the House, 1948, the year he was working his way into the Senate, Johnson studiously avoided voting on the issues that might have further revealed his rightest-special interest side. When the House voted on the motion to reject a Senate provision that would have discriminated against the admission of Jewish and Polish displaced persons—Johnson was absent. When the House voted on the unconstitutional and fear-buoyed Mundt-Nixon bill to combat un-American and subversive activities—Johnson was absent. When the House took up the Bulwinkle bill, which would have exempted railroad rates from the anti-trust laws and which had been the number one objective of the railroad lobby for the previous three years; and when the House voted on the Wolcott Housing bill, which contained mortgage and financial provisions that were a windfall to the real estate lobby but did nothing to provide low-cost housing or to clear slums—Johnson was absent.

But then he got his leg over the Senate sill, and another Johnson emerged.

He did not lead the Senate majority (which was finally whipped into a mob spirit, filled with a mob's sense of justice) to put down McCarthy until the Wisconsin senator had been so thoroughly discredited and repudiated by the best periodicals and newspapers in the country that it was very much to Johnson's political advantage to move in and do something. And then, of course, he moved for the wrong reason. Was he enraged because McCarthy had ruined decent government workers and professors from one coast to the other? No. If you read the one brief statement Johnson made against McCarthy you will see that he felt "the real issue [and the only issue he mentioned] . . . is whether the Senate of the United States, the greatest deliberative body in the history of the world, will permit abuse of a duly appointed committee. . . . If we sanction such abuse . . . we might just as well turn over our jobs to a small group of men and go back home to plow the south forty acres."

That certainly sounds like McCarthy had used some foul language. From the beginning, senators from time to time had with impunity called each other such things as "liars" and "polecats" and "dead stinking mackerel." What worse than this had McCarthy called the committee that Johnson was so incensed? He had called it the "unwitting handmaidens of Communism." These, said Johnson in righteous heat, were words "more fittingly inscribed on the walls of a men's room." Ah, would that our nation's public toilets were so high-toned as to carry such relatively classical messages!

Just as Johnson fell out with Texas' Governor Allan Shivers *not* over Shivers' racism or because he had led a crooked administration but because "he attacked me personally and my patriotism," so now Johnson was not angry with McCarthy for intimidating the country but because he had insulted The Club.

In 1959 Johnson supported retention of the loyalty oaths for students getting loans from the federal government. In 1954 he supported Eisenhower's proposal to force dissolution of organizations considered "Communist-infiltrated." The same years he opposed statehood for Hawaii and Alaska, going along with the Eastland arguments that Hawaii was run by Communistic labor unions (and with Eastland's unspoken argument that here would be four more votes against the filibuster). The same year, when the Senate confirmed the appointment of Joe McCarthy's protégé Robert E. Lee to the Federal Communications Commission (FCC), whose only experience in the field of radio was as master of ceremonies for H. L. Hunt's right-wing *Facts Forum,* Johnson was absent. But he said he favored the confirmation and would have voted for it if he had been there. He voted in 1950 against efforts to kill a $100 million loan to Franco. And the same year he voted for the McCarran Anti-Subversive Bill, which was denounced by most religious, labor and liberal groups as a grave frontal assault on civil liberties.

In short, Johnson's record has not been clean of certain traits which some around Washington, who want to perpetuate a relaxed society, believe have led and are leading the nation into dangerous riptides of absolutism and intolerance. Some, forgetting other eras, were shocked that he permitted presidential aide Marvin Watson to butcher the career of Abba P. Schwartz to satisfy the national right-wing's appetite or that he himself supervised the sacrificing of Adam Yarmolinsky to placate Southern right-wingers. Actually these things fit naturally into his record of dispensing with other careers for the sake of his own. Before McCarthy, yea, Lyndon had his great day at ruining a man.

This time it was done, not surprisingly, to ingratiate himself with the oil and gas fraternity. The episode is not mentioned much these days in Washington; the record of the event is hard to come by; the committee involved in the affairs says it has no more reprints for distribution and this is understandable. No doubt some high politicians would like the winds of time to wipe out the trail that leads back to 1949 and the place and the manner in which Leland Olds was, professionally speaking, murdered by Johnson.

Leland Olds, now dead, was born seventy-six years ago in

Rochester, New York. His father, George Olds, was for nearly fifty years a much beloved math professor, dean, and president of Amherst College; Calvin Coolidge, Harlan Stone, Dwight Morrow were among the many students who considered the Olds home their own.

As a student at Amherst, where he graduated *magna cum laude* in 1912, Leland Olds developed a philosophy which is today commonplace in what is known as the social gospel. After leaving school he went into church social work for a time, got sick of having to deal with trade unionists who weren't interested in helping the unskilled, and entered the Union Theological Seminary. For a time he preached at a little Congregationalist church in the low-wage section of Brooklyn. Disenchanted with the then-sluggish Church as a social force, he taught in college for a couple of years. But shortly after the United States entered World War I he was called to Washington to help prepare guidelines for the country's war labor policy. This launched him along a line of vigorous criticism and theorizing that was to take him into an outstanding government career and hot water. Over the years he sporadically carried out projects for Franklin Roosevelt and for progressive New York politicians. But he is best remembered today for the time he spent as a labor editor for the *Federated Press* between 1922 and 1929, and his time as Federal Power Commissioner from 1939–1949. The Golden Twenties were pewter to many millions of Americans; for them he wrote some rather fiery material that was syndicated in 100 different newspapers and periodicals. Those were the days when the radical pamphleteer and the critical novelist (Upton Sinclair, *et al.*) abounded; they were sorry times in many ways, the economic landscape fouled by child labor and bogus stocks and sweatshop wages.

The things Olds wrote then could have been matched or exceeded in indignation in the writings of many dozens of America's best authors. They were sentiments still being voiced proudly by the scattered ranks of the old Populist movement. For instance, early in 1927 he wrote of the injustice of the profit distribution by U.S. Steel Corporation:

> President Coolidge with his share of steel stock is entitled to about $900 of the 1926 profits. An unskilled worker in the steel mills would have to work more than 2,000 hours to earn as much for his family as Coolidge gets without a stroke of work.

And on another occasion he warned:

> The smaller corporations are survivals of a previous industrial order in which competition of independent businessmen was the rule. They will probably continue to appear in industrial statistics, allowed to survive to give the impression that the old order still exists. But the super-trust is the real order of the day and belongs in an entirely different category. It represents the development of state capitalism. [A warning which, with the continued sharp concentration of corporate control today, seems prescient indeed.]

And on other occasions he decried the "decay" of the church which at that time he felt was merely preaching "the principles of the exploiting class"; he denounced the American "dollar empire" [which Fulbright and Clark and Morse and Gruening are continuing to denounce on the Senate floor today, using the same terminology]; and he ridiculed the publicity given to John D. Rockefeller's gift of $1 million to the Metropolitan Museum of Art. He noted that Rockefeller owned nearly a half billion dollars in stocks, from which he received $12 million in annual dividends. "Give till it hurts means nothing to the money princes who govern industry, endow education, and generally distribute royal gifts to the glory of God and the admiration of the populace," wrote Olds. "They simply *can't* give till it hurts. They have too much. And if they could it would mean stepping down from the throne of exploitation to become a common man."

Ten years after Olds left the *Federated Press,* President Roosevelt nominated him to a seat on the Federal Power Commission (FPC). Five years later he was reappointed, and now, in 1949, his name went before the Senate for a third confirmation. The first time Roosevelt sent Olds' name to Congress not a word was raised against confirmation. On the second occasion, the subcommittee heard some state regulatory officials complain that Olds was too high-handed; at the last hour, Senator Moore of Oklahoma tried to block his confirmation by reading on the floor of the Senate some of Olds' radical-years writings, but the other senators waved him aside and Olds went through again without trouble.

Now on the third occasion Johnson was waiting. He was chairman of the subcommittee that handled the preliminary confirmation hearings. He also led the floor fight against confirmation. In the hearings there was ample testimony from both sides. Evidence was presented to show that during Olds' ten years on the Commission, he had squeezed more than $1 billion of water out of utility stocks; he had saved consumers a quarter of a *billion* dollars in rate reductions; he had introduced into regulation practice the concept of rates based upon the number of dollars actually invested rather than upon what the market will bear. On coming to the Commission in 1939 he had noted the national power shortage—which some denied—and helped beef it up in time for war production.

There were many officials, especially men devoted to rural electrification and cooperatives, who were there to praise Olds. James C. Bonbright, professor of business and finance at Columbia University and chairman of the New York Power Authority, called him "one of the most distinguished and outstanding men" in the field of public utility regulation. There were others who called Olds a tyrant. And there were some who did everything but call him Communist, basing their charge on his writing in the 1920's. George S. Benson, president of Harding College, was one who did. Johnson was another.

When Olds testified that his social crusading had stemmed from "a lot of thinking about what the effect would be if people really applied the principles of Christianity to their everyday business," Johnson came back with cold sarcasm, "Mr. Olds, if you care to, you may submit for the record any photostats of your writing indicating that you advocated a religious revolution . . ." Olds said he had been very impressed when, during a visit to the western Pennsylvania coal strikes in 1919, he had been inside a Catholic church with some of the strikers, and mounted police rode in and began to club them down. Johnson continued to mock him: "You may introduce any of the priest's writings you wish, Mr. Olds."

Olds agreed that his writings had been radical—"there's no question about that"—but that he had never approved of the approach of Karl Marx "because I felt that the road to harmony must recognize spiritual values and that ambition for power was an unwholesome influence in human affairs. I still believe that." He easily admitted that he had once advocated public ownership of utilities and the railroads, but he said he no longer felt that way.

LBJ: The point is this. You do not openly advocate public ownership of utilities, railroads, or resources today?

Olds: Do you want me to tell you what I do advocate today at this time, or later?

LBJ: I want you to answer that question "yes" or "no."

Olds: No, I do not.

LBJ: That is fine, that is what is important. [Later, on the Senate floor, Johnson was to say that Olds had not shifted his position.]

During his ten years as a labor editor Olds had written approximately 1,800 articles. He had no control over the subscribers; any paper that wanted to purchase the service could. One of the buyers was the *Daily Worker*.

LBJ: So far as you know, it is not a prerequisite of the *Daily Worker* for a man to be a member of the party in order that his articles might appear—was it?

Olds: I judge not. I certainly was never a member of the party or in any way affiliated or associated with an organization that was a member of the party.

LBJ: (*Apparently disbelieving*) They have no such requirement that you know anything about; is that right?

Olds: I do not know anything about their requirements. In general, I have never at any time been very favorably impressed with the *Daily Worker* type of journalism.

It was not enough for Johnson that Olds conceded the radical nature of his writings, or stated publicly that he had never believed the Marxist line, or that in his later years he had given up the notion of government ownership of utilities and some natural resources. Johnson had in mind forcing a more abject admission.

LBJ: Mr. Olds, do you repudiate those writings?

Olds: No, sir; I do not.

LBJ: Do you reiterate them; do you reassert them?

Olds: I am going to . . . tell you exactly what those writings mean.

LBJ: We are going to be able to judge what they mean. We will be glad to have your viewpoint upon what they mean, but this is the question I want to ask you: do you still feel as you did when you wrote those articles?

Olds: No. I have indicated that the change in the circumstances in this country and the change in my thinking that has gone along with it, would lead me to write some of those articles in a somewhat different way today.

(Later, on the Senate floor, Johnson would quote this passage with the observation: "The net result being that he would slant them differently today.")

Having failed to prove anything remotely Communistic about Olds, Johnson (whose closest friends and supporters in Texas would vote for Eisenhower in 1952 and 1956, and some of whom would vote for Nixon in 1960) attempted to prove Olds a treacherous party man. "In 1924," said Johnson, "Leland Olds left the Democratic Party—if he was ever a member—to vote for Senator Bob La Follette.

"In 1928, Leland Olds left the Democratic Party—if he was ever a member—to vote for Herbert Hoover" (a rather unique shift for a radical, but Olds had praised Hoover for having "a keen understanding of capitalist evolution, that is noticeably lacking in Al Smith").

What was all the fuss about? Why rake up these old stale ashes? It was no secret. On this issue the national press, most of the big papers, were against Johnson. The *Milwaukee Journal* summed it up neatly: "Natural gas, and natural gas alone, is the point at issue in [the] outrageous attack on Olds' nomination. Communism and all other charges are pure smear tactics." The *Kansas City Star,* not exactly a left-wing newspaper, remarked, "Human memory and gratitude are short, but a few persons in this area have reason to remember Leland Olds. He is the strong man of the FPC who stepped into the fifteen-year-old battle for lower gas rates in this region and won . . . It so happens that Texas is one of the gas-producing states leading the fight to undermine the authority of the FPC. Johnson, who went into the Senate as a liberal (Texas version), has appeared to be very much on the side of the pipeline companies . . ."

Olds had opposed bills such as the Moore-Rizley measure,

which attempted to remove independent producers of natural gas from FPC control; that is, it would have removed three-fourths of the industry from control and presumably sent rates sky high. Robert Kerr of Oklahoma, who came to the Senate with Johnson and was to remain his strong ally throughout, had a similar bill working in the Senate at the time, which Olds opposed. The greatest sin in the eyes of the gas companies had not been Olds' opposition to bills that would remove the industry from controls but his insistence that industry marketing was under the FPC in the first place. For most of his time on the FPC, Olds had not tried to regulate the price at which gas is sold to the pipeline companies. But after the Supreme Court case, Interstate Gas Company v. Power Commission, in which the Court held that such sales to the pipeline companies were matters for national regulation, Olds moved in.

It was this which set the Johnson avalanche in motion. By the time Olds' nomination reached the Senate floor, he was a goner. Some spoke in his behalf: Morse said Olds' was a typical case of a campus radical developing into a "sound liberal." Republican Senator Langer said he had looked over Olds' record and had found "it is good. It is the record of a man whom the public utilities could not control. It is the record of a man who has been honest, and who has been fighting in behalf of the common people of the country." Humphrey read into the record many editorials supporting Olds, and in the ringing Humphrey way proclaimed:

> There is not one iota of evidence that he was ever a Communist. In fact, he is a devoted American. . . . In the 1920's the American enterprise system should have been criticized, and anyone who conclusively criticized it should have a crown of diamonds. If there is any room in heaven for a politician, the politician who will be in heaven is the one who had the courage to stand up and condemn the exploiters of child labor and of adult labor, the exploiters of the widows who

put their money in phony stocks. If Mr. Olds had the courage
to stand up in the 1920's and say that he did not like that
kind of rotten business practice, God bless him. Those who
should be on trial tonight are those who did not raise a
finger of protest when millions of people were robbed. . . .
All they did was to talk about some kind of business confidence, and prosperity around the corner, and split up the
loot. If there is any divine justice those men will fry, and
Mr. Olds will have a crown.

It was a driving speech, vintage Hubert, full of protests
about the Senate "crucifying" Olds and "driving him into
the dirt" and "political double talk" and "pressure groups."

But the nation in 1949 had already been spooked by the
Red scare and it took a brave senator to vote for a man who
had been fingered, as Johnson fingered Olds in committee
and as he now did again, even more brutally, in the closing
hour of that day on the Senate floor. Johnson knew he had
the votes; and when Johnson knows he already has the votes,
nobody, but nobody, can rub it in with more vengeance.*
So long as the count is doubtful he will occasionally throw
out a compromising phrase; otherwise, never.

He began on Olds' accomplishments. Just a myth: "the
myth of Leland Olds, the knight in shining armor, doing
tireless battle with the dragons of 'special privilege.' It is the
myth of a humble, helpless man, naïve in the ways of political life, standing bare-headed and empty-handed before
some sinister political power. . . . *I will say I hope the vote
tonight for once and all will show to every man nominated
for high office that he has to do something besides jump on
the power lobby in order to deserve confirmation."*

---

* This bullying characteristic has been noticed in Lyndon since he was
a youth. H. M. Greene, professor of government and history at San
Marcos State Teachers when Johnson was a student, recalled on a
National Educational Television Network show: in debates in class,
"Well, he was, I would say, at times he would grow almost ruthless,
when he knew he had [his opponent] logically and had the advantage
of him, why he could become ruthless."

Johnson next accused Olds (contrary to evidence presented in committee) of circulating "vile, snide and unsupported whispers" about members of the Commission who disagreed with him. As for the argument that Olds' patriotism had been approved by the Senate on two earlier occasions, Johnson had his argument ready on that: "It is very clever of Mr. Olds' partisans to attempt to bind members of this Senate by events which never occurred. Is Mr. Olds to secure an exemption now from an honest, thorough scrutiny of his record, merely because twice before he has escaped scrutiny and because twice before he has been confirmed? *The Senate has, in the past, confirmed Henry Wallace for high office. Would he be confirmed today? I think not.*"

Johnson's momentum was now pushing Olds toward innuendos of subversion. Johnson noted Olds' "curious conduct" in administering the Natural Gas Act, and suggested that some of the things Olds had done to defend his position indicated he "must have something in mind" although "I shall not guess what Leland Olds might do in the future if he is now sanctioned again by the Senate."

It sounded ominous, and Johnson was not long in following it up with his clincher: Olds was a . . . no, not a Communist . . . "I do not charge that Mr. Olds is a Communist" although "I realize that the line he followed, the phrases he used, the causes he espoused, resembled the party line today . . ." No, not *exactly* a Communist, but "Leland Olds had something in mind when he began to build his political empire across the nation; he had something in mind when he began to smear and besmirch all those who disagreed with him; he had something in mind when he chose to force a showdown with the Senate over his power to write laws of his own; he had something in mind when he chose to disregard the clear language of the Natural Gas Act and plot a course toward confiscation and public ownership." (Something Olds had repudiated in committee hearing.)

The big cat began to play with his victim. He was glad *he* didn't have to defend the writings turned out by this "kid of forty." Johnson said no member of the subcommittee, least of all himself, accused Olds of actually being a traitor, but, still, "There were Americans of liberal views who expressed their thoughts and maintained their purpose without choosing—as did Leland Olds—to travel with those who proposed the Marxian answer . . . He spoke from the same platform with Earl Browder [Mrs. Roosevelt, commenting on this point made by Johnson, recalled that Robert Taft also spoke from the same platform with Browder on one occasion]. He accepted subsidy from the so-called Garland Fund, a fund created and expended to keep alive Marxist organs and Marxist groups. The managing editor of *Federated Press,* under whom Leland Olds worked as industrial editor, was Carl Haessler, a notorious leader of party-line organizations who sat out World War I in Alcatraz as a seditionist."

"By the way: he was sent to Leavenworth, and was so dangerous that he was sent to Alcatraz. When he came out *he joined up with* Leland Olds. Leland Olds knew who his friends were and for what they stood." So, from being merely a staff writer and subject editor, Johnson had promoted Olds to ringleader of the whole seditionist bunch.

It didn't last much longer. Shortly after midnight, the Senate voted to support Johnson's motion to deny Olds another term, and that was the end of the bouncy little man in steel-rimmed glasses who liked to play the cello, read poetry, grow flowers, take Boy Scouts on hikes, and who had for one decade of his life made the mistake of writing indignantly of what he called "the kind of open-shop capitalism which cracked workers over the head if they sought to organize."

Republican Senator Aiken, aghast at Johnson's tactics, predicted as the early morning vote was being taken, that "the effects of what is being done here tonight will echo down far through the years ahead of us, and will continue to plague those who accuse him much longer than the echoes of the Teapot Dome were heard. Certain public utilities of the country are out to destroy a man for performing his duty. I do not know of anything worse than that."

But it didn't work out that way. The next year Senator McCarthy took over, and in following his madness the public largely forgot what Johnson had done. Never again did the national liberals entirely trust Johnson, but even they did not tag him in the way they tagged McCarthy. As for the Texas liberals, it all seemed remote from them; anyway, they were entering their own period of home-grown McCarthyism which made the mere character assassination of one man seem almost tolerable. By and large, they would string along with Johnson for another eight years—until he all but destroyed *them* also.

It almost seems insensitive of the American people that they have failed to see Lyndon Johnson as he sees himself: all heart. How can they doubt him? Did he not carry on his person, and leave available in his Senate desk for ready reference, a personality guide list to remind himself—and judging from the well-fingered condition of the list when it was found, he often had reminded himself—"Give *spiritual strength* to people, and they will give *genuine affection* to you"? (His emphasis) How often he had said, in small gatherings and to large audiences, "My daddy used to tell me, 'Take care of the people and the election will take care of itself'." And how many sweating political crowds, swaying from the vertigo of campaign hokum, he had informed with emotional remembrance: "The motto of my 1920 graduating class at Johnson City High School was, 'Give to the world the best that you have, and the best will come back to you'."

And had he not, in 1960, promised a New York crowd that he would be "more liberal than Eleanor Roosevelt," which surely should be humanitarian enough to please anyone? And had he not, after a Senate session in which he came away exceedingly proud of himself, remarked, "If I should die, these bleeding hearts couldn't get their program out of committee."

However, if others just do not see Johnson as the do-gooder he sees himself to be, this may be explained by the fact that in the nation's subconscious, perhaps only darkly remembered now, there are those episodes that suggest that, where Johnson is concerned, what at first appears to be unction will usually turn out to be pure petroleum.

At the beginning of the 1955 session, Johnson had counseled his Democratic colleagues to stay low, keep quiet, and not stir up anything. The public, he said, was tired of headlines, controversy, partisan spats. He offered no program.

But the next year, at the opening of the 1956 session, to everyone's surprise (for by now he had the nickname Lyin' Down Lyndon) he was suddenly profuse with a rambling, duplicative "Program With a Heart." That's what he called it. It was filled with items which were not new proposals and, in fact, were known to be in the still-fluid Eisenhower program for that year. Nevertheless, for Johnson, who prided himself on his restraint in pushing ideas, it was an ambitious program, including the extension of social security coverage for women, a tax revision to help low income groups, a program to aid medical research, a low-cost housing program, and a program to relieve critical depressed areas. Thirteen points in all. Practically all of these ideas had been kicking around in the Senate for years, but everyone was so happy to see Johnson stirring that they did not belittle him for that. One item, Item No. 7 on the list Johnson distributed to reporters, was especially shopworn, having been handed around in Congress every year since 1947.

Federal regulation was each year drawing closer to his beloved natural gas industry; more precisely, it was closing in on that portion of the industry that meant the most to Johnson, the ten giant companies that owned most of the Panhandle and Hugoton Fields of Kansas, Oklahoma and especially Texas, fields representing one-fourth of the country's natural gas preserves. If he could throw up a Congressional wall between the industry and the Federal Power Commission, then the big companies could raise their prices. Just a *little* raise, to be sure, but every little bit helped. For instance, an increase of only five cents per 1,000 cubic feet would have meant about $390 million (consumer dollars) to Phillips Petroleum Company over the life of the preserves.

The year after he had destroyed Leland Olds, Johnson went to the Senate with a bill to exempt the industry from regulation. His choicest argument had been that the National Military Establishment wanted the bill passed. The Senate approved it, 44 to 38, and in the House Sam Rayburn came down from the Speaker's chair to make a personal, and successful, appeal to the House to go along. Only Truman's veto had saved the consumer that year.

In 1954 Johnson saw clearly that something must be done to save his backers, for that year the Supreme Court had, in Johnson's words, "done a shocking thing." It had ruled against Phillips Petroleum Company and, incidentally, had exonerated Leland Olds for the position he took in trying to regulate the natural gas industry all the way back to the well head.

The case, of some importance since the decision saves American consumers a minimum of $25 million a year, arose in 1948, when Olds was on the Federal Power Commission. At issue was the question of how far back down the pipeline the FPC had regulatory control. Gas suppliers (like Phillips) channel the product from the well to a processing plant, where the impurities are removed; after that the gas is piped to an interstate pipeline. Now, the question was, did FPC control stop with the interstate pipeline or did it go beyond that, past the processing plant, and to the source of the gas? A District Court having supported FPC jurisdiction all the way to the source, Phillips appealed to the Supreme Court.

In 1954, the Supreme Court upheld the lower court. Johnson went to the Senate, denounced the Court bitterly and put his colleagues on notice: "We must go into this matter thoroughly and take the necessary steps to assure ourselves that it is Congress—and not the Supreme Court—that makes our laws."

So he had returned in 1956 with the "necessary step," nestling deep in his "Program With a Heart": Item No. 7, which he called a "natural gas bill which will preserve free enterprise and of course provide legitimate protection to consumers." As described, nobody could quarrel with it. In actuality, however, the bill was drafted in such a way as to exempt the natural gas industry from regulation.

Only one other item in the "Program With a Heart" was passed that session and, in fact, *no* other item was pushed by Johnson. He moved the natural gas bill to the top of the calendar as the Senate's first business and apparently expended his energies all on it. Johnson might have more accurately called his program "Item Seven With a Heart."

There were some senators and outside critics who saw Item 7 in another light. It called for a "fair market price" without setting a criterion of fairness. Estimates of the windfall to the gas companies that would result from passage of the bill, at the consumer's expense, ranged from $1 billion to $12 billion. The industry itself would not help end these speculations; when Senator Douglas tried to get the cost and profit figures from the big oil companies, they told him they could not compute such things.

But there were other ways of estimating what the bill was worth to the oil and gas industry. Senator Alben Barkley said he had never seen so many lobbyists in Washington, and they all talked with Texas or Oklahoma twangs. Senator Hennings of Missouri said he had been warned "by some of the astute and knowledgeable observers of the American political scene that the power of the great oil companies, wielded today to influence the decision of national government by contributions to both parties in many parts of the U.S., is a menace to the proper functioning of free government." Senator Mansfield announced that "I have received a communication from one of the wealthiest oil men in the country asking me to vote in favor of the bill," and he said that was just the tiniest fraction of the total effort to have it passed.

Johnson, who was justifiably renowned for his coolness under fire on the Senate floor, brushed aside such talk. "Shoot," he told a couple of Texas reporters who asked him if there were any grounds for the innuendoes, "it's all a matter of appearances. When a gas and oil bill comes in here, everybody says it's crooked, for the same reason they think a girl on the street after midnight is probably up to something. But not me. I don't accuse a girl until I see her doin' more than walkin'."

On February 3, Senator Francis Case of South Dakota got up, cleared his throat half a dozen times, and said, "I rise to make a difficult speech . . . About a week ago, as I was signing out the day's mail, and talking at the same time to a couple of visitors, a long-distance telephone call came in . . . The voice at the other end of the line was that of a friend of mine in a South Dakota city, who said that a caller had left an envelope with him that was to be given to me— a contribution for my forthcoming campaign. My friend said he had opened the envelope and found it to contain hundred-dollar bills, twenty-five of them in fact. He said, 'What shall I do with it?' That would be the largest contribution I could remember for any campaign of mine. I was a bit startled."

All of Washington was startled too.

When it was discovered that the money originated with Superior Oil Company's President Keck (always generous to politicians, he had earlier given Joe McCarthy $2,000; he gave Eisenhower $5,000 that year and was to give Johnson $200,000 four years later) and thence through two attorneys before being dropped on Senator Case's desk, some thought the blatant intrigue of it all might rattle Johnson. It didn't.

"I, for one," he told his colleagues coolly, "feel no compulsion to establish my integrity by voting against this bill . . . Popular favor, quite as much as the coin of the realm, can lead men into paths of temptation." He was warmly applauded by the majority for this logic, and three days later, after what some of the more critical senators thought was unseemly hasty debate, Johnson hustled the bill to passage. Johnson had been asked by some senators if he would not like to hold off the vote until an investigation had been conducted to determine just how widespread, not to mention successful, efforts to buy support had been. He said he most certainly did not want to await an investigation. But, having the reputation of the Senate at heart, he would support an investigation for completion later on. Not a big investigation; not, in his words, "a general fishing expedition," not a "cow-catcher"; preferably one that would not last more than a month.

As newsmen continued to plague him with questions about his reluctance for a full dress investigation, Johnson was at last stung to reply at one news conference: "I think we ought to investigate the morals of some people in South Dakota for bringing this up."

In the East especially Johnson was criticized bitterly, and he responded bitterly, denying that he had tried to exert any influence on members or the President, although he conceded the obvious, "I realize that my state had a vital interest in it . . ." There was, for example, Humble Oil Company, Texas' largest oil company which competes with

Phillips as the largest producer of gas in the nation. But there is also Brown & Root, Johnson's oldest campaign contributors, which operates Texas Eastern Pipeline (Big Inch and Little Inch Pipelines) as well as Texas Eastern Production, producers of gas and oil.

For Brown & Root, Johnson has done much. On January 14, 1944, in company with Alvin Wirtz, attorney for Brown & Root and his own benefactor early in his career, Johnson went to President Roosevelt and stopped an investigation of the company by the Internal Revenue Service. This sort of helping hand had been offered by Johnson so many times to his supporters that he saw it as quite a normal action. Nor did he think it sporting of the press to point out that John Connally, his closest political ally in Texas, was a member of the steering committee of the General Gas Committee, which got together $1.5 million to pay for the lobbying. Nor did he feel that he had been done right by Eisenhower when he left him standing alone; Ike, perhaps hoping to convey the impression that Keck's gift of $5,000 to him was far below the going price, vetoed the bill.

The swift Senate investigation was held; small fines and suspended sentences followed when the lobbyists appeared in court. Now Johnson counterployed, announced that "We're going to have a strong elections bill this session," and named a special committee to investigate political activities, lobbying and campaign contributions.

Thereupon Johnson threw his influence against any legislation that would include contributions to primary elections —the only elections that counted in then one-party Texas— and, when the proposed reform came out of committee, let it die without reaching the floor. Thus ended, quite successfully for Johnson considering the potential damage, an episode which James Reston at the time saw causing "more apprehension in the Senate than anything that has come over the horizon of Capitol Hill in recent years." Reston reported Johnson had worked feverishly with minority leader William Knowland of California, also a gas-producing state, to "block the probe if possible, to limit it in any event, and to get it out of the control of the Senate Elections subcommittee."

All but successful on the first count and totally successful on counts two and three, Johnson could look upon the 1956 session, despite the death of "Item Seven With a Heart," as not bad at all, considering; and it was from maneuverings such as this, not from leading the fight for a comprehensive national program, that Johnson built his reputation in the Senate.

6 The Great *What?*

*I went with my father to visit some of the
"battlegrounds" of that war on poverty in
Appalachia. We saw children and grandchildren of
poverty. Sometimes, three generations of welfare
stood before us, pinched faces, strained eyes, peering
at this tall, broad-shouldered man who swooped
down from the skies and carried words of hope.*

—Lynda Bird, May, 1965

Not long ago, three new men who had been added to Johnson's speech-writing stable were listening to him explain what he expected of them: "I want four-letter words, and I want four words to the sentence, and I want four sentences to the paragraph. Now that's what I want, and I know you want to give it to me." At that moment Douglass Cater, who dabbles as a writer-in-residence and various other things, came in to show Johnson one of his latest speeches. Johnson scanned it rapidly and judged it to be "pretty good, Doug. You've got the idea. But you've got to get more PAY-thohs into it, hear? We gotta have more people livin' in wretched hovels and things like that. Doug, you've gotta get your hand *up* under the dress!"—accompanied by a descriptive gesture.

Shift scene: In a speech in San Antonio, President Johnson recollected how, as a little shaver, he used to follow his father around the ranch barefooted and, standing there in the hot sand of Blanco County and squeezing it up between his toes, he listened reverently while his father admonished him, "Son, if you are to speak for people, you must know them, and if you are to represent people, you must love them." As Johnson continued to talk it was clear that he looked upon himself—by inclination, genes, and training—as The Great Lover. Of mankind, of course.

Shift scene: Early in 1965, down on The Ranch, one of Lyndon's visitors was H. B. (Pat) Zachry, a multimillionaire builder from San Antonio who has often contributed heavily to Johnson campaigns and who has in turn been rewarded with some handsome federal contracts. During the visit Johnson started talking about what the millionaire could do to help the morale of the poor Latins on San Antonio's west side. "I wish you would tell the Mexicans to get out and work with the grass, prune the trees, work with the flowers," said Johnson, getting preachy, as he is wont to do. "Tell them that's how you got started, Pat. Tell them to work with the soil, Pat. Tell them that's where you started, with the soil—and now you're a millionaire. Tell 'em that, Pat. *They want to hear that, Pat. They want to be told that, Pat.* You started with the soil and now you're a millionaire."

It's that simple. Just because your father and your grandfather and your great-grandfather "worked in the soil" all their lives without getting a nickel ahead, that doesn't mean you can't do it! Just because your brother died of diarrhea and two of your sisters of *mal ojo;* just because everyone in your family and in all the families that travel with you are functional illiterates, that doesn't mean that you can't, with a little positive thinking, enjoy all the pleasures and hopes of a millionaire. Hit the migrant trail again—and remember Pat.

What kind of Great Society did you expect from a man who thinks like that? In his fancy, hand-tooled cowboy boots he no longer can squish the sands of Blanco County between his toes, so perhaps he is at a disadvantage. Whatever the reasons, and they are many, the Great Lover's hand under the nation's dress no longer arouses much excitement, though we've still got PAY-thohs aplenty and wretched hovels to spare.

By refusing to increase taxes during 1966, on grounds that must surely have been more political than economic, by refusing to put into effect any favored wage and price controls in an untamed war economy, by permitting interest rates to hit the highest point in forty-five years, who was Johnson hurting most? The poor, of whom there are a great many more than he seems capable of counting. In one press conference out of four he will allude to the great prosperity of America, while ignoring what is plain enough to everyone. James Reston, that great Calvinist with a heart, put the obvious into words: "Vietnam is hard on everybody, but it is harder on the poor than anybody else . . . The war in Vietnam has not produced the economic boom, but it has kept it going . . . No doubt it has provided more jobs as well as more profits," but it has taken its soldiers primarily from the poor * and those left behind were un-

---

* Some of them shaped up by the anti-poverty program. Of the Job Corps' first graduates, more than *one-fourth* went directly into the service. It is a very simple and politically acceptable form of sadism that forces the poor to fight hardest to defend what they've got least of. But it is a rather unique philosophy that considers military service a special privilege for the poor; yet that is the concept of the present administration, which three times in the last year lowered its selective service standards to bring in as many underprivileged young men as possible. Defense Secretary McNamara said he hopes to expand the program to "benefit" 100,000 substandard recruits next fiscal year. Thus the war on poverty becomes indistinguishable from just plain war.

able, because of lack of training or because of color or advanced age or sex, to benefit from the war boom.

Fifty per cent of the Negroes are, by government standards, poor; 20 per cent of the whites. Many of them are working; they simply earn nothing for their labor. Mollie Orshansky, in a Social Security bulletin issued in January, 1965, noted that the heads of "almost 30 per cent of all families called poor have been holding down a full-time job for a whole year." As its first step, the new minimum wage law passed in 1966 to the accompaniment of White House trumpets will raise *some* of the persons covered *almost* to a poverty level income. This is Johnson's "Better Deal"—as he first named his Great Society—and there can be no question that $1.40 guaranteed an hour is better that $1.25 an hour, though neither is a humane income, and not everyone covered will get even the $1.40 at once. Nor does the increase benefit nearly as many people as government propagandists have implied; they have said that 30 million workers are covered, but this is a veneer figure, a varnished, gleaming figure that means nothing because 80 per cent of those "covered" already are earning more than the minimum. In other words, the federal minimum wage as written still neglects most of the miserable poor. The bill, it is claimed, covers about seven million new workers with a beginning minimum of $1 an hour; six million of them are *already* earning more than that. Even if one calculates the potential pay increases up to 1971, no more than seven million workers will be touched by it, and by the time those five years have passed, because of the normal ballooning of the general wage and price levels, the 1966 law will only have enabled the marginal worker to drag his margin along behind. Put it in perspective: while the cost of living is going up at a rate of more than 3 per cent each year and food prices at a yearly 6 per cent, and while some industries are making 20 per cent profits, the Great Society's first increase to the federal minimum wage will, according to the House Labor Committee, add only 1.1 per cent to the total wages of those presently covered and .9 per cent to the wages of those being brought under the ruling for the first time.

Two years after the Civil Rights Act of 1964 was supposed to break down job discrimination, there are twice as many Negroes out of work as whites. But that, you say, is because they are poorly trained, and you are right. Why, then, did Johnson seek to cut his budget for vocational training? Why did the master builder of the Great Society come to the 1966 Congress asking only $2.3 billion for twenty-five Great Society programs, although Congress in 1965 had authorized $3.9 billion? Why ask Congress to cut the Higher Education Act's funds by 20 per cent? Why ask that the Appalachia program be cut by $100 million, that the funds for impacted schools be cut 50 per cent below what the Office of Education had said it would need? Why cut the regional medical program from $90 million to $43 million? Or neighborhood facility grants from $88 million to $25 million? Or the school lunch program by $19 million? Why seek to slash the school milk program by half, down $50 million? Why ask Congress to reduce the Rural Electrification expenditures by a half-billion dollars? * Why, of the 45,000 new government jobs asked for in his budget, were only five marked for the Narcotics Bureau, though the junkies and pushers are destroying whatever shriveled rind of civilization is left in the slums?

* At the time Johnson's budget was submitted, some unhappy observers believed he was just playing cute, that he really wanted the money appropriated and was cutting programs he knew Congress wouldn't follow up on. Congressman Michel, for example, said, "This is an old game the President is playing. He submits a completely phony figure which he knows the Congress in its wisdom will raise. By submission of a lower figure, he enhances his budget figure and throws the onus of raising the figure upon Congress, for he knows these very popular, worthwhile, on-going programs are not going to be sacrificed under any circumstances." But some of them *were* sacrificed. It is just as reasonable to assume Johnson wanted the cuts he asked for.

What did you really expect in a Great Society that budgets as much for government travel as is budgeted for the war on poverty? Which budgets *twice* as much for research and development of missiles alone, and *four* times as much for all military research and development, as for fighting poverty? What kind of Great Society should one anticipate from an administration that is well aware that persons earning less than $2,000 a year pay 38 per cent of their income in taxes whereas persons earning between $7,500 and $10,000 pay only 22.3 per cent of their income in taxes—but does nothing to redress the inequity?

The Great Society is revolution without change. Nothing indicates more clearly the bureaucratic staleness of its concepts than the fact that more than 1,500 permanent federal anti-poverty employees earn $10,600 or more. In the Washington regional offices of the Office of Economic Opportunity (OEO) more than 500 employees earn more than $14,600. The New York City poverty director earns $35,000 —as much as a cabinet member. Do not suppose that in this broad pyramid of pay-offs and goof-offs much of the money reaches the lowest level. If the flow of money becomes a muddy trickle by the time it hits the bottom, racial bias cannot be blamed altogether, for, though the *percentage* of Negro families existing on less than $2,000 annually is three times higher, the *number* of whites grubbing at that level in turn is three times higher than the blacks. The main difference, of course, is that the poor whites know that with a new suit of clothes and a great deal of luck, they may be able to scramble into the valhalla of the haves; the Negroes know that it will take not only luck but a conscious and massive hoisting from above to do the job. To them the anti-poverty war has become so important that their best critics are shaken by conflicting feelings—scornful of the program and what it is not doing, yet fearful that it will be ended altogether. It is a wretched show, but it is all they've got and from all indications it is all they are about to get for years to come.

And so we find men like Bayard Rustin, director of the A. Philip Randolph Center in New York, damning Congress for "pretending it's having a war on poverty and fiddling around with little projects, 79 per cent of which have been done for the last 200 years," and calling the anti-poverty thing "a bag of tricks"; yet when he was summoned to testify before Senator Ribicoff's committee he raged against Johnson's dismantling of the anti-poverty program as "not only stupid and dangerous but criminal, because it is criminal in that people who have power are now withdrawing the little carrot which was part of our effort to maintain some stability. . . ." For a moment the committee could not shut off the outburst— ". . . going to the moon while we leave all the unsolved problems in our ghettoes . . . a distortion, a fantastic distortion of priorities when the president of the United States can think he can get away with that kind of proposition. *He cannot get away with it!* What he will do is to bring into the society more frustration and more fear, and it ought to be stopped! What we ought to be doing is pouring more money into the war on poverty; it is only a trickle to begin with. And Negro leaders cannot be held responsible. . . ." Senator Robert Kennedy, who has developed the stratagem of trotting along behind and just slightly to the left of Johnson without wanting to appear to either attack or defend him, sat for a moment in shocked silence. What manner of basic courage was this? *Stupid and dangerous and criminal . . . he cannot get away with it. . . .* Kennedy, wanting no part of such impolite, revolutionary talk, whispered excitedly with Ribicoff and then, at his first chance, turned the questioning away from Rustin to another witness.

Rustin, one of the organizers of the historic march on Washington in 1963, certainly was expressing the traumatic disappointment felt by most Negro leaders in Johnson's rejection of their appeals. But the tragedy of Johnson's taking up their cause only to quickly abandon it is best seen not in the lives of the Negro leaders, for they have their glory whatever happens, but in the lives of the little-known Negroes trying to hold together the movement at the grass roots. They pinned great hopes on Johnson only a few months ago. In the autumn of 1964 I talked for an afternoon with one of Atlanta's old-line Negro political bosses; among militants he had for some time been criticized for trying to work things out with Atlanta's power structure, but with the coming of Johnson, scattering promises like appleseeds, he felt that his faith in the Establishment white man was being vindicated. This Negro was a preacher but Lyndon had become his god-made flesh. "If that man Lyndon Johnson came through that door right now," he told me grandly, "I would get down on my knees and kiss his foot! I surely would! I worship that man. I know, I know, he done wrong for many years, but now he's doing *right*. Even Jesus had to take the long way round to Calvary!" I talked to the preacher again in late 1966. He didn't have much to say.

What exactly does Johnson mean to do with these people? He will not train them. Of half a million girls eligible for Job Corps instruction, only 5,000 have been taken into the program. Nor, apparently, does he mean to let the poor work out their own problems. Community action programs, those which are supposed to invite the closest participation and control by the poor themselves (although as directed by the government this is generally an empty ideal), were slashed $166 million below their minimum requirements. Months before Congress took this action, rumors circulated that the Bureau of the Budget meant to hack great hunks off these programs, but the White House denied it. Then, when Congress began doing just that very thing, there was no protest and no effort to intervene on the part of Johnson or any of his aides. Even Los Angeles and Atlanta—places which produced two of the more memorable riots—lost approximately one-third of the money they needed to continue their previous programs.

In a speech at Newark on October 7, 1966, Johnson said, "Since 1961, the typical American family of four has had an increase of about $1,200 in real income. The $1,200 can reshingle the roof of their house and also pay for a color television set and an automatic washing machine. That $1,200 can finance a year at the state university for their son or daughter."

This is good campaign talk because it appeals the most to the great middle class; but it shows a calculated disregard for the impoverished. What he said was true enough; real incomes have risen since 1961, just as they have risen for many years. But the way he said it was, purposely one must conclude, very misleading. *The gap between the rich and the poor* has not been narrowed since 1961; since World War II the gap has not narrowed. If Johnson did not know it already, he could have sent over to the Bureau of Census and got Herman P. Miller's monograph *Income Distribution in the United States,* which would have told him, with supporting data, that "statistics show no appreciable change in income shares for nearly 20 years." All talk of the "typical" family having $1,200 more income is completely meaningless to the three million white families and 950,000 non-white families (Census figures) who now earn a *total* of less than $1,999 yearly. There are more than seven million families in the country now earning less than $2,999 a year. Are *they* the families Johnson sees improving since 1961 to the level that they can "finance a year at the state university for their son or daughter" with the growth in their pay checks?

The grotesque structure of the anti-poverty citadel, and its eventual collapse, was probably less the result of meanness than of myopia. It is difficult for Johnson to see America except as some kind of giant supermarket or army-navy store.

He has the vision of a superannuated clerk. While the gross national product more than doubled between the end of World War II and the 1960's, while there was an awesome outpouring of bigger and better bathtubs, motorboats, and television sets, and while more than a million people became owners of a vacation home—seven million family units, untouched by any of this, continued to wash about in the muck of measurable belt-tightening hunger. But Johnson apparently could not see it.

* * *

Since it is clear that the Johnsonian remedy has been misrepresented, we should not be surprised to learn also that we have not even been told the full extent of the ailment. Every time a reporter disturbs one of his press conferences with a query about unemployment, Johnson sails off on the wings of euphoria and returns with statistics to prove that unemployment is way, way down—under 4 per cent. It looks good. But as a matter of fact, numerous experts in this field, including Dr. Charles Killingsworth and Gunnar Myrdal, believe that unemployment in this country has been at the 8 to 9 per cent level for years. Many people hunt for work for so long, unsuccessfully, that they become discouraged and drop out of the market. They are not counted by Johnson. Neither does he say much about the "underemployed," just as frustrated although better fed: the millions who are working at jobs far below their abilities. It has been reputably estimated that this group constitutes 25 per cent of the labor force.

Of this latter group, let us suppose that there are many basic laborers who could hold a much higher job if they were not illiterate. This, of course, is a common situation. What has Johnson done about it? The James Farmer case is in point.

The federal government estimates that there are 11 million functional illiterates in the country (that is, people who by occupational standards can't read or write well enough to do any good) and 2 million who sign their names with an X. If the government says there are 13 million of these, that means there are probably 20 million. But in any case, there is virtually no government program to pull them out of their dark ditch. The Office of Education has a slender program coping with one-quarter million of them. Of course this means Negroes are hardest hit; 8 per cent of the Negroes are illiterate, 1.6 per cent of whites.

So along came James Farmer, then national director of the Congress of Racial Equality, with his own idea for helping the Negro to help himself. In December, 1963—this was in Johnson's elaborate "won't y'all he'p me?" period—Farmer visited the White House and said that what was desperately needed was a national literacy program (Johnson agreed) and that the ones to do the· teaching were the illiterates' Negro peers because Negroes on the bottom of the heap don't trust officials. Fine, excellent, wonderful, said Johnson; send me a memo.

Farmer did, both in October and November of 1964. This was nearly a year later and he had spent the time between laying his plans carefully. From Dr. Myron Woolman, head of the Institute of Educational Research, he had learned the mysteries by which any literate person can teach any illiterate without special teaching tools. It was a perfect bootstrap method for the catfish alleys of America. Farmer proposed starting with eighteen literacy centers around the country.

Johnson responded almost at once with a telephone call to Farmer telling him it was a great idea and to keep working on it. By the following August, 1965, Farmer had polished it up perfectly, had presented the plan to Sargent Shriver and had been given assurances that it would be funded. Farmer wasn't asking for a lot: just $785,000 to start off with. That's only ten times what Johnson paid for Luci's wedding. Aside from its many practical merits, the program was, as Dr. Sanford Kravitz, associate director of the OEO's Community Action Program, stated in his recommendation of the Farmer plan, "the first program that involves the latent strength of the civil rights movement in social involvement instead of social protest . . . Minimal educational skills are a necessary preliminary for moving out of poverty and out of the ghetto . . . You can buy literacy experts and administrators a dime a dozen. But how often can you get a great national leader like Jimmy Farmer to head a literacy drive?" Put bluntly, it meant that Farmer and a lot of other shiftless, trouble-making "niggers," as the South and much of the North, viewed them, were beginning to play heads up. In the preliminary, secret planning stage it was impossible to find anyone against the idea.

Late in December, 1965, news of the program and of Farmer's being tapped to head it was leaked to the press. And immediately the ring politicians moved in with their knives. They didn't like the program because it would have been set up to be independent of city hall. The Economic Opportunity Act states that community action programs shall be "developed, conducted, and administered with the *maximum* feasible participation" of the poor, and the Farmer program was going to be the outstanding, pilot program of that kind, to demonstrate that the poor can run their own show. Every hack politico in the country, the civic poltergeists like Chicago's Mayor Daley, began rattling the tables and thumping the walls in the haunted White House, to let Johnson know they wouldn't stand for that kind of independence. Johnson listened very attentively.

The next word from the White House came indirectly, but unmistakably. It came through Representative Sam Gibbons of Florida. Gibbons is one of those frightened knights with whom Johnson's Great Society suzerainty abounds:

knights driven by fear that middle-class realty prices may be chipped by some new neighbors. He is an archetype—the clean, decent, liberal hatchetman. He was one of the leaders of the crusade to purge mischievous Congressman Adam Clayton Powell, though in the midst of that crusade a newspaper inquiry disclosed that Gibbons and his brother were among the founders of a corporation that sold a reportedly defective site (it may cost a million dollars to fix up properly) to the Veterans Administration for a hospital; Gibbons' uncle handled the sale through the law firm of which the congressman is a member. Gibbons was indignant: white economics is surely different from black shenanigans on the beach at Bimini! So Gibbons isn't exactly pure. But there is one thing that can be said for him: his loyalty, yea, his abject devotion to Lyndon Johnson is as complete as that he felt for the phosphate companies and the moneyed power structure of Florida during the decade he served in its legislature. He was Johnson's floor manager for the original poverty bill and for subsequent appropriations relating to that program, and it can be accurately assumed that when he speaks on poverty matters, he is using a White House script.

Thus, through Gibbons, Johnson now spoke: "What in hell are we getting Farmer mixed up in a literacy program for anyway? . . . What does Farmer know about literacy anyway? Is he to be crowned liberator of the uneducated? I urged Mr. Shriver many times to slow down on projects like this . . . What we really need is more middle-class support for the [poverty] program. *Projects like Farmer's make it difficult to get votes.*" That was Johnson talking, all righ·. Meeting early in 1966 at the White House, Johnson, Gibbons, and Budget Director Charles L. Schultze killed the Farmer literacy plan that would have aided a million persons.

What did it mean? Was there a broader implication than just opposition to one Negro leader's ambitious plan to help his people? Ernest A. Ostro, the *Washington Star* reporter who did the most thorough investigation of this whole shabby episode, wonders "If a community action program as highly touted and widely supported as Farmer's can be scuttled, will any meaningful program that incurs politicians' disfavor ever be financed by OEO?" The answer is obvious.

Ostro also asks, "Does Shriver's action—or inaction—on the literacy project, along with other recent OEO decisions, foreshadow the collapse of independent community action in the war on poverty and the shifting of programs to existing agencies?" The answer to that is even clearer. The OEO is already being dismembered and distributed among the old traditional government offices—Labor, and Health, Education, and Welfare for the most part. It is probably just as well, considering the blatantly political use to which the Office of Economic Opportunity has been put. The comedian Dick Gregory, for instance, was arrested in Chicago in a civil rights demonstration; the woman who actually had bitten the cop was put on a poverty program at $175 a week and therefore wouldn't go to testify to help him. After Gregory's trial, at which he was convicted, she was fired.

In the field, the administration has worked effectively to snuff out supervision of anti-poverty programs by the poor: sometimes by buying them off, as in Philadelphia, sometimes by using a kind of brute economic heave-ho, as in trying to kill the Negro-run Headstart program in Mississippi and turning it over to the domination of Establishment whites who satisfy Johnson's old cronies John Stennis and Jim Eastland. (A backlash of bad publicity scared the administration away from completing this job of mugging.) Like so many other puffs in Johnson's life, the anti-poverty war will die, except in name. Through Gibbons, Johnson first revealed the clues to why. "The idea of building up a kind of new constituency on the basis of wealth or the lack of it was creating a caste system and a whole new layer of government," he said. "We can't create a special class of people on the basis that they're poor." Inasmuch as the special class—and a very broad and deep class it is—already exists, this could only mean that Gibbons (qua Johnson) was prepared to stop recognizing its existence, which is a vintage Johnson remedy for curing all ills.

* * *

Still, the concept of the Great Society is treated as a political reality, largely because labels have a strange way of getting believed. Kennedy called his rather nice, middle-class, ordinary thing a New Frontier, and everyone from Pablo Casals to Robert Welch took him variously at his word. Johnson is getting even more mileage out of "Great Society." Aid to schools! Medicare! Protection of the Negro's voting rights! That's *great!* But it isn't really. As William V. Shannon of *The New York Times* has reasoned unassailably: "An outside observer might point out that the bills now actively supported by Mr. Johnson round out the welfare state but they scarcely add up to a program for a 'great' society. Any civilized democracy is expected in the 20th century to educate its children properly, take care of its aged and ill, and guarantee equality in the voting booth."

Surely the United States—if it had not been held back by the wheeler-dealer precautions of such ambitious congressmen as Johnson—would have, years ago, qualified under Shannon's description of a civilized democracy. It seems a bit servile to be grateful to Johnson *now* for letting these things come about, in part, in often a trivial and unsatisfactorily fractional way, when for a generation he hedged his ambitions against them.

When, at last, he supported Medicare in 1965, it came out with the usual Johnsonian subsidization for industry. As approved by Congress, hospitals were supposed to be reimbursed for *reasonable costs only*—no profits. As put into effect by the Johnson administration, however, hospitals are allowed to ride high on the old profiteering cost-plus basis: they will be paid a profit of 2 per cent of their costs. The more they pad their costs, the more they profit. Furthermore, depreciation of facilities will be considered part of the cost. Here's a beautiful swindling of the taxpayer: first he finances the construction of the hospital through the Hill-Burton program, and then he is forced to pay for the building's depreciation. He pays twice. (The 2 per cent of *this* is a *third* payment.) It has already been discovered, by the way, that this depreciation money will *not* be spent on rehabilitating the hospitals but will in many instances go into a community's general fund (as in New York, for example), where the "hospital money" may be used for a new limousine for the mayor, or anything else.

One of the more manageable proposals in Johnson's State of the Union address in January, 1965, was for a "massive attack" on crippling diseases such as heart defects, cancer, and stroke. Many grants were to be given to America's best medical research scientists. Johnson started out talking in terms of a five-year attack costing $1.2 billion; but the American Medical Association did not like the program, and after its top officials met with Johnson at the White House he surrendered and sent them over to the Department of Health, Education, and Welfare to rewrite the legislation to suit themselves. The way Dr. James Z. Appel, then president of the AMA, put it, the President instructed HEW Secretary John Gardner to let them "make the bill less objectionable." They gutted it with twenty amendments. On Johnson's own instructions, the appropriation for the first year's attack-turned-rout was only $25 million.

But even these fumbling, half-hearted efforts at first aid and hanky-panky hospitalization came very late in his career. From 1937 to 1960 Johnson opposed helping old folks pay their medical bills. His priorities have never been exactly subtle; he was personally responsible for putting through Congress the man-on-the-moon program, which is expected to cost between $20 billion and $40 billion before the moon is walked upon; * but he refused to support one penny for medical care, which, even up to 1960, he was calling "socialized medicine." Many millions of Americans lived poorer, more fearful lives because of what he stood for and what he stood against.

From 1937 to 1960 Johnson opposed equal rights and equal opportunities for Negroes. "This civil rights program," he said in Austin in 1948, "is a farce and a sham— an effort to set up a police state in the guise of liberty . . ." From 1937 to 1960—long enough for a "nigger" to get borned in one of those fine shotgun shanties on Lady Bird's Alabama land, grow up eating neck bones, drop out of a nothing school by the third grade and go to work in the fields for $2.50 a day, and, finally attaining lustihood, drift off to the New Jerusalem of Harlem. Plenty of time. While a generation slipped away, Johnson calmly argued (as late as 1959), "I do not believe we have arrived at an answer until we have found the national answer, the answer all reasonable men can agree upon, and our work is not done until that answer is found—even if the process requires years of our lives." One can afford to be prodigal with one's life when it can be spent in the cool alcoves of the Petroleum Club, but the Negroes in Sunflower County may not, understandably, have the same heart for the long wait. Having known his opposition for so many years, many

* Dr. Philip Abelson, editor of *Science Magazine,* polled 113 scientists not connected with NASA and found that 110 were against the manned lunar probe as highly unprofitable. Dr. Warren Weaver, former president of the American Association for the Advancement of Science, called it "stupid." But perhaps the best question in regard to Johnson's moon jaunt was asked by Senator Douglas: "What is the advantage in getting there first, if there is no purpose in getting there at all?"

Negroes now seem incapable of believing anything that he promises them. Even after the 1964 Civil Rights Act, even with the promised 1965 Voting Rights bill being stirred languidly in committee, Johnson had to delay only a little at sending protection into Selma and the rights leaders were publicly and fulsomely describing him as they had over the years (with the exception of the 1964 moratorium on contempt). "I think Selma may make him understand," said one rights leader, "that Negroes voted more against Goldwater than they did for LBJ." That feeling, at least, is well integrated. When the ghetto Negro mother is forced to go to bed with the butcher for hamhocks to feed her children, the Johnson civil rights program suddenly becomes rather vacuous. A quarter century ago it would have been a leg up; it still might do much good if enforced in the South; but for Watts and Cleveland and Harlem, filled with the Negroes Johnson helped chase out of the South, civil rights laws are no longer enough. Still thinking in the woolly terms of his Pedernales plantation, he shows a dangerous thickness in coming to grips with the new situation. They wanted a civil rights law when he went to Congress in 1937; well, hadn't he finally given them a law? What more did they want? Seeking the answer—in one of the most pathetic gestures of his life—Johnson sent the Reverend Billie Don Moyers, dressed appropriately "rugged" (and accompanied by Secret Service men for protection) on a secret mission into the Negro joints of Baltimore. Moyers' report to his chief could be the epitaph for a lifetime of Johnsonian race relations: "We didn't even speak the same language."

Nevertheless, the legend persists that Johnson worked a "miracle" in 1957 in passing a civil rights act; it will doubtless persist for many years. And for even longer we will doubtless be hearing how it was not until *He* became president that a vigorous civil rights act came into being. The 1957 Civil Rights Act was a voting law which gave the

Attorney General no power to initiate lawsuits to protect the Negro's rights and allowed the Southerners to be tried by a jury if they were accused of violating voting rights. It was without substance. Of it Ralph Bunche wired President Eisenhower, "It would be better to have no bill than one as emasculated as that which has come out of the Senate." Urging Eisenhower to veto the measure, A. Philip Randolph called it "worse than no bill at all." This was Johnson's handiwork, his miracle, they were talking about. Not all were displeased with it. Richard Russell said, "This bill is not going to work any hardship on the people of Georgia." It surely did not. When Strom Thurmond filibustered the measure—the only Southern senator to do so, being so stupid as to think the bill would hurt the South—Herman Talmadge took the floor and bitterly denounced him for opposing it.

In 1959, the year before he was again to go before the national Democratic convention and ask to be nominated for the presidency, Johnson was still saying, as he had been saying all his life, that civil rights could not be enforced by law. Senator Douglas and sixteen other liberals ran aground of Johnson's opposition when they introduced a strong civil rights bill. This was only two years after the Little Rock riots, and the South was still dominated by politicians who threatened to set up a private school system, supported by tax gimmicks, if the public schools were integrated. The Douglas bill would have given the Negroes a way to fight back by providing federal funds for local schools deprived of state support; this bill would also have permitted the federal government to take the initiative in court proceedings on behalf of persons deprived of their civil rights; in other words, Douglas was again offering the Title III idea that Johnson had sliced out of his 1957 bill.

In contrast, Johnson's 1959 civil rights bill would have been another cover for inaction. Aside from extending the

life of the Civil Rights Commission to January, 1961—
nicely guaranteeing that no adverse report would be
brought in until after the election—it did virtually nothing.
Douglas offered realities where Johnson offered ectoplasm,
and the liberals in the Senate were somewhat bitter when
they discovered that once again the Leader was taking
them into the Southern conservative swamp. Writing in
Look magazine, Johnson helped smother the notion that
quick and firm remedies were needed; this was the year
before the sit-in movement began and all hell was to break
loose across the South. Said Johnson coolly, "The difference
between me and some of my Northern friends is that I
believe you can't force these things on the South overnight."
And to the Senate he said, the same year, that getting
tough with the South was altogether the wrong approach.
". . . the problem is being approached from the wrong
direction . . . Far too many of the measures that are proposed are efforts to punish people for the sins of their fathers.
There is in many of the proposals an underlying tone almost of blood guilt."

This opposition to any effective civil rights legislation
right up to the time he became vice-president makes one
wonder what "we" he was speaking of in his November 27,
1963, address to Congress, right after Kennedy's assassination, when he said, "*We* have talked long enough in this
country about equal rights. It is time now to write the
next chapter—and to write it in the book of law."

The evolution of Johnson as the mock champion of civil
rights began after the splintering of his hopes in 1956. He
got the message: victory lay in the cities, victory lay within
the union blocs, the black blocs, the immigrant blocs, the
big city bosses, with the independent voters, and if possible
with the farm blocs, though that was the last to worry about.
Johnson saw that he who gets the South gets naught. At no
time in the last fifty years, with the exception of Truman's

victory in 1948, was the Dixie electoral vote possibly responsible for the election of a president; except for 1948, the
South could have stayed at home. LBJ saw that he had to get
that magnolia blossom out of his lapel, and he coolly set
about it. He would pass a civil rights act. If necessary he
would pass two. Nothing to get the nation in a turmoil, just
something nice and American like saying a citizen should
be allowed to vote—without giving the Attorney General
the right to enforce it. And furthermore he had to do it in
such a subtle fashion that he could claim in Texas that he
wasn't doing it at all. The 1957 bill that he created fitted
that need perfectly, but when it failed to get him the nomination in 1960, he again lost interest in civil rights, and his
interest was not revived until his own presidential race in
1964. In the interim, Kennedy, with just the easiest help
from Johnson, could have passed a civil rights bill of his
own. If, in 1963, Vice-President Johnson had seized the
precedent set by Nixon in 1959 and in 1961, a few days
before he left office, of issuing an advisory ruling that a
simple majority could change the Senate rules, then the old
cast-iron cloture protections could have been weakened
enough to prevent the Southern filibuster from blocking a
strong civil rights bill that year. But Johnson refused to
accept the opportunity, and ruled with the South. Even so,
it was Kennedy more than Johnson who passed the 1964
act; or rather, the trauma of Kennedy's assassination did
it. Meg Greenfield, writing in *The Reporter* of December 19,
1963, was among many who saw that "Whether Johnson will
be able to maintain the memory of Kennedy's death as a
goad to further legislative action is the question hanging
over the Congress now. 'Congress is scared to death,' one
Republican remarked on the subject. 'There is more of an
interregnum here than there is in the White House. Nobody
knows what the effect of this has been on the public. That's
why they want to go home.'" Brandishing the still magic

martyrdom of Kennedy as a wand, Johnson led Congress easily past the civil rights act of 1964. It was hardly his victory. Senator Joseph Clark, in his book, *Congress: The Sapless Branch,* points out that "Some, like FDR or Lincoln were able to exert leadership because external events overwhelmed the legislative branch." The great depression and the Civil War did what the man possibly could not have done; the same was true for Johnson in 1964. Kennedy's death overwhelmed the legislative branch.

Johnson can deservedly claim the Voting Act of 1965 as his own, although he was notably unwilling to enforce the new Civil Rights Act in the redoubts of his Southern pals. The Attorney General's office has consistently refused to send a federal registrar into Sunflower County, home of Senator Eastland, though only 17 per cent of the 13,500 Negroes are signed up (if 70 per cent were registered they could control the county). The right to vote, as Shannon observed, is hardly a "great" innovation in a democratic society, but it is nice that Johnson finally came around to seeing the common justice of it; it would have been nicer if he had assigned federal registrars to more than 10 per cent of the 500 counties covered by the Act.

And that was as far as he would go. The Civil Rights Act of 1966 was a farce from the beginning. After being stripped of all helpful provisions—such as indemnification of victims of racist-inspired violence—it depended on the extremely controversial "open housing" provisions for its appeal. Both radical and conservative civil rights groups opposed it, on the ground that it would be almost impossible to get through Congress and was unnecessary anyway. In November, 1962, Kennedy had issued an executive order forbidding racial consideration in the sale of new Federal Housing Administration-insured or Veterans Administration-guaranteed housing, but this covered only 20 per cent of the total housing supply. By expanding the order to cover housing financed through any bank or savings and loan company protected by federal guarantees—something he did not need Congressional approval for—Johnson could have desegregated 80 per cent of the total housing supply. Instead, he chose the impossible route, and completed the sham by sending the bill to Congress *months* after he could even have made a decent fight for it. It died, unpushed, unmourned.

* *
* *

Home rule for the District of Columbia—the only major city in America where black power could become an immediate fact if its citizens were given the right to run their own affairs rather than having to look to South-dominated Congressional committees for guidance—was listed for two years by Johnson as a part of his Great Society program. He gave it little enthusiasm in 1965, and in 1966 he withdrew his support entirely, saying he would like to see home rule established but that it is "a matter for Congress to work out," which is the old well-understood signal on controversial matters that the White House doesn't give a rap what happens. A majority of the citizens of the District of Columbia are black, which is significant, but not nearly so significant as the fact that in most of the schools the color is 90–95 per cent black; Congress's inclinations being what they are, this means the schools are not exactly burdened with luxuries. Some have no money for libraries. One of these libraryless schools, Peabody, built in 1879 and marred by every year of its age, stands four blocks from the nation's Capitol and looks westward toward that gleaming edifice through 14 broken window panes. And in the summer where do the school kids cool off? Many of them swim in the civic fountains, where the water is not renewed and after a few days the small fry are floating around in fluid that is about 20 per cent spit and urine. There were seven public swimming pools in the District thirty years ago; today there are eight. When this was called to the President's attention, he replied that he felt so sorrowful about the situation that he had ordered sprinklers attached to the fire hydrants, as they had been attached in Chicago after the riots there.

There was one brief hour when Johnson sounded really great on the race-economic thing. That was in his commencement speech at Howard University on June 4, 1965, surely one of the finest manifestoes of fair play ever put on paper. He sounded fully aware of the scope of the problems and determined to deal with them. Whichever speechwriter handled that one, he certainly made Sahib Lyndon sound like the right man to lead the Negro through the thickets. It was a speech, as Floyd McKissick of the Congress of Racial Equality noted, "to make a rattlesnake cry." Johnson ended it by saying he would call a White House Conference on civil rights that autumn to get everything shipshape for the big move on Congress.

There was a slight delay. The conference didn't come about for another year. By that time—so deep into 1966 as to nullify any pressure the Conference might have had on the Capitol—it was plain to everyone that Johnson had lost interest, was totally preoccupied with Vietnam, and was beginning to respond to the white blacklash. The Conference opened deep in skepticism. The National Council of Churches' Commission on Religion and Race, for one, predicted it would be "a frivolous exercise which will accomplish nothing." The whole affair turned out to be a giant cauldron of Johnsonian tapioca pudding: overcooked, tasteless, rubbery. Particular grievances were smothered in the broad agenda of social ills—not enough economic security, welfare, housing, justice—with deadeningly vague remedies: more security, more education, more good housing, and more justice. Nobody could argue with that. What else was there to say? It had all been said on the sidewalks, in Negro churches, in marches, in sit-ins, in riots for a dozen years and more. As one delegate from Chicago observed, "If the conference had been held in 1950 it would have been forward-looking. Today, it's just ludicrous." FBI-types flitted around constantly, checking credentials so that no uninvited malcontents could get in and stir up an interesting discussion. The original ground rules permitted no resolutions from the floor and no voting. But behind Johnson's ideological Maginot Line the conference quickly began to die of boredom.

Some theorized that Johnson moved up his appearance from the last night to the first night because he feared giving the outside civil rights rebels an extra day to prepare a wild demonstration that might embarrass him. But a more likely reason for his change of schedule was that he saw it was necessary to stir some life into a conference that was beginning to sag dangerously.

The Council that had organized the conference for Johnson called for "nothing less than a broadly based 'crash' program that can significantly improve the life-chances of hundreds of thousands of Negro Americans . . ." but within a matter of months Johnson showed that features of the Civil Rights Conference program which he did not mean to ignore, he meant actively to oppose. The Council, for example, called for an increase in new home production from about 1.4 million to 2 million starts a year; Johnson's high interest rates soon dropped housing starts to the lowest level in a generation. The Council, for another example, called for much firmer enforcement of the school desegregation guidelines; yet when Commissioner of Education Harold Howe II did bear down on the enforcement, Johnson called him to the White House and told him to stop making pro-civil rights statements, and to go slower in pushing the Southern governors. Then in his news conference of October 10, 1966, at a time when Howe needed the most unflinching kind of White House support in the face of the nearly-hysterical opposition that was coming from the Deep South, Johnson instead hedged, saying that "I realize that in some instances there has been some harassment" by the Office of Education. A brochure of four of Howe's pro-integration speeches that had been prepared for wide distribution is still sitting in a Washington warehouse.

The last significant statements made by LBJ were in Chicago and Cleveland in July, 1966, when he reminded the Negroes that they constitute only 10 per cent of the population and must stand in line until "equality is given." His very words. *Noblesse oblige.*

Up to this point, except for the anti-poverty program, we really have not talked about what would constitute a creatively "great" aspect of society, but only of those things that should, naïvely, be taken for granted. What of the greatness? Shannon again has a good word on that: "A society seeking greatness has to concern itself more with the quality of its common life. On issues of this kind—as diverse as air polution, billboard control, the wastelands of television, chaotic suburban growth, tax reform and the anti-poverty program—the Johnson Administration has only begun to be tested."

Let us indulge in just a dash of testing here.

*   *
*   *

Ever since he was elected to the Senate by eighty-seven votes in 1948 Johnson has been suspected of a willingness to play fast and loose with campaign procedures, and this reputation did not diminish over the years as new rumors circulated of big contributions from special interests—interests for whom he seemed to display a special fondness in his legislative life. Nor did the Bobby Baker episode help to establish him as a puritan. So it was with both surprise and approval that the nation heard Johnson declare in his State of the Union message in January, 1966, a firm commitment to cleaning up campaign finances. Here—if it came about—would be the turning of a momentous leaf. The Great Society, he emphasized, stood for ethics in government and campaigning.

It was about time. Since he came to the White House, Democratic party financial matters were conducted with all the secretiveness of an outlaw bucket shop. Prior to 1964, the Democratic National Committee was frank about its income and expenses. But in Johnson's presidential campaign, secrecy became the keynote and it remained the keynote thereafter. A shifty atmosphere developed around national headquarters. In the first six months of 1965 the Democratic National Committee (DNC) reported spending $1,300,000 more than it took in. No explanation was ever given as to how it made up the difference. The President's Club alone reported spending $560,000 more than it received in 1965—with no explanation. The Citizens' Research Foundation of Princeton University said that the "lack of credibility" in some of the Democratic party's expenditure reports "is without precedent in recent years." It charged the Democrats with "secreting funds in certain states" where the Corrupt Practices Act could not get at them. Not only was the press refused answers to ordinary questions relating to DNC finances, members of the committee were also left in the dark. Affairs were run strictly by the committee treasurer and White House muscleman Marvin Watson, Johnson's aide Cliff Carter, and Committee Chairman John Bailey (who, as a hangover from Kennedy days, was a figurehead only)—and Johnson himself. After the 1964 campaign, Bailey told the committee only that the Democrats had wound up "with a great vote surplus and a sort of a little financial deficit." A year later clues began to emerge from discussions within the innermost John-

sonian sanctum that the "little deficit" came to more than
$4,000,000, which, if true, was the largest presidential cam-
paign deficit in history. None of the reports filed by law with
the Clerk of the U.S. House do more than add confusion
to the party's financial picture, and there were signs that
the filing data had been complicated to hinder investiga-
tions: contributors were listed by first initial rather than
by full name, sometimes no address was given, sometimes
the contributors were not listed at all. "These actions," as
the Citizens' Research Foundation pointed out dryly, "led
to a climate that could hardly foster confidence in the law
or in political finance management." During the first two
years of Johnson's presidency, complaints about corrupt
campaign practices were investigated by the Internal Revenue Service, the Treasury Department, the Post Office Department, the Civil Service Commission, and the Justice
Department. The FBI got in on it also. But of course no
reports of shady doings were made public.

Reform, if it was to come, would clearly have to come
from the President himself. So in his message opening
Congress for 1966 Johnson promised to push an elections
reform law that would require strict disclosure of all contributions, stimulate small contributions through tax in-
centives up to $100, and cut down on the proliferation of
phony committees behind which the big contributors customarily hide. His stated goal was to "make it possible
for those without personal wealth to enter public life without being obligated to a few large contributors." Perhaps he
had in mind the semi-illegal, but successful, effort only a few
months before by the Democratic National Committee in
publishing a blurb-book for the Great Society in which ads
had been sold at $15,000 a page to companies either regu-
lated by the federal government or which look to government contracts for much of their profits—companies such
as Lockheed, Sperry-Rand, Hughes Aircraft, Ling-Temco-

Vought, Alcoa, Harvey Aluminum, Xerox, Gulf Oil, American Airlines, Continental Can and many others. The rake-off of more than a million dollars had been accompanied by a great deal of critical comment in the nation's press, and Johnson was looking for a way to cancel that out. The proposed election law was his way of trying.

Or so it seemed until, with an amazingly obvious guarantee that no election reform would actually come about, Johnson bypassed both Senator Everett Jordan, chairman of the Rules Committee, and Howard W. Cannon, chairman of the subcommittee on elections, to select Senator Joseph Clark of Pennsylvania as the man to run with the bill. Clark is not only wholeheartedly in favor of reforming election laws, he is also in favor of reforming the Senate itself; his only failing is, however, a fatal one—his zeal for honesty and candor has left him way, way outside the Senate Establishment. No election reform bill could come close to passage without the aid of the Establishment, so of course with Clark carrying the bill it was dead to begin with, as Johnson of all people knew very well. Senator Cannon, showing his disdain for the bill, did not even hold hearings on it but instead called up a five-year-old bill of his own that would have done nothing but raise the statutory ceilings on spending to bring them closer to the realism of campaign costs. Just to make sure that Clark could get nowhere, Johnson sent his elections reform bill far too late for action.

It was all the rawest bit of tomfoolery. Meanwhile, the list of unusual contributions grew much longer. It was discovered that a $1,300,000 anti-poverty contract was awarded to Consolidated American Services, Inc. in 1964, although it was *not* one of the four firms recommended for the contract by Milton Fogelman, contract officer for the Office of Economic Opportunity. One of the prerequisites for the contract was to have a Washington operational office. ConAm had a one-man office. W. C. Hobbs, senior vice-president of the firm, gave $1,000 to the President's Club shortly before the contract was awarded; in 1965 he gave $1,000 to the Democratic National Committee, and in 1966 he gave another $1,000 to the President's Club. Two California brothers gave $12,000 to the President's Club, a generosity that some suspected of having a commercial rather than ideological basis inasmuch as one of the brothers, J. Edward Martin, was known to be a leader of the John Birch Society movement in that area. They have done a million dollars in government business during the past three years. Perhaps the most enchanting discovery of all was that shortly after top Anheuser-Busch executives and their wives contributed $10,000 to the President's Club, an anti-trust suit against the St. Louis brewery was dropped; and just to make sure that the beer barons understood that the government held no hard feelings for them, Assistant Attorney General Donald F. Turner accepted an invitation (as did Johnson aide Cliff Carter) to fly back to St. Louis in a company plane and be guest of the Busches at the All-Star game. This was less than a month after Turner dismissed the anti-trust suit; he insisted there was absolutely no connection. And there was also something of a stink when it was discovered that a $12,700,000 construction contract was awarded to the firm once headed by former Democratic national treasurer Matthew H. McCloskey, after he was allowed to lower his first bid and resubmit it beyond the deadline for receiving bids. The firm is now headed by his son, Thomas McCloskey. Old man McCloskey was charged a couple of years ago with slipping $25,000 to the 1960 Democratic campaign after he had been awarded a $19.8 million contract to build the D.C. Stadium. He constructed the Rayburn Office Building, possibly the most expensive office building in the world, at twice the original estimated cost. He was also involved in three Florida housing projects, costing $28.8 million, which promptly defaulted to FHA. No financial tie between McCloskey and Johnson has yet been made, and of course it could conceivably turn out that old Matthew is just lucky in business.

And there was in 1966 at least one episode brought out in Congress of civil service employees being shaken down for campaign contributions. Delaware's Senator Williams accused Johnson of knowing about the shakedown—"he must like it, he condones it, and I assume he wants it to continue. That statement stands until he helps us to pass [reform] legislation. Let him put a little arm twisting on the members of his party to help pass it, rather than telling them to use this subject in political speeches but not to vote for it."

If there was any arm-twisting, however, it was to recruit new members for the President's Club. One and all, their $1,000 membership fee gave them something in common—access to the presidential closet. As Cliff Carter once put it in a glowing sales pitch, members "are assured of a direct relationship with President Johnson." Some newsmen and congressmen continued to be skeptical of the motives behind the contributors. For some reason they did not believe that the executives of the Ling-Temco-Vought electronics corporation in Dallas—a corporation doing splendidly with government contracts since Lyndon became president—who contributed $25,000 to the President's Club under the name Citizens for Good Government were, really and truly, just out for good government.

There was a law passed on campaign finances—passed in the final hours of the 1966 session, without much discussion. It would let you assign a dollar of your income tax to the party of your choice. It will not deter the big contributors from continuing to subscribe to a membership in the White House Key Club. It will not demand cleaner accounting of party income and expenses. And in fact, there is considerable doubt that the act is even constitutional, since it sets the precedent of a taxpayer's specifying where his taxes will be spent.*

It was a typical Great Society reform, empty, awkward, slight, and mis-labeled. There were several other similar reforms.

* *
* *

Those who anticipate great accomplishments from the Highway Beautification Act of 1965 should temper their expectations with the reminder that none other than the Outdoor Advertising Association of America (OAAA)—whose membership accounts for most of the billboards—lobbied *for* passage of the act. Obviously the OAAA does not think the law will cut into the highway billboard business, and this is a good assumption since its toughest language is directed at the boondock stretches of the interstate and primary highway systems where only 15 per cent of the advertising on the grand scale is done anyway. The urban clutter will remain untouched. Such business losses as are incurred will be paid for by the government. The logical extension of this philosophy—that is, paying companies not to disfigure the countryside—would have the government paying muggers and felons to refrain from their midnight mischief; but inasmuch as the latter would help the poorer stratum and would smack of a guaranteed income, it will not likely occur to Johnson. That's the way the Great Society game is played.

Strip miners have left 800,000 acres of scarred land over a twelve-state area in Appalachia. Ninety-six per cent of

---

* The manner of passing this questionable "reform" was symptomatic, being made part of a legislative parcel that included a $2,000,000 windfall (a tax advantage) for the Harvey Aluminum Company of Torrance, California, some of whose executives are members of the President's Club. Another feature of the bill was the establishment of a depletion allowance for shell dredgers, among whom are some of Johnson's chums in Houston. After signing this ringing piece of legislative favoritism Johnson, understandably, would not discuss it with reporters, referring them instead to a mimeographed statement.

these mines were privately owned. How are we going to go about reclaiming the land—make the mine owners repair the monstrous damage? Oh no. The Department of the Interior has already suggested that the federal taxpayer lay out $250,-000,000 to do the job. Its excuse: "Many of the problems associated with past strip-mined lands are interstate in character. In particular: stream pollution from mine-acid drainage and sediment." Ah yes, the very thing the Department of the Interior already was supposed to be policing the industry to prevent. Well, it didn't; and now it proposes that the taxpayer pay for the previous industry-government collusion.

The Water Pollution Control Act of 1965 may do something to answer Johnson's own question, "Does our society need to tolerate filthy rivers?" But the manner in which the Act was implemented leaves some doubt. No sooner did Congress go home than Johnson began having new ideas. At the time the Act was passed, Congress thought it would be administered by a separate department in Health, Education and Welfare. But suddenly—at least it seemed sudden to Congress, which hadn't been given a hint of it up to the beginning of the 1966 session—Johnson got the idea that all of the water people should be in the Interior Department, so he sent a bill to Congress reorganizing everything to do just that. Interior Secretary Udall was called to the hill and asked to explain the new brainstorm; in his rather embarrassed words, it was just one of several ideas that Johnson got to "kicking around" and decided on, impulsively, after Congress left town.

Why the Department of the Interior, whose primary jurisdiction and influence is in the wide-open spaces of the Middle West and the West and not at all oriented to the urban problems of the East, where water pollution is most critical? When Johnson signed the bill, he made a little speech in which he said "there is no excuse" for industry's dumping acids into rivers and lakes, "nor any excuse—we should call a spade a spade—for chemical companies and oil refineries using our major rivers as pipelines for toxic wastes." So, why the Department of the Interior, whose Bureau of Mines, as Representative John Blatnik subsequently pointed out, has "known of acid mine drainage for years and has not done anything about it," just as the Department of the Interior's oil office has done nothing to inhibit the petroleum polluters, and just as the Interior Department's Bureau of Reclamation has done little to stop pollution from salt water? The Interior's various policing bureaus have, indeed, shown themselves to be just a bit industry-oriented when it comes to petroleum dumping, coal acid mine drainage, and the like. Which may, of course, *be* the answer to why the control of water pollution was shifted to a department whose main interests have traditionally *not* been human health standards but water conservation, of a sort. Seven months after the act had been passed, five years after he became Interior Secretary, Udall admitted he was ignorant of even a basic approach to the pollution problem. Asked if he thought the nation should have single or multiple standards of water quality control, he replied, "I am not really knowledgeable enough at this time to give you a flat answer." He almost sounded surprised that he might be expected to know. One thing seems already to be clear: when any massive control of pollution is attempted, the cost will be borne primarily by the general taxpayer rather than by the industries that are fouling the water. That's the way the talk already is going.

But since it must be done that way, then it should at least be done before the stench of solid feces and dead fish becomes so great as to obscure the purer odor of the chemical content; to this end, several congressmen proposed a $20 billion spending program over the next six years, to include $6 billion in federal funds—less than is now spent in Vietnam every three months—but Udall said that was too much; he favors spending only $3.45 billion, which, if used entirely on the Hudson River, might be enough to clear it up to a deep umber and remove the dead cats. Some experts estimate that the $20 billion figure would possibly cover the installation of modern municipal sewage treatment systems, but even that amount would still not begin to cope with the industrial waste problem.

Another of Johnson's false-front stores is being built as the new cabinet-level Department of Transportation. This looks like a place in which plenty of social defects can be shuffled, moved from office to office, and talked about for many months and years without anything happening. Some government officials have called it a "breakthrough," and perhaps it will prove to be that; it's too early to say what it will be. But a transportation department that has no power to regulate transportation is, surely, a very strange department of transportation. And that's the kind Johnson has put through Congress—a Department of Transportation minus the Interstate Commerce Commission, minus the Civil Aeronautics Board, and minus the Federal Maritime Commission, which are the three agencies that regulate all the fares, routes and rates on land, on the sea and in the air. As for the big city traffic problems, these will remain the jurisdiction of that other muscleless department, Housing and Urban Development. Also remaining free of the Department of Transportation is the most bountiful source of pork barrel known to man—the Army Corps of Engineers, which will continue to lacerate the nation with its increasingly weird canals and other waterways, all soberly dug under the guise of necessary inland transportation. Cabinet supervision might inhibit the Corps' creativity, which most recently includes plans for scooping a canal from Fort Worth, Texas, to the Gulf.

The Department of Transportation *can* claim to have

complete jurisdiction over the new highway safety program. But just what this will come to is somewhat in doubt, inasmuch as the DT's first Secretary, Alan S. Boyd, as late as May, 1966, was still pushing an auto safety bill that would do no more than give his department power to set up safety standards "if needed." Of course in this he had to represent Johnson's wishes and so it cannot be said that such a soft approach to regulating the auto industry came from his heart, but neither was there any indication that he felt otherwise. The administration continued to hold to this conservative line into the summer, by which time Ralph Nader's remarkably persuasive little book, *Unsafe at Any Speed,* had so triggered Congressional enthusiasm for some in-writing safety laws that Johnson was forced to shift to a tougher position; when the auto safety law was finally passed, Johnson, of course, was calling it "my bill." Later it was discovered that during the time the bill was under debate, Johnson was sitting on a report submitted by his advisers on consumer affairs that was very critical of the automobile industry for the way it makes, sells, and finances cars. For one thing the report scolds the industry for disregarding safety features; in other words, the release of the report would have made easier the passage of a vigorous safety bill. For some reason, Johnson didn't release the report until two months after Congress had gone home.

Safety in transportation simply isn't Johnson's desire. A few months before the *Yarmouth Castle* disaster (on November 13, 1965, the cruise ship bound from Miami to Nassau, burned and sank with the loss of at least eighty-nine lives), legislation was introduced to make foreign owners of cruise ships bring their fire traps up to U.S. safety standards—the highest in the world—or get out of the very lucrative U.S. cruise business. Johnson sent representatives of the U.S. State Department, the U.S. Maritime Commisison, and the U.S. Coast Guard to testify against the legislation. Came the disaster, and new get-tough legislation was introduced. This time Johnson counteracted it by sending up his own mellow bill which was passed, effectively killing the true reform legislation, and once again the travel agents and the foreign ship owners were safe. (Boyd, a Floridian with ambitions for returning to Florida politics, where the travel agent lobby is potent indeed, testified enthusiastically for the administration's do-nothing bill.)

In 1965, Johnson put together a transportation task force which was to come up with "something dramatic." The task force's report was, like so many other brainstorm reports of the Johnson regime, never released to the public and its general over-all findings and proposals never hinted at even in broad outline. Whatever dramatic upgrading of transportation was ever hoped for has been squeezed into the thimble of the new department.

It is strange how real wars can be set in motion and accelerated so much easier than ersatz wars. For instance, late in July, 1966, at the same time the administration announced that it was spending money on the Vietnam war so easily that it had far exceeded its previous estimates, it announced also that it just didn't seem to be able to spend money in that way on poverty, or at least not nearly as much money as Congress had given it to spend. During 1966, it said, it was unable to spend $206 million of the poverty allocation "because the present level of program activity wasn't reached as quickly as anticipated." Underscoring this was the announcement, at about the same time, that during fiscal 1966 there was a nine-month moratorium on recruiting for the Women's Job Corps because of a lack of billets; recruiting for the real army went on apace, with no lack of billets.

Of course, without planning vast sums of money are difficult to dispose of. This same strange plaint was heard again in August, 1966, when Secretary Gardner went before a Senate subcommittee to beg that restraint be exercised in spending on the critical urban problems and on allocations for school districts that serve predominantly low-income children. He pointed out that his department had gone the first year from spending nothing to spending $900 million to help impoverished schools but "we're just not geared up to go from $900 million to $1.8 billion."

But one may perhaps be excused for wondering how it is that after three years as president, to say nothing of the half dozen years when he was reputed to be the great shaper of the Senate, Johnson has still not presented the nation with any skeletal plans into which money could be poured for such obvious needs as those relating to medical care and urban rebuilding. Why is it that after all this Johnsonian leadership the federal government is still, as Gardner admitted, paying $6 billion a year straight into the pockets of slum landlords whose home-grown rats, like their own pocketbooks, grow fatter each day? Is building a better rat trap, or a ratless pad, so far beyond the scope of this Great Leader who has launched the nation, without consulting Congress, on the $5 billion venture of building a supersonic airplane that nobody but the aircraft companies want and which will, because of the sonic boom, probably be barred from overland flights? It takes planning, secret or otherwise, to spend big money; but Johnson seems most capable of masterminding plans that benefit big industry and big business, and he is rather adroit at throwing together plans for the Fairly Wealthy Old Pals, but he is helpless when it comes to planning for the poor.

Johnson will spend twenty times more on his favored moon race than he will spend during the next two years for meeting the swift decay of the big cities. As Senator Ribicoff pointed out during his 1966 hearings on urban miseries, rats killed or maimed 14,000 slum dwellers last year—some Harlem babies have had half their faces eaten away—but the federal government has marked only $27,500 for a rat-killing program, while it is spending $45 million yearly to control the yellow fever mosquito although not since 1917 has there been a yellow fever case in this country. It's easier for Johnson to continue an old useless program than to concoct a new useful one; but one sounds as good as the other on the campaign trail. Senator Kennedy pointed out that in New York City alone, substandard housing went up from 420,000 units to 520,000 units in the last five years. When Johnson interpreted this to be criticism of his efforts, he huffily replied that money to stop urban rot had been increased "one-third" during his administration. One-third of *what*?

These criticisms should not, however, be taken to mean that Johnson sees no value in pushing progressive programs. When it looks like a cinch, and when public opinion is driving strong in that direction, he will sometimes supply a helping nudge. The classic example of this was in the passage of the cold-war GI Bill in 1966.

Isn't that the bill Johnson opposed so bitterly in 1965? Isn't that the bill he sent Veterans Administration (VA) and Defense Department and Bureau of the Budget officials to testify against? Yes. And some beautifully wacky testimony they gave. There was Arthur W. Farmer, one of the VA's deputy chiefs, who argued that the vets of today do not merit such schooling because their term of service is shorter (actually, they serve an average of six months longer than the Korean vets, who had the GI benefits). Farmer's strength on the witness stand wilted when, under committee grilling, he admitted he didn't even know at what age men are now drafted!

And there was Brigadier General William W. Berg, who spoke for the Defense Department and for his Commander in Chief. Why did he not want a GI Bill? Because, said Berg, if the draftees knew they could get some schooling when they left the service, they might be less inclined to re-enlist. Of course, only 10 per cent of the draftees re-enlist as it is.*

Nevertheless, despite this opposition from the President's forces in 1965, Senator Ralph Yarborough of Texas got the bill through the Senate, as he had done on two other occasions, this time with the assistance of Senator Robert Kennedy of New York. They might have run into trouble in the House, as Yarborough had before, but this time LBJ saw the tide was moving swiftly against him and he adopted the GI Bill as part of his program. Why the about-face? Two reasons. First, it allowed him to take credit away from Yarborough, whom he dislikes very much, and from Kennedy, ditto. But the main reason was that all popular discussions of the Vietnam problem had moved from the rational sphere of foreign-policy debate to the emotional sphere of love-the-servicemen. Johnson will ride any national emotion. The time was right for a new GI Bill, and Johnson is always ready when the time is right.

When Harry Truman asked help for his national health insurance program, Johnson's response was: "I want no part of socialized medicine . . . The democratic answer to this form of socialism is more hospitals, more doctors, more nurses." He did not lift a hand to help, even behind the scene, until the field had been plowed and fertilized and planted and contoured for twenty-five years—by others—and finally the time was right for him to step in and reap the crop. And with just the same deliberate sense of timing he reaped the civil rights crop. Now he was ready to put his name to the cold-war GI Bill, and carry away the credit.

---

* Some administration witnesses who testify in favor of a budget cut are required to use the most embarrassingly dumb arguments. For instance, to support Johnson's proposed reduction of the school milk program, the government witness testified that the program was set up originally to help dairy farmers, not children, and since dairy farmers don't need help any more, the program is useless.

That's how, in the midst of confusion and double talk, legends of the Great Leader are made. That's how, incidentally, the nation will get peace out of Johnson, if it ever does. When he hears that the people *really* want peace, he'll give it to them.

7 Lyndon Über Alles

*Johnson has ruined morally all who deal with him at
home and he will ruin all who deal with him abroad.*

—I. F. Stone, October, 1966

It is time Lyndon Johnson got credit for sticking to something until he carried it off. Those who had followed his
career were quick to conclude, when it became clear that
he was discarding the idea of creating a Great Society, that
ol' Lyin' Down Lyndon was tired of another project and
was ready to lie down again. Although such recriminations
were deserved, he has at the same time failed to receive full
measure of credit for creating almost single-handedly the
Vietnam-United States war. In a superficial, partisan way,
it is sometimes called "Johnson's War," but those who call it
this probably never realize how accurate they are.

It *is* his war. Not since William Randolph Hearst and
Theodore Roosevelt combined talents to produce the Span-

ish-American War has a major conflict been so deliberately contrived. And whereas it took two of them to turn out a war that killed only 385 Americans, Johnson almost alone has produced a war that already has killed more than 5,000 Americans.

The following three sections are devoted to a proper recognition of this great militarist, his motives, and his methods for trapping us.

* *
*

Of all the eerie echoes that inhabit the haunted White House, none raises the nape hairs with such delicate horror as Lyndon's talk of peace. "Our passion is peace," says Lyndon, the very same Lyndon in whose presidency the sales of arms and military equipment to foreign countries by the Pentagon has risen threefold, from one-half billion dollars a year in 1963 to $1.5 billion a year (this does not include what we have *given* away through military aid), making us history's greatest hucksters of mischief. From the year that Johnson became Democratic leader in the Senate until the present time, this country has given or sold to other countries $35 billion worth of arms; we have done it very democratically, however, selling to both sides: to India *and* Pakistan, to Israel *and* the Arab nations.

The time has come, in this anno LBJ, that "the heavy industrial-business-Pentagon investment in military-space spending is almost out of control." This happens to be a quote from Representative Don Edwards, president of Americans for Democratic Action, but many in and out of Congress have noted the same crisis. What Eisenhower warned was coming has arrived with Johnson; that is, a blank check for the military. At a recent press conference Johnson recalled what he considered to be one of the wisest bits of advice he ever received from his friend Sam Rayburn. Johnson had committed the momentary apostasy of questioning a decision of the generals. Rayburn rebuked him: "Lyndon, if these people in the Joint Chiefs of Staff, and a man of General Eisenhower's military experience, don't know more about this than us civilian legislators, then we've been wasting a lot of money on West Point all these years." Johnson never forgot it, except when Ike tried to economize. There were times over the years when he complained that the generals "only know two words—spend and bomb," but after he finished his mild complaint he went along with them, spending and bombing. In 1966 the Pentagon had at its disposal $100 *billion,* including unspent previous appropriations—more than *twice* what Congress set aside during the year for all civilian expenditures put together; *twice* what the country spent at all levels—local, state, and national, elementary, secondary, and university—for education.

In an undeclared war, against one of the smallest and most backward nations in the Far East, with not a Tojo or Hitler in sight, opposing the most rudimentary of military machines, we are spending at a higher annual rate than in World War II.

We have arrived at this through a natural progression of LBJ hysteria. At the outbreak of the Korean War, which he called more significant than World War II, Johnson demanded all-out legal mobilization of reserve troops, national guard, draftees, civilian manpower, and industry—and hang the expense because "this is not a bookkeeping war." When Humphrey said that he, too, was interested in fighting a proper fight but wondered "what has happened to these funds, this $13 billion or $14 billion" that had been appropriated to the Defense Department, Johnson brushed him aside. "I do not wish to go into that question at this time," he said, "I do not wish to attach blame to any individual or group" for lack of preparedness, especially the Pentagon. If the generals were not given *all* the money they wanted, without hounding them with bookkeeping, then the question might well be asked, "Is this the hour of our nation's twilight, the last fading hour of light before an endless night shall envelop us and all the Western world?" On that wild rhetorical note Johnson helped launch military spending on an upward curve that, with the exception of a brief and insignificant economy dip after the Korean War, has continued up to the present.

At a Cook County fund-raising gala not long ago he said, "I leave you with the assurance that we love peace and we seek it every hour of every day" (last verse of Lyndon's Epistle to the Chicagoans). There *was*, Mayor Daley observed, a scriptural cadence to it. And to the American Alumni Council meeting in White Sulphur Springs, West Virginia, Johnson explained his reason for ordering a World War II-level of explosives to be dropped on tiny North Vietnam: "To prove the use of force to conquer others is a losing game." He explained that he was using weapons and bombs "as a former schoolteacher who turned to politics only to learn that all of life is a classroom. All my life, I have taken seriously the warning that the world is engaged in a race between education and chaos." He was destroying North Vietnam to educate it and save it from chaos.

In such utterances some insist that they detect a schizoid wheeze. But the illusion of madness comes not from what Johnson says or from his actions, but from the juxtaposition of what he says and does against the backdrop of our expectations.

With a two-gun angel of mercy running Washington, logic must marshal itself along Prussian lines or understanding will be scattered. Humor, too, must come to attention before moving off in a snappy *parademarschshritt*. Would you believe, for example, that a White House Conference on Disarmament was held in the spring of 1965 without discussing ways to disarm (as Senator Clark pointed out in the final hour and was ruled out of order), or that the

U.S. Arms Control and Disarmament Agency hired six
former consultants for the Departments of State and Defense
to write a report on why it would be *impossible* to disarm?

No, Lyndon Johnson is not insane; he is merely a common Southern precinct militarist, perfectly willing and
certifiably able to use militarism for anything from winning votes, to exploiting the pork barrel to, if need be,
blowing up half the world in corn-pone pique.

This side of Johnson, for some reason, keeps surprising
people and angering them because it is a surprise. On the
same night Johnson gave his speech in Chicago, Barry
Goldwater also delivered a speech there; Inez Robb said she
was "halfway through the Johnson speech before I realized
I wasn't reading the Goldwater pronouncement." She was
so shocked she thought of going to Johnson and making
him "say it ain't so that this great democracy is subtly being
transformed into a military oligarchy wherein the Commander in Chief is President by right of military office and
not vice versa, as provided for in the Constitution."

This is not an unreasonable worry, but Miss Robb is
certainly slow in noticing this neofascist side. His career
has been so dedicated to the aggrandizement of the military
that he even sees space exploration, heavily directed by retired military officers and adaptable to military use, as a
kind of Chester Gould comic strip way of ruling the universe.
Early in 1958 he told his Democratic troops that they must
stop at nothing to see that the U.S. captures space, the
"ultimate position—from which total control of the earth
may be exercised . . . Whoever gains that ultimate position gains control, total control, over the earth." *The New
York Times,* among others, scolded him for such opiated
"frightening images of American spatial imperialism."

Shortly after World War II, we are informed in *The
Lyndon Johnson Story,* Johnson was afraid the U.S. military
machine would be dismantled. He worried Rayburn with

his fears so often that the Speaker appointed him to the new Postwar Military Policy Committee, where he could help see that it didn't happen. He was also put on the Joint Committee on Atomic Energy.

The nonuniform generalissimos of Capitol Hill are usually thought of as those Southern hotheads Mendel Rivers, chairman of the House Armed Services Committee; Richard Russell, chairman of the Senate Armed Services Committee; John Stennis, who wallows in several armed services–space assignments; and Strom Thurmond, master sergeant of the Dixie guard.

Johnson was seldom thought of as one of their kind, yet none of these could match his talents as a pentathlon militarist. *All* his enthusiasms and experience as a representative and senator were bound up with the military and more efficient war-making: he was a member of the House Naval Affairs Committee, a member of the Senate Armed Services Committee, chairman of the Senate Preparedness Committee, chairman of the Space Committee, a member of the Appropriations Subcommittee for the Armed Services.

Aside from his fellow legislators, his chief cronies came from the brass, the admirals and generals hanging around the Capitol corridors for a reason. When it was Scotch-and-water time, Johnson turned to them and to his semi-service buddies to share it—Russell, whom he often likened to a Daddy; and William Knowland, the silly right-wing senator from Formosa, whom Johnson once hugged and breathed upon as "my trusted and treasured friend"; and Stennis and Eastland and the other Southern belligerents who swung like Romulus and Remus from the tits of the military appropriations bill, growing fat.

Johnson apparently has not been unaware of his man-on-horseback tendencies. In 1960, in a unique moment of candor, he observed, "I don't think I have the disposition, the training, or the temperament for the presidency." He needs, as he must have known, the disciplinary drag of many coequals ("I am a man of Congress," he said at the same time) to hold him in check. As Chief Executive the deep yearnings get out of control. In his concepts of boundless executive privilege, of textbook patriotism, of narrow dissent, of the simplistic revenges that for him constitute diplomatic negotiation—in various ways Johnson has displayed throughout his career (except in the humble pie period of his vice-presidency) the usual attitudes of one who, if he were in a position to indulge the dark side of his nature, would be something of an *El Supremo*. The fact that Johnson is an insecure man, and in some ways even a shy man, probably heightens the pleasure of the prospect.

Eighteen years ago he forecast the role he apparently sees himself in today. In a speech to the Senate on March 9, 1949, he predicted that the precious last-ditch fighters for freedom against a tyrannical president would be a stubborn minority in the Senate. Tyranny from whence? "A man elevated to the office of the President has virtually unlimited powers of influence over his countrymen. His own personality is a force of great impact upon all the people of the nation and, in fact, upon the people of the world. Add to those powers directly his, all those less-conspicuous powers of his aides, his administrative agencies, and the multitude of channels which feel his influence, and you have a force no other representative government has ever entrusted for long to one man.

"If on occasion you grant to this titular head of government the further intoxicant of an overwhelming majority of loyal supporters in the legislative branch, then you have a force well-nigh irresistible. The distinctions between executive and legislative are difficult to preserve under such circumstances; mere memoranda become laws, and laws become mere memoranda."

The further intoxicant of an overwhelming majority of

loyal supporters in the legislative branch was his for three years, and there have been times when, raging against the feeble dissent within the Senate to his Vietnam policies or strolling down the White House corridor, head back, laughing, arm-in-arm with his pretended opposition, Everett Dirksen, he has indeed sounded intoxicated to some witnessing reporters.

Looking out over the crowd at Omaha last July, he drove another spike through his drawl and clubbed down all opposition. "Only twenty months ago," he shouted, "the people of America held a great national election and the people of forty-four states of this union . . . gave me a directive and voted me a majority for the presidency of this country . . . Now there are many, many, many who can recommend and advise and sometimes a few of them consent. But there is only *one* that has been chosen by the American people to decide."

The Chosen One! He feels himself to have become what he foresaw eighteen years ago, "a force well-nigh irresistible."

In that wildly wandering, historically cockeyed press conference on June 17, 1965, Johnson revealed his concept of his powers as president. He does not, he asserted, need Congress's approval in order to use the army *any*where and *any* way he wishes. He does not need, he said, the Tonkin Gulf resolution to authorize his waging a war in Vietnam. "The authority of the president is very clear and unquestioned without a resolution. The Commander in Chief has all the authority that I am exercising. Any time they [Congress] want to take the authority the resolution gives me, they can take it away. *It is just an expression and they just approved our position that we were taking.*"

Congress can approve but it cannot disapprove his actions? He did not always hold this unique interpretation of its powers of consent. He saw the legislative branch, while he was in it, as at least coequal with the executive branch, especially in setting military policy. Even if a nuclear test ban came out of the Geneva disarmament conference, Senate approval, said majority leader Johnson in April, 1960, might not follow. Today he views the legislative branch as the executive's tool, and he exultantly rubs it in that "the Congress approved . . . the determination of the president as Commander in Chief to take all—all—all necessary measures to repel any—any—any armed attack" anywhere. So much for Congress's traditional war-making powers.

To be able to say to one man go, and he goeth, and to another man come, and he cometh; to be able to get the same response from whole nations; the open-end whim, the chance to change one's mind, and then flip back again, without apologizing; to be as secretive, and petulant, and arbitrary as a Nero; to go forth and proclaim, and withdraw and countermandate—it's a great life for the well-to-do burgher's son from Johnson City, able to keep whole kingdoms on edge.

How else does one explain Johnson's complete lack of a policy, a fundamental directive, a basic tone, a skeletal ethic for treating with other nations? "We are living in a world with 120 nations," he said shortly after becoming president, "and we have got 120 foreign policies." This was a conservative estimate. He is the mad genius of the *ad hoc*.

In the early 1950's he was sounding like a Dr. Strangelove, ready to drop The Bomb on Moscow and be done with it. Once we were in the Korean War he wanted to plunge in, get it over with, globally, plan world-wide military strategy and then lock horns with Russia. "How tragic, how horrible it would be for the free world or the West to squander its young manhood in futile, indecisive little wars before the real enemy is engaged," he said on December 12, 1950. Later he warned Russia, "We are tired of fighting your stooges. We will no longer sacrifice our young men on the altar of your conspiracies. *The next aggression will be the last* . . .

*We will strike back, not just at your satellites but at you.
We will strike back with all the dreaded might that is within
our control and it will be a crushing blow."*

That raging was done on November 12, 1951. Three
months later he was again ready to bomb. "We should announce, I believe, that *any* act of aggression, *any*where, by
any Communist forces, *will be regarded as an act of aggression by the Soviet Union.* We should keep strength ready,
the strength we are now building. If *any*where in the world
—by *any* means, *open or concealed*—Communism trespasses
upon the soil of the free world, *we should unleash all the
power at our command upon the vitals of the Soviet Union.*
That is the policy we should build toward. That is the
policy we should maintain—for one year, for five years, for
fifteen years." Johnson is unable, fortunately in this case,
to maintain a policy for one year, much less fifteen, or Vietnam could easily be construed as excuse to "unleash all the
power at our command upon the vitals of the Soviet Union,"
or Peking.

Controlled by Kennedy's sanity, Johnson at least publicly
was able to act like he accepted the close and present danger
of Russian missiles in Cuba with the appearance of equa-
nimity. Late in 1962, in response to critics who said Kennedy
should blockade Cuba, Johnson said that "stopping a Russian ship is an act of war . . . Some people have more guts
than brains. We're still trying to explain our sending troops
to Nicaragua." Such temperance was mere parroting of
Kennedy; his *own* feelings he expressed in the secret councils at the White House, where, just before the 1962 elections, while others who sat around the table were preoccupied with dread thoughts of a possible war-triggering error,
Johnson—and Johnson alone—coolly suggested that a tough
line in Cuba would sure help the Democratic candidates
get elected.

On his own again as president he reverted to an unmistakable militarism, though this depends considerably on whether he is in a campaign year. In a presidential year he is a dove; in 1960 he said Nixon was wrong when he "made a hot-headed proposal that American soldiers should be sent to fight in the jungle" of Vietnam. Johnson's peace-keeping remarks of 1964 have, justifiably, been tied like empty cans to the tail he now says he will not "tuck and run" with. Two months before the election he vowed he would start dropping bombs "only as a last resort" and with the awareness that bombing North Vietnam would be "likely to involve American boys in a war in Asia with 700 million Chinese."

But the election safely past, Johnson again began practicing the fast draw. By April 17, 1965, he was ready to announce that by God, no matter what fire it brought on our heads in return, "whatever the risk and whatever the cost," he was ready—as in 1951 and 1952—to go all the way. "If the price of ending aggression is blood and men, we are ready to pay that price." He seems far more emotionally receptive to the idea of war than any of his recent predecessors: Kennedy, the Navy officer of heroic exploits; Eisenhower, the General of the Hour; Truman, the brassy artillery captain. Johnson has nothing to put beside those records.

A hundred years ago, they say, grandpa Sam Ealy Johnson had his horse shot out from under him at the Battle of Galveston. If it really happened, he was the last of the Johnsons to spend much time in the vicinity of unfriendly shot and shell. Daddy Sam Ealy, Jr., spent World War I farming and serving in the Texas legislature, where he made several speeches urging folks to temper their patriotism with understanding for those who did not feel so ill toward Germany (there were quite a few Germans in his district, and some of them liked the Old Country). And then came Lyndon, who, with the exception of one month in the South Seas and one day within sight of the enemy, spent

World War II either behind a Navy desk in San Francisco or back on his old beat in Congress. Between Johnson's straggly military record and his rampant militarism there may, of course, be some causal connection; a headlong drive to compensate, perhaps.

In any event, when the people handed him the mace in 1964, Johnson resumed his character of international wildness. Joseph Kraft specified Johnson's "capacity for immoderation" as "the real source of uneasiness about the President." Kraft, who is not given to sensationalism, believes that because "power excites him, and success even more" and because "he is subject to self-intoxication," there is nothing comfortable in the thought that we are "living in a delicate world under the direction of a leader capable of excess." This sounds a great deal as if he were speaking of the Goldwater many feared in 1964, but it is the much more dangerous Johnson of 1964 who was capable of disguising his intemperance in that campaign. Five years before his race for the presidency he had said in a speech, "I remember twenty years ago—in 1940—a great American president called me to the White House. He said, 'Lyndon, I have accepted an engagement for you—to keynote the convention of Young Democrats at Louisville, Kentucky. What I want you to tell those young people is this: there will be no danger to freedom in America *if young Americans are as fanatical about freedom as Hitler's young Germans are about Nazism.*' " He added, "This I believe remains true today."

Five years earlier he had given another excellent clue to the actions that could have been anticipated from him in Vietnam: "Yet there is a very clear conclusion we can all draw," he said in a Senate speech on May 11, 1955, "there are only two alternatives to winning the cold war—hot war or slavery." Two years before that, he had made much the same sanguine prediction: "It is foolish to talk of avoiding war," he said. "We are already in a war—a major war . . .

Someday, somewhere, some way there must be a clear-cut settlement between the forces of freedom and the forces of Communism."

Johnson's predilection for the strongman role has rendered him incapable of effective cooperation with other countries on a multilateral basis; if he can dominate them, very well, but he will not work as a coequal with them. Thus on December 10, 1963, when he was confronted with the question of whether to recognize a military junta in the Dominican Republic, he summoned Humphrey, Morse, Fulbright, Dirksen, Under Secretary Ball, Hickenlooper, Valenti, and Manatos to the Cabinet Room and asked for opinions. They were all for recognizing the junta, except Morse, who advised Johnson: "You should call in your democratic friends in Latin America and get their advice. You should call in the president of Chile, the old president of Colombia and the new president, the former president of Venezuela, Betancourt, and the new president, the old president of Costa Rica and the new president. You should call in the president of Peru, Terry, former Governor Muñoz Marin of Puerto Rico and the president of Mexico.

"If you had them here, they would be unanimously opposed to recognizing the junta. If you recognize the junta, you will cause more coups. You're just buying trouble."

After the meeting broke up, Johnson called Morse into a side office and said he wondered if he were doing right but that he felt he would have to follow the advice of the State Department. This kind of apology has led some senators to pity Johnson as "a captive of the 'classic wisdom' of the State Department," in Senator McGovern's words. He is not captive; he has always favored the strong military dictatorship over the weak but reform-motivated democratic regimes in Latin America. The last military take-over in Argentina was hardly announced before he had given it recognition; financial aid was promptly offered the Castelo

Branco military junta in Brazil. In Mexico City in the spring of 1966, he said, "despots are not welcome in this hemisphere," yet he has co-operated with every right-wing despot in the hemisphere.

Typical of his response to struggling democrats was his stirring up of the Senate by introducing a resolution opposing Colonel Arbenz, who was *elected* President of Guatemala in the early 1950's and who tried to take some of the United Fruit Company's idle farm lands and redistribute it among the peasants; in the United Nations that great patriotic puritan Henry Cabot Lodge, who is now bringing Johnsonian Democracy to the Vietnamese, fought back Arbenz' appeals for help; that sort of thing kept up until Arbenz was overthrown by a CIA-directed armed attack.

Ike must have had a miserable time coping with Johnson in times of international stress. He hints at this in his book *Waging Peace,* when he recollects that:

> These encounters also revealed something about the character and interests of the legislators. Sam Rayburn, for example, was always anxious to make certain that the United States would do everything possible to negotiate. Senator Lyndon Johnson, on the other hand, appeared to be anxious to be able to take some action, visible to the world, to indicate we had—or the Senate had—strengthened our Armed Forces.

This was apropos an incident in 1959, during which Ike had to stroke Lyndon's head and soothe him by "reiterating my confidence" that the U.S. had enough atom bombs not only to obliterate Russia but to choke the entire world in fallout.

Johnson was always talking about a hell-for-leather Hoot Gibson approach to settling world affairs. "There's an old saying down in Texas," he once told the Senate, "if you know you are right, just keep on coming and no gun can stop you," which, whatever the soundness of the advice for a saloon brawl, somehow struck some senators as inadequate for guidance in negotiating with other countries.

It is not just talk, but a style of action and a conscious style. Remarking on Johnson's sensitivity to allusions to the Kennedy style, a Johnson acquaintance told Ed Lahey of the Knight Newspapers Washington Bureau, "During the Dominican crisis, the President gritted his teeth and said, 'I shove it down the throats of the Communists in Santo Domingo—that's my style.'"

Mrs. Johnson once put it another way: "Lyndon is unrelenting."

* * *

To make the conspicuous assumption that Johnson is temperamentally capable of plunging into any conflict still does not explain *why* he would want to. The answer to that comes again from his background, not from any ideological logic.

Knowing from long experience that the best way to pay off campaign backers is via the military pork barrel, he went instinctively to the biggest pork barrel of them all, war, to keep a nation working and prosperous and content with his administration.

It was the natural thing for him to do. If you were a cactus-patch politician who had moved into the Washington stream during the days when FDR was proving the invincibility of a combined welfare-war program; if you were the shrewd kind of mechanic who quickly caught on to the gimmickry of the Roosevelt program without picking up the philosophy behind it; if you, furthermore, were convinced, and wisely so, that this nation would put up with anything but joblessness; if your long experience in office had convinced you that the easiest way to prime the pump was through defense spending; and if coupled to that was a basic disposition to "shove it down the throats" of your selected victim—wouldn't you probably hunt up a nicely-paced drawn-out war as just the ticket to prosperity? A war too far removed from sight and understanding to be successfully criticized by more than the intellectuals; with a race of people that is unknown to most Americans and therefore unlikely to attract much sympathy; rising out of a dispute that was fuzzed and clouded by old, esoteric treaty alliances? Vietnam was perfect.

Johnson needed a war that would last a while. A half dozen Dominican Republic-type flurries would not do. He needed a war that could be held in check, yet stretched to any desirable term, escalated and de-escalated at will. For an example of this need: when members of the superelite Business Council held their fall meeting at Hot Springs, Virginia, they predicted that toward the end of 1967 there would be a sharp slowdown of the economy; indeed, a group of economists headed by Walter Hoadley, senior vice-president of the Bank of America, forecast virtually a halt in economic growth in the butt months of 1967. They based their pessimism on the belief that the war might then be over. Neil McElroy, chairman of the board of Procter & Gamble and Ike's Secretary of Defense, said with simple fatalism: "Wars do come to an end—or get hot." Now, at this point, if Johnson had been fighting in, say, Cuba, he couldn't have bluffed the issue; but Vietnam is beautifully plastic. Five days after the business leaders made their sad forecast, the Pentagon made a forecast of its own, calculated to put the business community at ease: pay no attention to the rising toll of enemy troops, the Pentagon said in prominent news stories, the United States is still in for a long, hard war.

The manipulative quality of the Vietnam conflict is the only logical reason for our being there. It is ridiculous to think that Johnson would go half way around the world to imbed the nation in the muck of a militarily hopeless war— as his administration has conceded it to be—simply to save from some nebulous brand of Communism a piece of real estate that has been of little exploitative value (not, of course, our reason for wanting to save an Asian or South American country) to anybody but rubber companies. If we paid $500 an acre for the land—which is more than Johnson's friends are paying per acre for the proposed parkland across from the LBJ ranch—we could *buy* North *and* South Vietnam for $40 billion, or considerably less than we will spend in two years to fight over half of it.

If Johnson is so terribly eager to save some little patch from Communism why does he start with one that requires de-moth-balling a hundred Liberty ships? Why not start with one that is only 90 miles away? Or how about Mexico, a wadeable distance, which has a great many socialistic traits and, since it virtually disbanded its army years ago, would be easy to conquer, despoil and rebuild (only 300 miles from Brown & Root's headquarters in Houston)? Or if, by some strange reversal of character, he preferred to clean out a small pot of fascism, there is always Haiti within barging distance. A little farther, but much closer than Vietnam, is the fascistic government of Argentina, newly established over the complete destruction of the university system and all pretense of freedom. (LBJ *did* say he "regretted" this.)

There are many more convenient places for Johnson, Global Reformer, to begin; but of course Vietnam is much more preferable *because* it is so far away, so difficult to deal with, so difficult, with its bogs and jungles, to fight over and through.

Further indication of the mercenary motive behind Johnson's desire to save Vietnam is that it did not come about until he was President. If a country was worth saving from Communism in 1964, it must have been worth saving in 1954, yet in that earlier year, when Eisenhower was confronted with the proposal that he send troops to Vietnam, he said he would not do it without support from Congress.

Johnson advised him against it.* If salvation in 1964, why not in 1961? Robert Trumbull's report to *The New York Times* of Vice-President Johnson's trip to Asia that year records that "according to accounts of Mr. Johnson's conferences by persons who were present, the idea of sending American troops to fight on behalf of the governments under siege by the Communists in South Vietnam and Thailand never came up for discussion. It had been discovered at a much earlier stage that the Asians questioned the desirability of bringing in white soldiers to fight Asians. The Asians were said to believe they had sufficient manpower to do the job alone if given the equipment and training."

If he advised Eisenhower against sending troops, and as Kennedy's emissary did not even bother to discuss sending troops, why did a massive buildup suddenly become so appealing? Idealism cannot supply the answer. Johnson has never been known to act out of idealism. He ballooned the war for a practical political reason: because now *he* had a personal interest in keeping the industrial-military pot boiling with profits. But first, the election. He had learned the method from Roosevelt: the promise not to send troops before the election, the plunge after. "We are not about to send American boys 9,000 or 10,000 miles away from home to do what Asian boys ought to be doing for themselves," he had said thirteen days before votes were cast in 1964. In three months he was bombing North Vietnam, the buildup was under way and a lasting prosperity was just around the corner.

There was, however, one awesome risk: China's 700 million, with nearly 20 million trained for war. On Septem-

---

* Nevertheless, this was such abnormal advice for Johnson to give that, possibly to put his metabolism back in balance, he railed against the British proposal to partition Vietnam as "a doctrine which smacks strongly of the appeasement at Munich" and he saw, or pretended to see, it as possibly "the beginning of the fall of all Southeast Asia . . ."

ber 28 and again on October 21 of the election year he had taken ominous note of that fact, adding, "We could get tied down in a land war in Asia very quickly if we sought to throw our weight around."

With the bombing of North Vietnam and the U.S. troop buildup, would the Chinese pour down and ruin everything? It could only end atomically and his name would be a curse. By June 17, 1965, there were 71,000 fighting American troops in the war, more than three times the number of the preceding December. If China put up with that many, Johnson knew he could inundate Vietnam with his troops. But there was dreadful danger in the escalation. Late in June, 1966, Merriman Smith of UPI said that Johnson's friends were very worried about his sleeping habits. He was waking at three and four in the morning, calling the White House intelligence center for a report on Vietnam, and then tossing sleeplessly the rest of the night. The *London Observer*'s correspondent noted the same effects: Johnson was "showing visible strain . . . working compulsively . . . his overwrought mind leaps from one subject to another . . ."

Then China had its internal flap, which seemed enough to keep it preoccupied for a time without seeking troubles elsewhere, and Johnson's ploy was home safe.

It was his very own war, his by creation and by bluff, and he deserved credit for the prosperity. One could sense his contentment. It was a rare speech thereafter that did not refer to the "longest period of uninterrupted prosperity in our history." There were still nuisance criticisms to deflect; it was unfortunate that 20 per cent of the Americans in Vietnam in 1965 came down with a venereal disease; it was regrettable that his construction friends had wasted an estimated $150 million; it was discouraging that an estimated 20 to 40 per cent of our aid supplies to Vietnam were stolen and wound up either on the black market or in the hands of the enemy; it was an inescapable unhappiness that four Vietnam civilians were killed by our troops for each Vietcong. But we reimburse, we recompense: an average of $35 per Vietnam killed, up to $85 for each rubber tree killed. Anyway, as anyone who is not "callous or timid" must know, these things are just the normal tediousness that one must put up with to save a country.

And, he promised, if Vietnam would hold still for the despoliation, he would later be around with the second-stage, the equally profitable stage of rebuilding, and he would make "the Mekong Delta bloom like the Tennessee Valley." Like the god Shiva, Johnson is both the destroyer and the preserver—acting on the omnipotence that there is pucka profit in both.

* *
* *

A large measure of Johnson's time in the Senate was expended in efforts to circumvent President Eisenhower's modest plans for curtailing the military. The establishment of NATO, the building of the atomic bomb by Russia, and finally the Korean conflict had all worked to establish events and an atmosphere in which, by the time Eisenhower came to office, it was extremely difficult to hold back the ambitions of the Pentagon; yet Eisenhower vowed that he would have "security with solvency" through what he called the "New Look" at military policy, which would include recalling many troops from overseas and a sharp reduction in troop numbers.

The death of Stalin and a much softer aspect in Eastern Europe made these goals appear reasonable and possible. Over the next two years Ike succeeded in cutting defense spending by $10 billion, despite heavy lobbying by the military. On May 19, 1953, Eisenhower went on radio to seek public support for his military economies, arguing that defense could not be founded on "sudden, blind responses to a series of fire-alarm emergencies, summoning us to amass forces and material with a speed that is heedless of cost, order and efficiency."

But the buildup of the Congressional hawks was under way. That was the year Johnson came to the Democratic leadership through the help of Richard Russell and Walter George, and Johnson was time and again to prove his gratitude not only to the Georgians personally but to the military clique inside and outside the Senate. To Eisenhower's original defense budget in 1955 was added $356 million to push the production of B-52 bombers. Most of the military airfields are in the South, and planes are needed to keep them open. For the 1957 budget, after George complained that "we are not keeping pace with the Russian air force" (later this was found to be false) $800 million for building B-52's was added to Ike's budget.

In 1958 Johnson showed that he considered the military, aside from its other virtues, to be a wonderful WPA-type outfit. In March, when there were 5.2 per cent unemployed in the nation, Johnson's only proposed solution was to step up military construction and procurement. He was quite open and unabashed in his military pump-priming. "I want the Senate to have assurances on behalf of the Senate Preparedness Committee," he said, "that we are going to continue to urge faster decisions on the Department of Defense. *These decisions would be followed by contracts which would do a great deal to put men and women back on the payrolls.*" Earlier in the year he had written Secretary of Defense Neil H. McElroy, urging more military construction "in areas where there is substantial unemployment." His letter mentioned nothing about assigning the construction on the basis of military needs.

His unabashed willingness to boondoggle sometimes reached almost comical proportions. When Russia sent up Sputnik in 1957, Johnson's Preparedness Subcommittee grabbed its shields and spears with loud clangor and alarums, and started an investigation to find out why the United States was lagging in space. The investigators came back with recommendations for strengthening the Strategic Air Force, strengthening the ground and naval forces, and stepping up the production of ballistic missiles—though there was no explanation of what this pump-priming in the midst of the 1957–58 recession had to do with space exploration.

At this point the generals and retired generals, the colonels and the retired colonels, the starred and eagled guerrilla lobbyists began to cluster under the Capitol dome and squirt through the Congressional office buildings in high-pressure streams. It was too much to keep secret, and few of the participants tried. It was all so open and successful that Johnson's friend, James J. Ling of Ling-Temco-Vought, Dallas—whose sales had been skidding—had even publicly urged a group of Southwestern business executives that they had better all get into the lobbying act; *he* was going to. Some of the peaceful congressmen were complaining, however, first in mutters and later in loud indignation. Newsmen asked Eisenhower about the munitions lobby. Did it actually exist? Was it effective? "Obviously," said Ike, "political and financial considerations" influenced defense decisions "aside from the strict military needs." Representative Hebert of Louisiana called for hearings, got them, and found that there were indeed swarms of retired officers working for defense contractors—186 for General Dynamics, 171 for Lockheed, 92 for North American Aviation, etc.— and that some of the larger Georgia aircraft companies had been flying high-ranking officers to the Bahamas for fun and games, and that the Air Force was privy to much of the wheeling and dealing of the contractors.

A bill to regulate the activities of retired officers passed the House. In the Senate, Johnson, giving the military establishment the last year of his allegiance as majority leader, saw that the bill was properly laid to rest without even a quiver of action.

*
*   *
*

One of the crispest accounts of the natural good luck that falls to military contractors who know Johnson concerns a Texas company.

Transport Company of Texas (T.C.T.) was awarded a "housekeeper" contract for the Kwajalein Island bases in a way that some people thought was queer. Because T.C.T. had made a "feasibility study" of the Kwajalein problem—at government expense and at a cost 50 per cent higher than they originally bid to do the study—a panel from the Bureau of Aeronautics recommended that the housekeeper contract be *negotiated* directly with T.C.T. rather than open it to competitive bidding. The company's "reputation" was given as one reason for the panel's decision; *Fortune* reporter Herbert Solow, who did much of the investigation into this shadowy episode, pointed out that although the company's record for turning out quality work was impeccable, its president, Edgar M. Linkenhoger, had once had to pay the government $200,000 to settle what had begun as a federal tax-fraud complaint. (One member of the panel that recommended Linkenhoger's company later went to work for him.)

But it wasn't long before news leaked out of what was happening; other companies began to complain and forced the Navy to call for bids after all. The Navy's capitulation showed little gracefulness. It gave the twelve responding companies a huge, complex stack of job specifications and allowed them only six days within which to submit bids. The bids were to embrace not only Kwajalein but were for housekeeper work on Guam and Midway also. No time was given for the other companies to inspect the job sites—as

T.C.T. had done—because the actual contract-letting was only eight days away.

The hardships being what they were, only six of the twelve companies bid on the work. Most of these were thrown out by the Navy panel as "unresponsive." Nevertheless, T.C.T. did not win the three-island bid. Pan American did.

T.C.T. had lost the war, it seemed, but not the battle; for at that juncture Rear Admiral Joseph Dodson, assistant chief for procurement, did an unusual thing. He broke up the award. Pan American, he said, had too much of the Navy's work already; besides the Navy had a "moral obligation" to T.C.T. because it had already done the government paid-for study. So he gave the Kwajalein contract to T.C.T. after all.

This flowered into a most profitable deal. When the contract was extended, the housekeeping costs shot up to $13.3 million, with T.C.T.'s total cut reaching the million dollar mark.

T.C.T. President Edgar Linkenhoger of Corpus Christi was an old, old friend of Lyndon Johnson. Another stockholder, John E. Lyle, Jr., served in Congress from 1945 to 1954, and throughout was a close ally of Johnson. The third major stockholder was oil man Sid Richardson, LBJ crony and faithful campaign contributor. Lyle and Linkenhoger were close political allies, too, of George Parr, in whose bailiwick Johnson received the desperately needed 87-vote majority that put him in the Senate in 1948.

No specific favoritism was ever tied to Johnson on this contract. But Sam Houston Johnson, Lyndon's brother, had worked for Linkenhoger as a "consultant" before moving on to Washington to join brother Lyndon's staff as a $16,000 clerk. His duties for Linkenhoger, he said, were confidential.

Reporter Solow said one Navy officer was told by a T.C.T. official during the dickering period, "We are in like

Flynn, because Linkenhoger is a good friend of Lyndon Johnson." Johnson denied even knowing the bidding or the contract-letting was taking place. Linkenhoger said, ". . . It's a hell of a long story. It's none of the public's business."

Franklin Jones, a wry East Texas lawyer who helped found *The Texas Observer,* is given credit for the maxim, "To understand Johnson, you have to get down to the Brown and Root of the thing." The mutual interests of B & R and Johnson are, of course, well known. Johnson claims credit for the establishment of the Corpus Christi naval air training base, and the shipbuilding yards at Houston and nearby Orange in World War II; but he has denied any personal persuasion in getting the Corpus Christi contract for B & R, or the contracts to build 359 destroyer escorts at the Texas shipyards, or the very profitable defense construction jobs in Texas and Spain and in the South Pacific.

It would be unreasonable to conclude that (1) because Johnson has for years been a powerful man in Washington and (2) because Brown & Root has during the same period become probably the largest construction company in the world, partly as a result of great defense and other federal contracts, both in this country and abroad, this adds up to something crooked. A politician must get his campaign money somewhere, so why not from Brown & Root, as Johnson has done for more than a quarter of a century? Brown & Root probably does as conscientious a job for the government as the next contractor.

Still . . . it is worth noting that Lyndon Johnson, George Brown and the late Herman Brown made an awfully effective team. For instance, there was the little matter of the National Aeronautics and Space Administration (NASA) Space Center in Houston. Why build it out in the middle of that great dreariness, twenty-two miles from the heart of Houston? Why, indeed, build it in Texas at all rather than in Florida, where billions of dollars already had been poured into developing the nation's launching pad; or in Houston rather than at one of the other twenty cities that wanted the NASA operations so much?

The answer to that lies in Johnson's friendship with George Brown. At the time the NASA site was selected for Houston, and Brown & Root was chosen to build the Space Center, Johnson was head of the Space Council. But also important in the decision was Congressman Albert Thomas of Houston, chairman of the appropriations subcommittee controlling NASA's budget. The late Thomas was a classmate of George Brown's at Rice University and they were very close over the years; Brown established a chair of political science at Rice in Thomas's honor. Brown is chairman of the board of trustees at Rice and has been for a long time. Humble Oil Company, Texas' largest oil company and now a subsidiary of Jersey Standard, has always looked upon Rice as "its" school: the late Harry Weiss, who ran Humble, was on the Rice board of trustees; Walter Fondren, Sr., a founder of Humble, donated the money for the Fondren Library at Rice; Weiss donated the money for establishing Rice's department of geology; a large proportion of each Rice graduating class used to go on the Humble payroll (this is not so true any longer). Johnson's high regard for the oil industry of Texas, and especially for the big companies such as Humble, is of course a matter of heavy record in the Senate.

So there was considerable satisfaction in the hearts of Johnson, Thomas, Brown, Rice, and Humble when NASA came to Houston. Of course, there was some profit, too, in addition to Brown & Root's cost-plus-fee on the $90 million project. Humble Oil gave the 1,000 acres (through Rice) that the government accepted as the nucleus of the Manned Spacecraft Center homestead. Measuring it by present-day land prices, this was at least a $5 million gift. But Humble was not exactly hurt by this benevolence; it is the largest landowner in that area (one knowledgeable resident estimated Humble owns a minimum of 50,000 acres in the vicinity) and with the coming of the Space Center, this land's value went up to more than five times what it had been. And prices have just begun to climb.

Too, the presence of the Space Center has brought new life and value to Humble's possessions along the ship channel only a few miles away, and here Humble has built a large industrial park, Bayport. This ship channel was touted to the public as one of the main reasons the Space Center was brought to Houston: easy access to the Gulf for transporting giant spacecraft. But that was, at best, mistaken propaganda. There never were any plans for blasting off from Houston, and therefore no need for the ship channel.

One other to profit by the Space Center development was Jack Valenti, former employee of Humble Oil and more recently President Johnson's aide, whose advertising firm had the contract for the nearby Clear Lake City housing development. Rice University, too, did all right. It has become almost an arm of NASA. It is the first university in the country with a space science department giving space science degrees; it is the first university in the country given contracting powers by NASA; and it has received several million dollars for satellite manufacturing.

All of this makes George Brown very proud, and doubtless makes Johnson proud, too; the LBJ pork barreling has often been quite openly justified in the name of science, education, and most often, patriotism; and, of course, no good American will quarrel with *that.*

Other close friends of Johnson's, men such as H. B. (Pat) Zachry of San Antonio, another multimillionaire builder, have earned great wealth from federal contracts, but none equals the patriotic-scientific-educational good luck of Brown & Root. For another example, there's Mohole, although

Mohole, as the B&R-LBJ teamwork sometimes does, developed into a disturbing affair, rife with speculations of favoritism, waste, and political kickback.

When Project Mohole—which was supposed to discover a way to dig through the earth's crust under the ocean about 100 miles from Honolulu—was dreamed up at a breakfast of geophysicists nine years ago, it was thought that it could be completed for between $5 million and $20 million.

At first the project had about it the pure aura of research. But shortly after Phase I was completed—that is, the $1.5 million test run that proved the feasibility of drilling in the bottom of the ocean from a free-floating vehicle—the scientists were pushed into a secondary role and businessmen took over. One congressman later charged that direction of the project was given to "high-powered businessmen who had never drilled a hole bigger than a cesspool anywhere in the world before," but this wasn't quite accurate. Brown & Root had dug holes deeper than a cesspool; they had drilled many oil wells.

With the accent now sharply shifted from science to business, the costs of the project shot up dramatically. The National Science Foundation (NSF), which was supposed to be supervising the Brown & Root work, was muffing the job. Periodically some official of NSF would pop out of his office to proclaim publicly, with a long face, that the costs were rising a bit sharper than anticipated. The last of these pop-out estimates was $127 million. Things were clearly out of control.

From the beginning the National Science Foundation's role in this was smudged. The NSF is not set up to administer programs, but only to hand out money for basic research. For some reason, it stepped out of its traditional role—possibly, some suspected, to act as a buffer for certain wheeler-dealers—and became the administrator of Mohole, a job which it did with remarkable clumsiness. It ran into trouble in 1962, and probably laid the groundwork for the eventual Congressional execution of Mohole, when by a secret and widely criticized arrangement it awarded the contract to Brown & Root, although a panel of experts had recommended two other firms. Brown & Root's bid was not the low bid. In fact, it was 50 per cent higher than the low bid.

At first the NSF refused to reveal the contractual maneuverings, saying this would not be "in the public interest." Only after the *Los Angeles Times* and California Senator Kuchel raised a national howl and President Kennedy intervened and ordered the information made public did most of the hanky-panky come out. *Most* of it, not all.

For its work, Brown & Root was guaranteed $1.7 million, which is a nice fee, but not much compared to its annual income of more than $300 million. The great profit to Brown & Root would have come from another source, which is discussed later. Senator Kuchel said "politically powerful" selfish interests had intervened on behalf of Brown & Root. Nobody ever learned for sure who the "politically powerful" interest was, but there were a lot of similar guesses.

By 1966 Congress was tired of the disappearing act, watching a steadily growing stream of funds go down what one called Operation Rathole, and when it was revealed that George Brown and his three married daughters and their husbands had given $25,000 to the President's Club, and that just a few weeks later Johnson made a personal appeal to Congress to appropriate more Mohole funds, Congress used the coincidence as an excuse to kill the project.

George Brown said it was "ridiculous" to think that the contributions were connected with Mohole, and he was right. It is ridiculous, as everyone in Texas knows, to think that after all the money Brown has sunk into his political career, Johnson would be much impressed by another $25,000. Anyway, Brown would get his fixed fee, whether the project continued or not. He wasn't interested in that. But Brown & Root was very interested—as was the entire oil industry—in learning how to drill deep under the ocean from a floating rig.

Johnson's support of the project was a payoff, all right, but on a much broader scale. First of all it was a payoff to the oil industry. There is far more oil under the oceans than remains to be discovered on the continents. It will cost many millions to develop the floating platforms and the drilling tools to explore for this oil. No industry can better afford to pay its own way, but why not let the government pay for it? Exactly. And thus Mohole.

Secondly, it was a specific payoff to Brown & Root, but *not* just in the percentage-of-cost of one project. When the National Science Foundation was being criticized for favoring Brown & Root over lower bidders, who were oil companies, NSF director Alan T. Waterman excused their action by saying that they had not wanted to give any oil company a competitive advantage over the rest of the industry by what it learned in the Mohole Project. His implication was that Brown & Root had nothing to do with the oil industry and could not profit from learning how to dig ocean wells.

Later, uncommented on as to its Mohole significance, every share of stock in Brown & Root (George Brown stayed on as president) was purchased by Halliburton Company of Dallas, the world's biggest supplier of oil well services—cementing, formation testing, fracturing, the works. With the secrets of the Mohole technique in hand, Brown & Root (Halliburton) would be really ready to take command.

Oddly, the vast benefits to the oil industry—and to those like Brown & Root who are not only participators in the industry but service it—were hardly mentioned in Congressional debate. Only Senator Moss of Utah seemed inclined toward candor in this matter. "The engineering effort being expended on Project Mohole," he said, "will not bring scientific knowledge alone. The knowledge gained in developing new tools, techniques, and equipment will increase the depth capability of the oil industry by 40 per cent . . . The new drilling technology developed for Project Mohole will find immediate application wherever drilling, coring, and sampling are done, whether on land or sea." That's what Mohole turned out to be; the thing backed by the "politically powerful" interest and/or Johnson, and on which the government had spent $55 million before Congress called it quits, was nothing more than a laboratory for the oil industry.

But Brown & Root had no time to mourn the loss of Mohole, which George Brown called "a drop in the bucket." It was already deeply involved in one of its great patriotic ventures, this one perhaps the most patriotic of all—building South Vietnam into a suitable arena for war.

For this venture it joined with Raymond International of New York; Morrison-Knudsen of Boise, Idaho; and J. A. Jones Construction Company of Charlotte, N. C. Jointly known as RMK/BRJ, they set out to do their bit for the Johnson Doctrine, and for a healthy slice of a $900 million contract. It was the largest contract of its type ever awarded, which is not surprising, inasmuch as most wartime work of this sort is done by military construction units—the Army Corps of Engineers and the Navy Seabees—at a fraction of the cost. The contract was awarded in 1962. Like Mohole, it started small—$15.3 million. By the time Congress caught on to what RMK/BRJ and friends were up to, the contracts— for everything from a new embassy to miles of airstrips— had crept past the three-quarter *billion* dollar level.

Just as Johnson had warned against making the Korean War a "bookkeeping war," somebody apparently had decided not to make this conflict a bookkeeping war either. For the first two years, the giant consortium was audited by one man; then, between June, 1964, and September, 1965, this staff was increased to two Navy auditors. Between the latter date and January, 1966, when some disgruntled con-

gressmen moved in, the auditing was done by six Air Force
officers and one Army enlisted clerk. They were, of course,
swamped. The Government Accounting Office found that
they had actually looked over only about one-seventh of the
claimed cost reimbursements, and the backlog was increasing daily. At this point, the total waste is anybody's guess.
Some congressmen believe the consortium has already lost
or wasted—or watched, as the Vietnamese stole—$125 million
in materials.

Bertram L. Perkins, resident chief of the consortium,
agreed that they had "recruited people with a butterfly net"
for the construction work. Roughly one-tenth the work
force, or about 4,500, are said to be Vietcong; and the Defense Department has not denied it. For RMK/BRJ it
doesn't matter; the cost-plus contract is as profitable working with Vietcong as with anyone else.

A certain kind of profit, in short, will follow those who
follow Johnson, as the Vietnam war proves once again, but
really in no unique way. Defense contracts have risen more
than 30 per cent in the past year; of these Texas reaped
a lusty $2.5 billion. For Christmas of 1966, the Pentagon
placed $186 million orders for aircraft fuel. Chemical com-
panies—in which the Houston area abounds—had sold more
than $10 million in defoliants for use in Vietnam by mid-
1966. But itemizing the good times is endless. Aircraft, rubber, oil, petrochemicals, cotton—*every*thing was doing just
fine, like Lyndon had planned. "Let us," he said in Bangkok,
"renounce the works of death—and take up the tasks of the
living." Beautiful thoughts coupled with beautiful profits
equals the Johnson Doctrine in Asia.

* * *

To wage a war, a strong man must have an easily enlarged
army and a marketable provocation. Johnson has managed
both the men and the timely fuss with adroitness, but of the

two, his deft outmaneuvering of all efforts to kill or change the draft has been the most masterful.

By 1964 there was developing around the nation a great wave of resentment toward the draft. Columnists, editorial writers, specialty reporters, professors, and politicians were beginning to talk seriously of whether the draft was really necessary and, if so, if it couldn't be radically changed and improved. The previous summer President Kennedy had ordered the Pentagon to review draft provisions with an eye to possible major changes by 1967. The Pentagon was ordered especially to weigh the possibility of abandoning the draft.

A few days after Congress reassembled in January, 1964, Senator Kenneth Keating of New York introduced a bill to create a fourteen-member Presidential Commission on the administration of the draft act. Four similar bills, along with an exact duplicate of the Keating bill, were introduced in the House on March 3. And on March 11, Representative Thomas Curtis of Missouri introduced a bill to create a select joint congressional committee on American manpower and national security.

By now it was clear to everyone in Washington that the old draft was in trouble. When mossbacks like Bennett and veteran liberals like Gruening join forces on the same reform bill, something is going to move. The support for it was not only bipartisan but radically bi-ideological: the cosigners were Republicans Case, Cooper, Kuchel, Scott, Beall, Javits, Morton, Bennett, Allott, Miller, Prouty and Simpson; Democrats Gruening, Douglas, Neuberger, Nelson, McGovern and Bartlett.

The proposed Keating Commission would exist for two years, hold public hearings, and come to a fast and public conclusion. It would leave the control of the draft in the hands of Congress, where constitutionally it belonged.

Just as the steam was being poured on, President Johnson

cut it off. He didn't want Congress obstructing his plans for 1965, when he would increase the manpower in Vietnam fourteenfold. In an April 18 press conference, he announced that he was launching a comprehensive executive review of the draft, including the possibility that it might be eliminated within *ten years*. The study would be conducted secretly by the Department of Defense. Just why the Pentagon needed to embark on *another* study, when under orders from Kennedy it had been conducting one for nearly a year already, was not made clear by Johnson, but it was generally accepted as an obvious maneuver to kill the congressional study, and it succeeded.

The public has a short memory of congressional acrobatics or it might have been startled at Johnson's turnabout on this occasion. Here he was turning the decision on the draft problem over to the very men who have the most vested interest in preserving it, and expanding it. When Eisenhower had tried to pull that very thing in 1959, he was thoroughly denounced by leaders of the Senate for attempting to pre-empt Congressional duties. Senator Richard Russell, lavishly praised by Johnson for his wisdom, said in response to Ike's move: "Congress has the responsibility. It will not escape it by giving to the executive department the power to appoint a commission to review the matter. Is the President likely to appoint a commission which will support the view of Congress and will be somewhat critical of his position? Or will it not be more likely to sustain the view of the President? It is about time that we got away from attempting to meet every problem by the appointment of a commission . . . Usually we end by getting the same recommendations from the commissions that we have had from the Department of Defense on the same subject. It is really a new way of asking for the views of the Department of Defense." Apparently both Johnson and Russell had changed their minds in the intervening five years.

Eleven days after Johnson's press-conference axe had fallen on the 1964 Congressional reformers, Senator Russell wrote Defense Secretary McNamara asking his opinion of the Keating bill. McNamara, to no one's surprise, replied that the Keating study wasn't necessary because all the necessary data would be collected by the Pentagon in its study and, in short, "the establishment of the proposed Congressional commission would not, at this time, best serve the purposes for which it is designed."

Having booted any responsibility for a draft change or even a close look at the draft beyond the election year he was in, Johnson turned savagely on Goldwater, who had launched his campaign with the suggestion that "we could do away with the draft now and proceed on a voluntary basis," if military pay was increased. It was, Johnson implied, one helluva cowardly way to talk.

After the Pentagon "study" dragged on for more than two years, a new wave of criticism splashed across the White House. With the stepped-up quotas for Vietnam came charges that the draft favored young men with enough money to go to college, picked on the poor in general and on the Negroes in particular, and was administered unfairly, chaotically, and inconsistently by local draft boards. These same criticisms were being voiced in Congress where new demands were made for a Congressional probe of the draft. Some Congressmen suggested that youth be allowed to substitute a hitch in the Peace Corps.

Johnson got wind of one serious proposal by Senator Gruening to stop draftees from being sent to Vietnam in August, 1965, and moved in to cut it off. He did not want Congress to get a taste of running the selective service program. Looking back on the episode now, Gruening wryly acknowledges that Johnson outfoxed him. He remembers the method like this: "I had made a speech praising the Johnson domestic policy, an unremarkable speech that found its place amongst a barrel of the same kind of pap that goes into the Record every day. But the next morning Johnson called me at home and praised me fulsomely. I should have suspected then that something was wrong. Johnson said he would like to talk with me about Vietnam. He invited me to a briefing the next Monday. Bundy and Maxwell Taylor and McNamara and the usual brassy turn-out was there, and Johnson told them that he had consulted with me and would again (he hadn't consulted with me in any way)."

With that opening wedge of flattery, Johnson called Gruening back to the White House a couple of days later to discuss Vietnam. "I asked the President not to interrupt me for ten minutes. I didn't want him punching my chest or slapping my knee or doing those other things he likes to do to keep you rattled and off balance. So he sat very patiently and listened to me for about nine minutes and then I said I was going to stick an amendment on the appropriations bill the next day that would forbid the sending of draftees to Vietnam without Congressional consent. Johnson threw up his hands and said, 'Oh no, don't do that. If we don't have the boys out of there by January, you can do it.' But he definitely left the impression with me that the boys *would* be out by January. Later I learned that this was not his true expectations and that more draftees were being sent in even as we talked." Having got what he wanted out of Gruening, he didn't invite his "counselor" back.

But with the antidraft movement appearing to be approaching an effective momentum from other directions in the spring of 1966, Johnson pushed the Pentagon on stage, finally, with the results of its study—more than a year past the deadline Johnson had set. It had spent $1 million and had assigned thirty-five men full time to the study; but when a résumé of its investigation (but no definitive report) was finally issued, it contained no data other than a few

charts. It came to no conclusions other than a flat and unsupported claim that the draft was still needed.

It was so obviously a hoked-up job that even Johnson
scarcely gave it a second look. Instead, on July 3 he announced—insisting that it was only "coincidental" to the
rising complaints from the public—that he was appointing
still *another* study group, this one to be called the National
Advisory Commission on Selective Service (NACSS).

Loud raspberries followed the announcement. John Mc-
Claughry, an aide to Senator Prouty, summarized the
thoughts of these skeptics: "Johnson may not be the inven-
tor of the phantom committee, but he is rapidly becoming
a master of its use. Several Congressmen or Senators—it
doesn't matter of which party—get interested in what they
believe to be a serious problem. They agitate for a serious
study effort, by a select committee of Congress or by a special presidential commission. Bills are introduced, speeches
delivered, letters sent to the President stating the urgency
of the matter and pleading for its support.

"But for reasons of his own the President does not want
the issue aired. The solution: with much fanfare the President establishes a phantom committee. On paper, the committee makes a frontal assault on the problem it faces. In
practice, the committee does little or nothing. Its main purpose is to quiet the demands of Congress by assuring the
public that something is being done."

Such is the skepticism of sophisticated young men after
they have lingered in the shadow of the Capitol for a time.
How could he call the National Advisory Committee on
Selective Service a "phantom committee" when it is made
up of such people as George E. Reedy, Jr., Johnson's former
press aide; Warren G. Woodward, now vice-president of
American Airlines but a former employee of Johnson's at
KTBC and a campaign manager for Johnson in the old
days; James Henry McCrocklin, president of Johnson's alma

mater, Southwest Texas State College; Oveta Culp Hobby, president of the *Houston Post* and a very intimate political ally of Johnson's for two decades; as well as such renowned "doves" as John McCone, former director of the CIA, and Thomas S. Gates, former Secretary of Defense?

The NACSS was asked to come in with some conclusions by June, 1967, when the Selective Service Act must be renewed. Thus, by the time this third study of the draft is completed, four years will have elapsed since Kennedy got it all started, and the public is not yet in possession of any investigative details.

At his next press conference after announcing the appointment of the NACSS, Johnson was asked, "What is your appraisal of the defects and shortcomings of the military draft as it is now administered?" Johnson refused to say. He had seven months of the Kennedy-Pentagon study to refer to as well as the two-year study which *he* had jockeyed through the Pentagon, but he said he had no answers and that, anyway, "I don't want to prejudge the study that is in the process of being made." In other words, three years of study had taught him nothing, but perhaps a fourth year would. It was a transparent stall past another election.

Data supporting the Johnson-Pentagon study, from which the rather meaningless résumé was made, remains classified in Pentagon files, if it exists at all. Congressmen who have asked to see it have been refused. Eventually, of course, Johnson will elaborately ask Congress to take back the problem he filched from it in the beginning. Now that he has built a war of such size that it will guarantee its own supply of manpower, he needn't be worried by reform. He is over the hump of belligerency, and there is no horizon behind. The hoax of the super-secret Pentagon study and the appendage fraud of the pro-Johnson citizens panel have allowed him to stall as long as he needed. Now if Congress wants to take on the problem of manpower fairplay in the middle of a war, all right, he may be willing to turn back the problem just as he found it, untouched.

* * *

The provocation which Johnson used to seize the war-making powers from Congress occurred on August 4, 1964, under circumstances that have never been fully detailed by military authorities. There was considerable open discussion by non-Communist officials at the United Nations as to the possibility that the episode was contrived merely for the sake of supplying Johnson with the excuse he had long waited for.

Only ten days before this reputed attack, Johnson had said, "the United States seeks no wider war" but that "provocation could force a response"—an interesting forecast of what was about to occur, as there had been no rash of provocations that could explain such a comment.

General Khanh, South Vietnam's dictator at that time, had been demanding that the United States carry the war into North Vietnam; there had been street rioting by South Vietnamese making the same demands of this nation. It might seem strange that South Vietnam, whose 400,000-man army could not contain 25,000 Vietcong, considered itself in a position to demand anything from anybody, but such was the case.

Shortly before the "provocations" that launched Johnson merrily into the north, General Khanh and U.S. Ambassador Taylor met at a party at a country estate outside Saigon and —according to Senator Morse—"stories coming out of that meeting were to the effect that they had resolved their differences." What was the agreement? Perhaps that was explained by what happened next.

On July 31, South Vietnam PT boats bombed two North Vietnam islands in the Tonkin Gulf about three miles off the mainland. U.S. officials in Saigon knew it was going to take place but failed to notify officers of the 7th Fleet, some of whose ships were patrolling the area. Morse stated in the Senate that secret testimony later given before the Foreign Relations Committee was a "complete admission" that the Pentagon also knew the bombing of the islands would take place, but did not notify the 7th Fleet.

So when the U.S. destroyer *Maddox* cruised by shortly after the trouble on the islands, North Vietnam PT boats went after it. The *Maddox* retreated to sea after an exchange of shots. Two nights later, the *Maddox,* now accompanied by the destroyer *Joy,* was allegedly attacked once again. The only reported damage to the *Maddox* was a broken search-light.

There were altogether too many aspects of this encounter that were never explained. It was, as many commentators pointed out, a suicide attack. And which side fired first? Defense Secretary McNamara never did make that clear.

No sooner was the second assault allegedly made than bombers from the 7th Fleet immediately carried the war to North Vietnamese territory, attacking the PT bases and putting the enemy's fleet out of commission in one assault. Johnson, too, was quick to act. Congress promptly considered a resolution giving him power to take all the action anywhere in Southeast Asia he wanted to take.

It was not exactly a spontaneous resolution. Johnson had been carrying it around in his pocket "for weeks," waiting for the first excuse to present it to Congress. If it is hard to believe that LBJ would pull a sneaky trick like that, one should refer to "Lyndon Johnson *vs.* the Ghost of Jack Kennedy" in the November, 1965, *Esquire* magazine. Way, way down in that article, in a brief paragraph telling what a genius Johnson is at timing, is the information about his packing that resolution around until he had an excuse, actual or contrived, to use it. The author of the article is Tom Wicker, chief of *The New York Times* Washington bureau.

A very knowledgeable man, Tom Wicker. Little goes on in the White House that he doesn't know about. It may seem unusual that such momentous information—information that would indicate Congress may have been suckered by the Commander in Chief—did not appear for months and then made its appearance buried in the middle of a routine profile in a "man's magazine." Well, those things happen in Johnson's Washington, even when the best of newspapers is involved. Asked specifically about that statement, Wicker said his source was the most high.

The day after Congress voted to give away its war-making powers (only Gruening and Morse dissenting, Morse warning that "those who vote for this will live to regret it," as about fifteen senators did indeed), stories began to appear, based on "new" Pentagon evidence, that the North Vietnamese attack on the *Maddox* was based on "confusion" (Richard Fryklund in the *Washington Star*) and "bumbling" (Murray Marder in the *Washington Post*) rather than on any conscious scheme to diminish U.S. prestige.

Congress, it appeared, was the victim of a Johnson stampede. He had the draft and he had the power, and now all he needed was an irrevocable step, moving out into the quicksand part of the war. This he put off until after the election and after the festivities of the inauguration. Then, on February 7, 1965, he ordered the "retaliatory" bombing of North Vietnam to begin. Another rather fishy incident had supplied him with another good excuse.

Though manpower commitment was still slight, the Pentagon had for months been yearning to bomb North Vietnam.* Months before, Johnson had promised it would be done. In the summer of 1964, while the U.S. voters were being persuaded to look upon candidate Johnson as a peacemaker, he was giving assurances to Premier Khanh that, to help stabilize the government of South Vietnam, we would bomb North Vietnam as soon as the imagery of the election

* See *The London Observer*, May 23, 1965.

had faded.* Later the administration admitted that it was for morale-boosting—rather than for any expected military advantage—that disposed Johnson to send out the bombers. All semblance of simple reprisal vanished, of course, when the bombers kept going out. It was obviously escalation of the most vigorous sort.

The episode which Johnson used to excuse the bombing was itself shadowy enough to arouse permanent suspicions that contrived negligence on the part of our allies, if not our own military leaders, was necessary to bring it off. It happened at Pleiku, which is roughly 200 miles south of the arbitrary boundary separating North and South Vietnam. Successfully passing through the guardline of South Vietnamese troops, who were strangely hard of hearing that night, the Cong (using an American-made mortar which they had taken from, or been given by, the South Vietnamese) blasted into a barracks in which U.S. troops were sleeping. Eight American soldiers were killed.

That was the excuse Johnson was looking for. With only brief recesses, his "reprisal" bombers have been flying ever since. He sought to explain his refusal to stop the bombings by saying that it was the only way to slow down the infiltration of troops from the north. Yet after seventeen months of bombing, the White House had to admit that there were 100 per cent more North Vietnamese troops in South Vietnam than when the bombings began. In mid-1966, when he escalated again by pounding the fuel dumps of Hanoi and Haiphong, Johnson's excuse for doing so—to hamper transportation southward—was again shown to be, if not an outright falsehood, at least an effort to mislead.

Defense Secretary McNamara had told Johnson the oil dump bombings would have little effect. Indeed, McNamara had told *every*body. At a Senate hearing in February, 1966,

* See *The New York Times,* May 20, 1966.

he was asked by Senator Ervin: "And you are telling us, am I to infer, that you could wipe out the entire industry of North Vietnam, and have no effect whatever upon their capability to prosecute the war?"

McNamara: It might affect their will to do so. In my opinion, it would have *no measurable effect* upon their capability to furnish the supplies they are presently supplying to the Communist forces in South Vietnam . . .

The portion of fuel used by their trucks could be obtained even though we were to mine the Haiphong and Hon Gai harbors. *And, if they got no fuel for trucks, they have demonstrated many many times before that, in the Orient, they can move the quantities of supplies now being moved into the South by animal and manpower.*

Senator Ervin: Don't you think a massive air attack on North Vietnam would have a vast effect on the will of the people to continue to fight?

McNamara: No one can be sure how they would react. I do not believe that it did in Japan and I do not believe that it did in World War II, and I do not believe it did in Korea . . .

Nevertheless, even with this advice from his chief civilian military adviser, Johnson decided, for what was widely believed to have been strictly home-consumption political purposes, to smash the North Vietnam petroleum facilities, something that Senator Morse was not alone in describing as "shocking outlawry." A few days later Johnson announced the inevitable poll: 85 per cent of the U.S. favored his decision.

McNamara was not the most accurate adviser the President could have had (he had predicted in 1963 that "the major part of the U.S. military task can be completed by the end of 1965"), but on this occasion he happened to be right. The raids on the fuel dumps and on practically every military target in the North did nothing to stop the southward flood of troops. McNamara reported in August, 1966, that despite the much heralded Johnson onslaught, the monthly infiltration of the enemy was *twice* what it had been a year earlier.

Having established the U.S. in the war with such overwhelmingly successful confusion, Johnson still had to pull an occasional fast one to keep all peace efforts from succeeding. The start of the post-Pleiku bombings, in fact, was the second wave of the anti-peace manipulations. Only forty-eight hours earlier Premier Kosygin had arrived in Hanoi, after stopping over at Peking to see how much co-operation he could get from the Chinese in arranging a cease-fire in Vietnam. He brought no strong proposals but he brought *some* proposals, and he talked Ho Chi Minh into earnestly considering them. The start of the bombings, of course, ended all that.

But Johnson's first, and much more significant, move to block peace had come in the autumn of 1964. Many times Johnson has said, "I will go anywhere anytime to talk peace with anyone" and that "we are ready now, as we always have been, to move from the battlefield to the conference table." But this is just another part of the seemingly mad, but actually very shrewd, posturing. In the fall of 1964 he had a chance to sit down with Ho Chi Minh, before the big build-up, before the bombings.

Donald Grant of the *St. Louis Post-Dispatch*, reporting from the United Nations, was the first to get wind of this episode. In an April 18, 1965 story he said it was believed that the enemy had offered to negotiate the previous year. Two months later Johnson, apparently having noticed the increased flow of rumors out of the UN and hoping to counteract them with one of his whoppers, said, "our information is when we asked them [the North Vietnamese] to come into the United Nations last August [of 1964], after we said you bring these people in and let's try to work through the United Nations, they weren't the slightest interested—the North Vietnamese were not."

Then, with an astounding show of gall even for one of his arrogance, Johnson said that an emissary from the United States to Hanoi on the previous February 15 had reported Ho Chi Minh unwilling to negotiate. Johnson failed to point out that this little feeler was made only nine days after the U.S. had embarked upon its program to bomb North Vietnam out of existence!

It was four months after Donald Grant's news beat before another newspaper took official notice of the same whisperings at the UN, and then only the *New York Herald Tribune* did so, front-paging it on August 8. The administration said the story was wrong.

Just prior to the *Herald Tribune* revelations, Eric Sevareid had reported on CBS Radio (but not on CBS television, which for some unexplained reason made no use of the astounding news) that he had learned "from unimpeachable sources that U Thant, working with Mr. Adlai Stevenson, twice took initiatives to get peace talks started and twice was rebuffed by Washington." Sevareid revealed that in the fall of 1964 Hanoi had agreed to allow one of its officials to meet with an American emissary in Rangoon, Burma, for preliminary peace talks, but that "the American election held up progress on this. *Later, Secretary McNamara stopped it on the argument that the Saigon government would have to be told, would be demoralized and come apart still further.* U Thant was represented as being bitterly angry about this.

"Later, last winter [1964] U Thant, under heavy criticism from other nations in the UN not only proposed a cease-fire agreement, but *offered to let Washington write its terms, even to the extent of drawing a cease-fire line clear through Laos.* Again, the Pentagon was opposed and Secretary of

State Rusk did not take up the proposals." Still the administration denied any such goings-on.

Not until Sevareid three months later put it all down in detailed fashion in *Look* magazine did Johnson, Rusk, and McNamara admit that they had indeed more than a year earlier snubbed all efforts by the United Nations leadership to bring about negotiations between a willing Hanoi and an unwilling Johnson.

Thus on two occasions in the early, changeable portion of the war Johnson took steps—which he later admitted taking —to stave off peace and escalate the war for one reason only: to bolster morale in the corrupt and disintegrating government of South Vietnam. The constancy of the Johnson administration in refusing to treat any peace efforts seriously is too blatant to be without significance.

A Canadian emissary made a special mission to Hanoi to lay a possible groundwork for negotiations; after Assistant Secretary of State William Bundy returned from Ottawa where he had had a briefing on this mission, the administration said the Canadian effort wasn't worth following up on.

A Rumanian deputy premier, after visiting Hanoi and Peking, went to the American ambassador in Bucharest to talk about the possibility of negotiation. The administration said it was such a tenuous offer as to be worthless.

Then UN Secretary General U Thant said that if the U.S. would break off bombings altogether, he thought he could get the peace talks going. Hardly had he made this proposal before Johnson ordered the bombing of Hanoi and Haiphong.

Most of the nation's press failed to see or to draw any conclusions from this series of violent obstinacies. But the *St. Louis Post-Dispatch,* the greatest voice of opposition to the Vietnam war, called it "a curious coincidence, if nothing more, that every American escalation of the war has appeared to come at a time when Hanoi was sending peace feelers, or international efforts for peace negotiations were afoot." It was as close as the *Post-Dispatch* could come to saying what was increasingly evident: that Johnson was determined to protract the war that he had helped create.

The miracle of the Vietnam war is that Johnson and his advisers have painstakingly constructed the most awesomely intricate temple of falsehoods, a delicate structure of the flimsiest of fabrications—and yet, though there have been some very hard assaults made against it, still it has not quite fallen. Perhaps it is held up by the nation's pride; nobody wants to witness the total and ugly embarrassment that would result, for all of us as well as Johnson, if we were to publicly and nationally acknowledge the deception and unfair play of which this administration has been guilty in the waging of the Vietnam war. Senator Gruening, among others, notes these duplicities:

—After repeated assurances that he was not seeking a military solution to the war, Johnson quickly eliminated all other possible solutions.

—He said he was in Vietnam simply to help a legitimate government defend itself. There have been eight heads of state in Vietnam since Johnson became president; which was the legitimate one? As for the Vietnamese eagerness to "defend" the military oligarchy, that was well illustrated in 1966 when there were 116,858 desertions from the South Vietnamese army.

—He promised not to "go north." Then he dispatched thousands of sorties into the northern realm. Then, having broken the promise to stop short of the 17th parallel, he indicated he was there only for a brief retaliation. The brief retaliation has lasted two years.

—He claims to be winning world support. Except

for nations such as Thailand and South Korea, which have become vassals to our military encampments, no Asian state has sent troop support. The really important anti-Communist Asian nations, such as India, Pakistan, Burma, and Afghanistan, are pointedly absent from the fighting. Support in Europe is equally hard to find. After Johnson had made a personal hard-sell appeal to the Franco government (for which as a senator he had helped obtain millions of dollars in aid), Spain reluctantly agreed to send four ambulances, with crews; no more. Turning to Latin America, Johnson instructed each U.S. ambassador to recruit with firmness, reminding the host government of our past largesse. The recruiting drive was remarkably unsuccessful. Brazil agreed to send coffee.

—It all began with a distortion of fact. In his State of the Union message to Congress in January, 1965, Johnson laid the groundwork for the horrors ahead. He said that U.S. troops were in Vietnam because "ten years ago we pledged our help. Three presidents have supported that pledge. We will not break it."

What pledge? In a letter to Diem on October 23, 1954, President Eisenhower had noted, "your recent requests for aid to assist in the formidable project of the movement of several hundred thousand loyal Vietnamese citizens away from areas which are passing under a *de facto* rule and political ideology which they abhor." Eisenhower promised aid for that: moving displaced persons. No more. Other aid —but he did *not* mention military aid—*might* be given later, he said, provided the government of Vietnam followed through on "needed reforms" and thereby "be so responsive to the nationalist aspirations of its people, so enlightened in purpose and effective in performance, that it will be respected both at home and abroad . . ."

The stipulations were not met. The Diem government, and all succeeding governments, bulged with corruption and antidemocratic psychoses. Two and a half months before he died, President Kennedy told Walter Cronkite of CBS that the stipulations laid down by Eisenhower for our help were nowhere in evidence. "I don't think that unless a greater effort is made by the government to win popular support that the war can be won out there," he said. "In the final analysis, it is their war. They are the ones who have to win it or lose it. We can give them equipment, we can send our men out there as advisers, but they have to win it—the people of Vietnam—against the Communists. We are prepared to continue to assist them, but I don't think the war can be won unless the people support the effort, and, in my opinion, in the last two months the government has gotten out of touch with the people."

After committing vast military projects and heavy troop support to Vietnam, when Johnson tried to hang the initial commitment around Eisenhower's neck, Ike backed off and insisted that he had offered *only* economic aid. When he left office there were only 600 U.S. military men in Vietnam. Under Kennedy—and notably on the advice of his and now Johnson's chief warlord, McNamara—this number grew to 20,000; but from Kennedy's remarks it is plain that he contemplated no increase, and possibly a pull-out. In any event, Kennedy spoke only of "advisers." Nothing that he said, nothing that Ike said or wrote, committed American fighting men to an Asian fight. This commitment was made first and only by Johnson.

Precedent was one thing he lacked the most. In 1961 a critical situation had been solved in Laos by permitting the domestic Communists to have a hand in the government. Johnson, then vice-president, took part in all of the National Security Council discussions leading up to that decision. Why, then, does Johnson oppose so adamantly the participation of home-grown Vietnamese Communists in their own government?

One will never find Johnson without an excuse for spreading what Senator Morse calls "the pious cloak of humanitarianism to disguise our nationalistic aims in Southeast Asia." Not long ago in a speech to the Northwestern University Alumni Association at Evanston, Under Secretary of State George W. Ball declared: "If the Vietnam war were merely what the Communists say it is—an indigenous rebellion—then *the United States would have no business taking sides in the conflict* and helping one side to defeat the other by force of arms." That was one of the many lines of propaganda which the White House altered.

All evidence points to a strong element of civil warring in Vietnam. After touring the front, Senator Stephen Young returned to report to the Senate, "I learned from General Westmoreland that the bulk of the Vietcong fighting in South Vietnam were born and reared in South Vietnam. I learned from General Stillwell and other generals that 80 per cent of the Vietcong fighting the Americans and the South Vietnamese in the Mekong Delta south and west of Saigon were born and reared in that Mekong Delta area. This is a civil war in which we are involved."

Against such proof, however, Johnson has raised an unanswerable answer: there is no difference between wars. Addressing the nation in April, 1965, Johnson conceded, "Of course, some of the people of South Vietnam are participating in attacks on their own government," but the next month Johnson took care of this in a speech at Baylor University, handing himself carte blanche to enter any country's disputes: "... *the old distinction between the civil war and international war has already lost much of its meaning.*"

He has been very frisky at changing the rules in the middle of the game, not only by redefining civil wars but by reinterpreting our own Constitution. Article VI of the U.S. Constitution commands that "all treaties made, or which shall be made, under the authority of the United States, shall be the supreme law of the land." Supreme law; nothing over it. No panicky Tonkin Gulf Resolutions; no post-Pleiku fiats. No whimsical promises made in Melbourne on a political barnstorming tour—nothing. The Constitution states that our treaties with other nations are to guide us as though they were part of our own law.

If Johnson had been content to obey the Constitution, our troops would not be fighting in Vietnam today—unless (1) we had got permission from the United Nations or (2) we had officially declared war against somebody. There is no other constitutional way to be there. One of our supposedly most respected treaties is the United Nations Charter. Article 33 of Chapter 6 commands: "The parties to any dispute, the continuance of which is likely to endanger the maintenance of international peace and security, shall first of all, seek a solution by negotiation, inquiry, mediation, conciliation, arbitration, judicial settlement, resort to regional agencies or arrangements, or other peaceful means of their own choice." Far from seeking negotiations, "first of all" or any other time, Johnson *rebuffed* the top UN official's efforts to negotiate.

Johnson violated the UN treaty and therefore the U.S. Constitution; there is no other way to interpret his action. In place of adherence to the most solemn pledge a nation can make, Johnson has substituted, in Senator Gruening's outraged phrase, "that dubious, conditional, qualified, tentative offer of help to a vanished South Vietnamese chief of state."

(As a matter of fact, he violated the Constitution twice, because he also violated our membership in the Southeast Asia Treaty Organization, whose compact, Article I, restates the obligation to pursue negotiations by the UN formula.)

* *
* *

Having shown himself independent of all national rules and treaty restrictions, having held at bay all secret negotiators until the military buildup had locked the U.S. into the war, having inflated the national economy with the typical wartime prosperity that silenced wide support of ideological dissent, Johnson now allowed himself time to joust with his Congressional critics.

To detract from the headlines that were coming out of Senator Fulbright's hearings on Vietnam—and for no other discernible reason—Johnson concocted a moment's notice meeting with Premier Ky (putting his arms around the little chap whose one and only acknowledged hero is Hitler) in Honolulu, which stirred editorial writers in this country to embarrassed appraisals of the Texas psyche and stirred new rebellions in South Vietnam, but which poor Hubert Humphrey saw as having "as much significance for the future of Asia as the Atlantic Charter had for the future of Europe."

And yet, in a perverse way, who knows? For in the same interview Humphrey, who is all too unhappily known now as the parrot in Lyndon's blue room, identified the Johnson statements in Honolulu as "The Johnson Doctrine" for Asia and revealed that around the White House, Vietnam is looked upon as "almost like the first voyage of an explorer into a new land. The ship has almost been storm-tossed on the shore, but we are there." And then he added with stunning candor: "We are going to be in Asia for a long, long time." Somehow it did not seem to harmonize with Johnson's own statement, "We seek no new territory."

Equally chilling was the quasi-official revelation in William S. White's column that what was happening in Asia was the culmination of Johnson's secret global ambitions, going back to his vice-presidential days: "President Johnson's newly proclaimed Asia Doctrine, in which the United States for the first time formally accepts its full responsibilities as the leading Pacific power-in-fact, has been in his mind for five years." Many in and out of Congress joined Fulbright in "an uneasy feeling that we are drifting—through such pronouncements—into the adoption of a Monroe Doctrine for Asia." Many also joined Fulbright in wondering if Johnson, in proposing also a Great Society for Asia, "ever thought of asking the Asians if they really want to join the Great Society."

It was too late for sarcasm to have much effect on Johnson. He was too far gone to stop. And besides, when it came to sarcastic knifings, he had the advantage of being able to plant very easily with the press any rumors about his opposition that he wanted to plant. Thus there came into being the anecdote, widely reprinted and retold, that Senator Frank Church was upbraided by Johnson about a speech critical of the Vietnam policy. According to the legend, Church is supposed to have replied, "I didn't go any further than Walter Lippmann," and this pricked Johnson into saying, "Well, Frank, the next time you need money to build a dam in your state, you better go to Mr. Lippmann."

Church, whose reputation for truthfulness is certainly as good as Johnson's, says no such thing, or anything even remotely like it, ever occurred. He says what *did* happen is that after the anecdote first appeared in a New York newspaper, he was at the White House and Johnson asked, with a look in his eye indicating he also had seen the story, "Well, Frank, how are all the dams in Idaho?" and Church answered, "Just fine, Mr. President, and the next one we build, I think we'll name the Walter Lippmann Dam." To Church, the planting of the story by the White House indicated that Johnson "was trying to threaten the dissenters, trying to suggest the kind of punishment that *could* be taken against us."

Other plantings began to push through the soil, but without bearing much fruit. The White House put out the story that Johnson had rebuked dissenter Vance Hartke by saying,

"You were just a two-bit mayor of a two-bit town, and I
made you a senator." Hartke denies that any such remark
was ever made to him; and he also points out that if it were
made behind his back, it just goes to show Johnson's weakness for fantasy, since Hartke was already nominated before
Johnson spoke up for him in 1958, a year which supplied
the recession on which many new Democrats coasted into
office without needing the help of Washington's power elite.

Meanwhile Johnson was criticizing those who would not
"put away childish, divisive actions," and suggesting that
those who challenged his position were, actually, betraying
American soldiers. And on this petty haggling note Johnson
set out to demand from his fantasy empire of the Pacific the
trust and acclaim he could not get at home. He began, as is
his custom, with a humble, peaceful tone, decrying in
Honolulu those "voices of extremism and apostles of mili-
tancy," but by the time he reached South Vietnam for a
144-minute stopover he was in a sic-'em mood ("Bring back
that coonskin on the wall"), and by the time he passed
through Alaska on his last lap he was ready to tell his opposition around the world that they could take their notes
pleading for negotiation and "you can put that in your pipe
and smoke it."

The robustly crass bully boy was riding again. He *would*
have his way, whatever the cost. "We don't ask for much,
but what we ask for we are going to get, we are going to
keep, we are going to hold." (Just one more border adjust-
ment! The phantom intruders of Poland and Ethiopia were
moving again.) European reporters, made more sensitive by
the abrasion of excessively ambitious men, saw more easily
what was going on. Peregrine Worsthorne of the *London
Sunday Telegraph,* who followed Johnson's chariot through
Asia, wrote home, "I suspect that this Asian trip has both
given him a taste to play the king and determine the part of
the world where he will make his bid for immortality."

The same taste, the tendency toward arbitrary rule, had earlier been noted by the aide perhaps closest to Johnson, Billie Don Moyers: "The Presidency 'stands across the path of those who mistakenly assert that democracy must fail because it can neither decide promptly nor act vigorously.' That office is now occupied by a man with a talent for power. If he fails, we all fail. If he succeeds, we all succeed."

This is a new concept of the presidency. We are not accustomed to thinking, as Johnson and his band in the White House now think, that the destiny of the nation depends upon the destiny of one man. It would, of course, be convenient for Johnson if we did think so. Then we would not dare to judge the fact that as president he has used the FBI to get a report on the sex life of a senator; that the long arm of El Ranchero reached out, through the Secret Service, to interrogate an employee of the Tennessee Valley Authority who described the president to an acquaintance as "tyrannical, dictatorial, domineering and overbearing"; that twenty-eight pickets were arrested on orders of the Secret Service when they greeted Johnson in Indianapolis with signs carrying no more radical a legend than a quote from Senator Hartke, "Escalation Breeds Escalation"; that federal employees are required in some Washington outposts to pledge their personal support to the President's bond drive or sign their names to a confession of error ("I do not accept my responsibility to support the President in this savings bond campaign"). Student groups that oppose the Vietnam war suddenly find themselves of considerable intimate interest to the FBI. The Subversive Activities Control Board is percolating again. He is watching us, and he is not always happy in what He sees, although He does try to sound Christlike about it, publicly praying for His opponents on one occasion, "Father, forgive them, for they know not what they do."

Well, it is too late for that, his forgiving us or our forgiving him. For better or worse, we know each other now, and can only stare at each other for the rest of the term. The discomfort is no longer made more agreeable by mystery; we know him too well. At the time of the 1964 Democratic convention in Atlantic City, Douglas Kiker said there were three questions which keep chewing at the minds of Johnson-watchers: Would his ego disrupt his administration? Would he command a loyal response from his peers? Would he have only a vague vision of the direction in which the nation should go and the way he intends to lead it? For many months the answers have been in: His ego has stifled all but the stoutest, or the dullest, or the most recalcitrant souls in Washington. He has commanded far more fear than loyalty. And the legislative program which once passed for vision has now degenerated into puff and pork barrel.

The strength that Johnson could have used for great humane achievements is consuming itself, as the old cycle catches up with him again: great promise, over-ripeness, spoilage.

See page 145.

* The intricacies of this deal were revealed to me by an executive of a medium large oil company that was prevented from participating in the import program by a technicality that was, because it brought about an $83 million loss, rather resented.

He thought they at least deserved the pleasure of revealing the true way in which the import program came about. So he gave me a note penned on personal stationery by one J. Edwin Hill, who died in January, 1960. Hill had been production manager and an officer and director in Richardson's corporate empire. Oil men ordinarily do not tell tales on each other. But after Richardson had died, and shortly before his own death, Hill, at the urging and in the presence of the old friend who must be nameless here, wrote out in longhand the source of Mr. Anderson's good fortune, as well as the agreement between Richardson and Eisenhower.

For persons interested in the jazz of oildom, here is his account of how Richardson made the arrangements for the cool million:

1. Stanolind Oil Company, Kirby Oil Company, Phillips Oil Company, and Sun Oil Company held farm-out property belonging to Richardson in Texas and Louisiana.

2. Richardson asked those companies to assign a royalty interest to F. J. Adams, a Fort Worth oil man who had been a vice-president of Gulf Oil Corporation. Adams' role was simply that of a go-between.

3. Adams assigned his royalty interest to Anderson for one dollar and "other valuable interests."

4. Anderson sold his interest in the property to Dalada Corporation for $900,000, half cash, half from future earnings. (Dalada was run by Toddie Lee Wynne, an old friend of Richardson's who accompanied him to a stag dinner at the White House in November, 1954.) Also, Anderson had already earned $70,000 in production before the sale.

5. Finally, Perry Bass, Richardson's nephew (John Connally's law partner), bought back Dalada's interest.

Thus the property went full circle, with Anderson grabbing his $970,000 as it went past.

If you refer back to Richardson's step No. 1, you will see that Stanolind was one of those helping Anderson to make a million. Stanolind (later absorbed by another Standard subsidiary, Pan American) was a wholly-owned subsidiary of Standard of Indiana. Standard of Indiana is among the top six to benefit from the import program. Phillips, you notice, was another benefactor; Phillips got the Puerto Rico franchise, in violation of the formula agreed upon.

Index